THE
SONS
OF
BEN

Noctes atque dies patet atri Ianua Ditis.

Unto this Island and great Plutoes *Court,*
none are deny'd that willingly resort,
Charon *or'e* Phlegeton *will set on sheare,*
and Cerberus *will guard you to the doore:*
Where dainty Devils drest in humane shape,
upon your senses soone will make a rape.
They that come freely to this house of sinne,
in Hell as freely may have entrance in.

Mrs. Holland's brothel as shown by the frontis-piece of Nicholas Goodman's satirical pamphlet *Hollands Leaguer.* . . . (London, 1632). The Latin—"Night and day the gate of gloomy Hell lies open"—is from Virgil's *Aeneid* VI, 127. The verses are Goodman's own.

THE⅊ SONS ⅊⅊ OF BEN⅊

Jonsonian Comedy in Caroline England

BY JOE LEE DAVIS

UNIVERSITY OF MICHIGAN

Wayne State University Press   Detroit   1967

TO SHIRLEY,
PAM, RANDY,
AND SANDRA

Preface

 Ben Jonson is now coming into his own as one of the greatest dramatists of the English Renaissance. During the past decade a series of books on his dramatic work—John J. Enck's *Jonson and the Comic Truth* (1957), Edward B. Partridge's *The Broken Compass: A Study of the Major Comedies of Ben Jonson* (1958), Jonas A. Barish's *Ben Jonson and the Language of Prose Comedy* (1960), C. G. Thayer's *Ben Jonson: Studies in the Plays* (1963), and Robert E. Knoll's *Ben Jonson's Plays: An Introduction* (1964)—have hewn a many-faceted interpretative capstone to adorn the solid structure built by a long line of earlier scholars and critics. The twentieth century has not restored Jonson to the place above Shakespeare where the later seventeenth and early eighteenth centuries seem to have wrongly elevated him as a consequence of their neoclassical prejudices. But what has occurred is that nineteenth century romantic Bardolatry, which tumbled Jonson from his pedestal into generally unread and unperformed oblivion by the earlier 1900's and advanced beyond his the claims of other Elizabethan and Jacobean contemporaries of Shakespeare, has now somewhat spent its enthusiasm and

7

yielded to a sober judiciousness that has brought Jonson back as second to none but Shakespeare himself.

Inevitably this change in Jonson's fortunes directed some attention to the so-called "Sons of Ben" in comedy—that group of minor dramatists of the Caroline period who sought to ape his comic practices while also, after the fashion of small fry, picking up tricks from their betters generally. This is a somewhat heterogeneous group consisting of Richard Brome, William Cartwright, William Cavendish, William Davenant, Henry Glapthorne, Peter Hausted, Thomas Killigrew, Shackerley Marmion, Jasper Mayne, Thomas Nabbes, and Thomas Randolph. Considerable specialized research has been done on all of them, as my Notes and References and Selected Bibliography show. But what is needed is a guide to their thirty-two comedies that is addressed to the general reader and non-specialized student of the drama, that is humanistic rather than antiquarian in intent, conception, and execution, and that provides an adequate historical background. It is such a guide that the present volume seeks to supply.

Chapter One—No Time for Comedy?—is an attempt to present the peculiar historical circumstances surrounding the rise and disappearance of this still virtually forgotten body of comedy. It shows that the Caroline milieu was dominated by two forces—Puritanism and Platonism—gravely and even fatally antagonistic to the spirit of true comedy but for that very reason offering it a challenge; then it sketches other aspects of the period that intensified the challenge, to the point of calling forth the Sons to their gallant efforts, despite the certainty that these efforts would be damned and doomed. Chapter Two—Thalia's Double Image—examines two of their plays that stand apart from all the rest as embodying the theory of comedy that helped shape their efforts. Chapter Three—More Than One Father—sketches the already well-established English comic tradition—the achievement not only of Jonson but also of other major and of near-major dramatists—that sustained the Sons' efforts right up to the end, when the Civil Wars and Cromwell's rule wiped out both their actual and their fictive worlds. Then follows a series of chapters analyzing play-by-play each phase

Preface

of their extensive comic production: Chapter Four—The Learned Sock—their adaptations and imitations of classical comedy; Chapter Five—The Sentimental Sock—their anticipations of the later comedy of sensibility; Chapter Six—The Stuffed Sock—their ventures into predominantly native, as opposed to classical, farce; Chapters Seven and Eight—The Sophisticated Sock, I and II—their development of a nascent comedy of manners or comedy of wit somewhat analogous to the later Restoration coterie comedy. Chapter Nine—A Concluding Note—sums up my findings and offers a brief judgment of the place that the Sons of Ben as a group should occupy in the history of English comedy.

J.L.D.

ANN ARBOR

Acknowledgments

I wish to thank the regents of the University of Michigan for granting me sabbatical leaves during the first semesters of the academic years 1950–51 and 1957–58 for the purpose of doing much of the research and writing for this book. I owe a special debt to Professor Paul Mueschke, my just-retired colleague in the Department of English of the University of Michigan, for arousing my interest years ago in the Caroline Sons of Ben in comedy and in guiding my earliest labors on the subject. To three chairmen of this department—the late Louis A. Strauss and Professors Louis I. Bredvold and Warner G. Rice—I am deeply grateful for many kindnesses and much encouragement. I desire also to make acknowledgments to the following: Professors Howard Mumford Jones and Oscar James Campbell, and the late Morris P. Tilley and Hereward T. Price, for helpful suggestions when as a graduate student I first became involved with Jonson and the Sons; Professor W. H. Hickerson, of the Department of English of Lake Erie College, for generously sharing with me insights into Caroline drama gained through his research on Shirley; Profes-

11

Acknowledgments

sor Sue Maxwell, of Bradley University, and Miss Marion Jones, of the University of London, for making available to me upon request their useful unpublished studies of Marmion; Dr. Louis B. Wright and his staff for courtesies they showed me during my brief period of study at the Folger Library in Washington, D.C.; various staff members of the University of Michigan General Library for facilitating my labors; the editors of *PMLA* and *Studies in Philology* for permission to borrow from articles of mine originally published in their pages; and Alexander Brede, Chief Editor Emeritus of the Wayne State University Press, for ridding my manuscript of many shortcomings that without his scrutiny would have appeared in this book. For those that do appear, no one mentioned in these acknowledgments is accountable: the responsibility is wholly mine.

Contents

Chronology

$\mathscr{A}$n asterisk indicates considerable uncertainty as to date. Hyphenated dates refer to inclusive years and describe a *terminus a quo, terminus ad quem* situation in the case of specific plays. Unless otherwise noted, dates for plays are of first performances. Dates are in New Style (i.e., beginning the year at January 1), except that it seemed desirable, for precision's sake, to indicate some January–March dates in Old Style (i.e., beginning the year at Annunciation Day, March 25) in parentheses with the N.S. year after the bar, e.g. (O.S. 1631/2). The order of items under a given year is sometimes approximate only. I have found Alfred Harbage, *Annals of English Drama 975–1700*, revised by S. Schoenbaum (London, 1964), most helpful, even when I have not strictly adhered to it.

I PRE-CAROLINE

1596   *Jonson's *A Tale of a Tub* composed in a version now lost. (See also listing under 1633.)

1597   *Jonson's *The Case is Altered* (probably composed earlier). Chapman's *An Humorous Day's Mirth.*

15

1598 Jonson's *Every Man in His Humour.*
1598–99 *Chapman's *All Fools* composed.
1599 Jonson's *Every Man Out of His Humour.*
1600 Marston's *Jack Drum's Entertainment.*
    Jonson's *Cynthia's Revels.*
1601 Marston's *What You Will.*
    Jonson's *The Poetaster.*
1601–02 Chapman's *May Day* composed.
1602 *Chapman's *Sir Giles Goosecap.*
1603 Death of Queen Elizabeth.
    James VI of Scotland becomes James I of England.
    Marston's *The Dutch Courtesan.*
1604 Chapman's *Monsieur D'Olive.*
    Marston's *The Malcontent.*
    *Heywood's *The Wise Woman of Hogsdon.*
    Marston's *The Fawn* composed.
    Dekker's *Westward Ho.*
1605 Chapman, Jonson, and Marston's *Eastward Ho.*
    Dekker's *Northward Ho.*
1604–06 *Middleton's *A Trick to Catch the Old One* composed.
    *Middleton's *A Mad World, My Masters* composed.
    *Middleton's *Michaelmas Term* composed.
1604–07 *Middleton's *Your Five Gallants* composed.
    *Middleton's *The Family of Love* composed.
1606 Jonson's *Volpone.*
    *Beaumont and Fletcher's *Wit at Several Weapons.*
1607 *Beaumont's *The Knight of the Burning Pestle.*
1608 *Chapman's *The Widow's Tears.*
1609 Jonson's *Epicoene.*
1610 Jonson's *The Alchemist.*
    *Dekker and Middleton's *The Roaring Girl.*
1611 *Middleton's *A Chaste Maid in Cheapside* composed.
1613 *Beaumont and Fletcher's *The Scornful Lady.*
    *Fletcher's *The Wild-Goose Chase* composed.

1614	Beaumont and Fletcher's *Wit Without Money.*
	Jonson's *Bartholomew Fair.*
1616	Jonson's First Folio published.
	Death of Shakespeare.
	*Middleton and Rowley's *A Fair Quarrel.*
	Jonson's *The Devil is an Ass.*
1620	Thomas May's *The Heir.*
1621–22	*Massinger's *A New Way to Pay Old Debts.*
1623	Shakespeare's First Folio published.
1625	Shirley's *Love Tricks* (O.S. Feb. 11, 1624/5).

II CAROLINE

1625	Accession of Charles I, Mar. 27.
	Theaters closed for about eight months by plague.
	Marriage of Charles I to Henrietta Maria.
1625–26	Randolph's *Aristippus.*
	*Randolph's *The Drinking Academy* composed.
1626	Jonson's *The Staple of News* (O.S. Feb. 1625/6).
	Massinger's *The Roman Actor.*
1626–28	*Randolph's *Hey for Honesty, Down with Knavery* composed.
1627	Digby's *Loose Fantasies* ("Private Memoirs") composed.
1628	Shirley's *The Witty Fair One.*
	Ford's *The Lover's Melancholy.*
1629	Jonson's *The New Inn* (O.S. Jan. 19, 1628/9)
	Charles I's third and climactic dissolution of Parliament.
	Brome's *The Northern Lass.*
	*Brome's *The City Wit.*
1630	Theaters closed for about seven months by plague.
	Randolph's *The Muses' Looking Glass* as *The Entertainment.*
1631	Marmion's *Holland's Leaguer.*
1632	Hausted's *The Rival Friends* (O.S. Mar. 19, 1631/2).
	Randolph's *The Jealous Lovers* (O.S. Mar. 22, 1631/2).

Shirley's *Hyde Park*.
*Massinger's *The City Madam*.
Jonson's *The Magnetic Lady*.
*Brome's *Covent Garden Weeded*.

1633   Prynne's *Histrio-Mastix* published (O.S. Jan. 10, 1632/3).
*Nabbes *Covent Garden* (O.S. Feb., 1632/3).
*Marmion's *A Fine Companion* (before June).
Jonson's revised *A Tale of a Tub*.
Nabbes' *Tottenham Court*.

1633–34   *Sir Richard Baker's *Theatrum Redivivum* composed.

1634   Davenant's *The Wits* (O.S. Jan., 1633/4).

1635   Cartwright's *The Ordinary*.
*Brome's *The New Academy*.
Davenant's *News from Plymouth*.
Shirley's *The Lady of Pleasure*.
Davenant's *The Platonic Lovers*.
*Marmion's *The Antiquary*.
Brome's *The Sparagus Garden*.

1636   Glapthorne's *The Hollander* (O.S. Mar. 1635/6).

1636–37   Theaters closed by plague from May 1636 to October 1637 except for a short period during late February and early March (O.S. 1636/7).

1636–38   *Glapthorne's *Wit in a Constable*.

1636–39   *Brome's *A Mad Couple Well Match'd*.

1637   Jonson's death, Aug. 6.
*Brome's *The English Moor*.

1637–38   *Mayne's *The City Match*.
*Brome's *The Damoiselle*.

1638   *Jonsonus Virbius* published.
Randolph's *The Muses' Looking Glass* (revised from 1630 performance) published.
Nabbes' *The Bride*.
Brome's *The Antipodes*.

18

1639–40   *Brome's *The Court Beggar.*
          *Killigrew's *The Parson's Wedding* composed.
1640   Charles I calls Parliament back into session after his long
          period of absolutist rule.
          Meeting of Long Parliament.
1641   Brome's *A Jovial Crew.*
1641–42   *Cavendish's *The Varietie.*
1642   Theaters closed by an ordinance of Parliament Sept. 2, al-
          though the Cockpit, the Red Bull, and the Fortune con-
          tinued to disobey the ordinance and offer occasional per-
          formances during the ensuing years.
          Beginning of the Civil Wars with the indecisive Battle of
          Edgehill Oct. 23.

The Eleven Sons

*A*uthoritative biographical sketches, as well as bibliographies, of the Caroline Sons of Ben in comedy are to be found in Vols. III–V of Gerald Eades Bentley's *The Jacobean and Caroline Stage.* The following brief addenda bring together, for convenient reference, a few miscellaneous facts about their lives and works insufficiently stressed or not mentioned in my text and notes. (The dates of plays are of first performance unless otherwise noted, and all years are N.S.)

BROME, RICHARD (c. 1590?–1652 or 1653) The oldest and most prolific of the Caroline Sons of Ben and the one most closely associated with Jonson as his servant or "man." Wrote plays for the Blackfriars, Red Bull, Salisbury Court, and Cockpit theaters. In addition to the eleven comedies discussed in the text, wrote several more romantic comedies or tragi-comedies, including *The Queen's Exchange* (1631–32), *The Novella* (1632), *The Love-sick Court* (1633–34), and *The Queen and Concubine* (1635–59), the third of these being possibly an anti-Platonic parody-burlesque, and collaborated with Thomas Heywood in *The Late Lancashire*

Witches (1634). Was author or co-author of a number of lost plays, including *The Lovesick Maid* (1629), the great popular success of which was in striking contrast to the failure of Jonson's *The New Inn*.

CARTWRIGHT, WILLIAM (1611–43) Attended Westminster School with Thomas Randolph and Jasper Mayne. Entered Christ Church, Oxford, as a gentleman commoner in 1628. Received his B.A. in 1632 and his M.A. in 1635. Took orders in 1638. In 1642 became Reader in Metaphysics to the University. After a short imprisonment in 1642 for his Royalist activities, served as the University's Junior Proctor. Won great popularity at Oxford as preacher, poet, and lecturer in philosophy. In addition to his one comedy discussed in the text, wrote three tragi-comedies—*The Lady Errant* (1628–43), *The Royal Slave* (1636), and *The Siege* (composed 1628–43).

CAVENDISH, WILLIAM (1593–1676) The second son of Sir Charles Cavendish. Pursued sport at the expense of his academic studies while at St. John's College, Cambridge. In 1612 spent a year abroad with Sir Henry Wotton, Ambassador to Savoy. Became Viscount Mansfield, Baron Cavendish of Bolsover, Earl of Newcastle, and Baron Ogle. At his country estates lavishly entertained King Charles in the summers of 1633 and 1634. Was appointed tutor to the young Prince Charles in 1638. During 1642–44 was in command of Royalist forces in the north. Was made Marquis of Newcastle in 1643. Fled to the Continent after the disastrous Royalist defeat at Marston Moor in July 1644 and eventually joined the Queen at Paris. In 1645 married his second wife, Margaret Lucas, later famous as the Duchess turned writer. Lived from 1649 to 1660 at Antwerp, establishing a riding school there and publishing his first treatise on horsemanship. Returned to England with Charles II and was restored to most of his estates as well as being created Duke of Newcastle in 1665. Was a patron of Jonson, Brome, Shirley, Davenant, Dryden, Shadwell, Flecknoe, and

Hobbes. In addition to *The Varietie,* wrote several comedies in collaboration with others, including Shirley, Dryden, and the Duchess of Newcastle.

DAVENANT, WILLIAM (1606–68) The son of a tavern-keeper and mayor with a last name spelled in a bewildering variety of ways. May have been the illegitimate son of Shakespeare, who is reputed to have been a frequent visitor with the Davenant family. After holding minor posts in noble households, became the boon companion of Sir John Suckling. Incurred the following misfortunes: fifteen years of indebtedness to an incorrigibly dunning tailor, syphilis and mercury-poisoning consequent to its treatment, and conviction for the murder of a hostler or tapster. While waiting for the King's pardon, wrote a masque for the Queen that gained him fame and favor at Court. Managed Beeston's Boys Company at the Cockpit theater for a short period after June 27, 1640. Served with the King's army in and near Oxford and was knighted in the summer of 1643. Later made himself useful as royal messenger, supply officer, and member of the commission that took Prince Charles from Jersey to Paris. Sailing for America in 1650 as the appointed Lieutenant Governor of Maryland, was captured in the Channel and imprisoned in the Tower of London. After pardon by Cromwell in 1654 and a stay in France, returned to London and formed a company in 1656 to give operatic performances at the hall in the back part of Rutland House and at the old Cockpit theater in Drury Lane. During the Restoration became manager of the Duke's Company that performed plays at the Salisbury Court and Lisle's Tennis Court theaters. Remodeled the latter, known as the Duke's Theatre, to provide a stage equipped with moveable scenery and with living quarters for actresses. In addition to the three plays discussed in the text, was author of other comedies produced during the Restoration, the famous heroic poem *Gondibert* (1651), numerous shorter poems, masques, and tragedies, and several Shakespearean adaptations.

23

GLAPTHORNE, HENRY (1610–43?) The son of a gentleman who became bailiff to Lady Hatton, the wife of Sir Edward Coke. Attended Corpus Christi College, Cambridge, briefly as a pensioner. Probably served for a while as some nobleman's groom-porter. Wrote for the Phoenix and the Globe and probably the Salisbury Court theaters. In addition to the two comedies discussed in the text, was author of a sheaf of poems, the pastoral drama *Argalus and Parthenia* (1638?), the tragi-comedies *The Lady's Privilege* (1632?–40) and *The Lady Mother* (1635), and the tragedy *Albertus Wallenstein* (1634–39). Probably wrote another extant heroic play, *Revenge for Honour* (1640?), as well as four lost plays of the same type.

HAUSTED, PETER (c. 1605–45) B.A., Queen's College, Cambridge, in 1624; M.A. in 1627. Remained at Cambridge until about 1633, concerning himself with dramatics. Was curate of Uppingham in Rutlandshire from 1634 to 1638. Later became vicar of Gretton and rector of Wold, both in Northamptonshire, and served as chaplain to the Earl of Northampton. Was dragged from his pulpit, menaced by a mob, arraigned, and temporarily committed for preaching too vigorously against nonconformity at Great St. Mary's in Cambridge in 1634. Was created a D.D. at Oxford in 1642. In addition to *The Rival Friends* and *Ten Sermons* (1636), wrote a Latin play, *Senile Odium* (1631?). Prepared the inscription for the monument that Sir Christopher Hatton erected to Thomas Randolph in Blatherwycke Church.

KILLIGREW, THOMAS (1612–1683) The fourth son of Sir Robert Killigrew. Had one brother (Sir William) who was a courtier and playwright and another (Dr. Henry) who was a clergyman and also a playwright. Became a page at Charles I's Court in 1625. Married one of Queen Henrietta's maids of honour in 1636 at the Queen's house at Oatlands. In 1635 visited France and Italy, probably as gentleman attendant to Walter Montague, the Catholic convert. On his return lived in the Covent Garden

24

Piazzas. Between 1639 and 1641 visited Paris, Geneva, Basle, and Rome. Served as messenger for the King for a year after the beginning of the Long Parliament. Was arrested and confined to London, then given a pass to the Royalist army in July 1643. Probably left England with the Queen and was for many years messenger and minister for members of the royal family on the Continent. Married a Dutch heiress in 1655 and entered the service of the States-General. Returned to England with Charles II and became manager of the King's Company, which acted at such theaters as the old Red Bull, Gibbon's Tennis Court, and the new Theatre Royal. Shared a kind of Restoration theatrical monopoly with Davenant but was less successful, partly because of his extravagant living. In addition to *The Parson's Wedding,* wrote the tragi-comic trilogy *The Prisoners* (1635?), *Claracilla* (1636), and *The Princess* (1637?); the tragedy *The Pilgrim* (1646?); the elaborate two-part dramatic romances *Cecilia and Clorinda* (composed 1649–50) and *Bellamira Her Dream* (composed 1650–52); and the two-part autobiographical comedy *Thomaso, or the Wanderer* (composed 1654).

MARMION, SHACKERLEY (1603–39)   The son of a Northamptonshire country gentleman with the same first and last names, both spelled variously. Received his B.A. in 1622 and his M.A. in 1624 from Wadham College, Oxford. Saw military service in the Low Countries between 1625 and 1629. Was arrested in July of 1629 for assaulting and wounding one Edward Moore in a highway fracas not far from the Phoenix theater. Became Sir John Suckling's valued friend and fellow-adventurer. Wrote for both the Salisbury Court and the Phoenix theaters and was boon companion of Randolph, Nabbes, and Brome. In addition to the three comedies discussed in the text, was author of one of the finest long poems of the period, *Cupid and Psyche* (1637) and may have collaborated with John Clavell in *The Soddered Citizen* (1629–30), a comedy.

MAYNE, JASPER (1604–72)   Attended Westminster School with Thomas Randolph and William Cartwright. At Oxford took his

25

The Sons of Ben

B.A. in 1628, his M.A. in 1631, his B.D. in 1642, and his D.D. in 1646. Wrote occasional poems and began a translation of Lucian's dialogues. Held livings at Cassington, near Woodstock, and at Pyrton. Was chaplain to the Earl of Devonshire, in whose household he was companion and disputant of Hobbes. During the Restoration enjoyed several benefices—Canon of Christ Church, Archdeacon of Chichester, and Chaplain in Ordinary to the King. In addition to *The City Match,* wrote one tragi-comedy, *The Amorous War* (composed 1628–48).

NABBES, THOMAS (c. 1605–41) Probably matriculated at Oxford in 1621 but must not have stayed for a degree. May have been tutor or secretary for some nobleman near Worcester. Wrote for the Phoenix and Salisbury Court theaters. Settled down as a family man in the parish of St. Giles in the Fields—the parish of the Phoenix theater. In addition to the three comedies discussed in the text, wrote numerous commendatory verses, a hack contribution to a history of the Turks, the tragedies *Hannibal and Scipio* (1635) and *The Unfortunate Mother* (composed 1639, published 1640), and the masques *Microcosmus* (1637), *A Presentation Intended for the Prince His Highness on His Birthday* (published 1638) and *The Spring's Glory* (published 1638).

RANDOLPH, THOMAS (1605–35) The eldest son of the steward of Sir George Goring and Edward, Lord Zouch. Attended Westminster School with Cartwright and Mayne. Received his A.B. in 1628 and his M.A. in 1631 from Trinity College, Cambridge. Rivaled Hausted in Cambridge dramatic activities. Began to write for the Salisbury Court theater while still at Cambridge. Tutored the son and heir of Captain William Stafford. In addition to the five comedies discussed in the text, wrote the monologue *The Conceited Pedlar* (1627), the pastoral drama *Amyntas* (1630), and numerous poems, among them a fine elegy for Venetia Digby and a tribute to Sir Kenelm Digby.

26

THE
SONS
OF
BEN

CHAPTER
ONE

No Time for Comedy?

Sons born of many a loyal Muse to Ben,
  All true-begotten, warm with wine or ale,
  Bright from the broad light of his presence, hail!

*W*hen Algernon Charles Swinburne wrote these lines in his sonnet on "The Tribe of Benjamin," he was thinking of both dramatists and lyric poets of the Jacobean and Caroline periods who acknowledged Jonson to be their inspiration. It is well to stress at the outset that "Sons of Ben" in the present study is limited to writers of stage comedy of the Caroline period, that it excludes poets who did not write plays, and that it does not refer to pre-Carolinian or post-Carolinian writers of comedy, such as Nathan Field, on the one hand, or John Wilson or John Crowne, on the other, who were to some extent Jonson's imitators. Arbitrarily, the term embraces only eleven writers, all admittedly minor.

Different worlds shaped these writers' experience of life and conception of their craft. Thomas Randolph and Peter Hausted of Cambridge and Jasper Mayne and William Cartwright of Oxford were "amateurs of town and university." Shackerley Marmion, William Davenant, Thomas Nabbes, Henry Glapthorne, and Richard Brome were professionals identified with the popular theaters. William Cavendish and Thomas Killigrew were primarily courtiers.[1] All had, however, at least one trait in common when they wrote comedy, and that was a zeal to follow Ben Jonson more diligently than they did other masters, not only in their superficial quarrying for situations and characters but also fundamentally in their strategies of illusion and meaning. They took very much to heart this item of his advice to writers:

> The third requisite in our *Poet*, or Maker, is *Imitation*, to bee able to convert the substance, or Riches of an other *Poet*, to his owne use. To make choise of one excellent man above the rest, and so to follow him, till he grow very *Hee*: or, so like him, as the Copie may be mistaken for the Principall. Not, as a Creature, that swallowes, what it takes in, crude, raw, or indigested; but, that feedes with an Appetite, and hath a Stomacke to concoct, divide, and turne all into nourishment.[2]

This dictum has come down to us in his *Timber, or Discoveries* of 1641, but they doubtless had it direct from the oracle in the flesh and in his cups.

For it is more or less certain that virtually all of them carried their discipleship further and were members at one time or another of the constantly changing nondescript group of poets, playwrights, and merely conversational wits who met so regularly with the aging Jonson at various taverns of London, or in his lodgings near Westminster Abbey, until shortly before his death in 1637, that they came to be widely dubbed "The Sons of Ben" or "The Tribe of Ben," as if they were actually a kind of institution, a combined drinking academy, literary society, and philosophical confraternity. What their sessions were like is suggested by an often-quoted stanza in Robert Herrick's ode for Jonson:

No Time for Comedy?

Ah Ben!
Say how or when
Shall we thy guests
Meet at those lyric feasts
Made at the Sun,
The Dog, the Triple Tun?
Where we such clusters had,
As made us nobly wild, not mad;
And yet each verse of thine
Outdid the meat, outdid the frolic wine.[3]

An even more vivid description occurs in one of the plays of Shackerley Marmion appropriately entitled *A Fine Companion,* in a scene where the young wit Careless explains volubly to his lady love that he has just come from the Apollo Room of the Old Devil Tavern:[4]

From the heaven
Of my delight, where the boon Delphic god
Drinks sack, and keeps his Bacchanalias,
And has his incense, and his altars smoking,
And speaks in sparkling prophecies; thence do I come!
My brains perfum'd with the rich Indian vapour,
And height'ned with conceits, from tempting beauties,
From dainty music and poetic strains,
From witty varlets, fine companions,
And from a mighty continent of pleasure,
Sails thy brave Careless.[5]

But whether these "brave" Sons of Ben or such of their greater fellow dramatists as Philip Massinger and James Shirley were well advised in their efforts to keep comedy alive on the Caroline stage may have seemed even to some of their more sympathetic contemporaries a moot question. The atmosphere of the age was changing subtly from that of the Elizabethan and Jacobean periods in that forms of high sobriety present but not prevalent then were deeply affecting the psychology of both the aristocratic and the middle classes whose patronage was essential to the performance of plays. Puritanism in its many modes,

31

spreading among the yeomanry and gentry of the countryside, the artisans and merchants of the towns and cities, and even some lords of the realm,[6] joined incongruously with the exotic cult of Platonism fostered at Court by Queen Henrietta to make it appear that this was no time for comedy.

Why such should have been the case becomes clearer if we borrow a theory set forth by L. J. Potts in his unpretentious but profound essay on *Comedy*. After an extended citation and analysis of a part of Act III, scene 1 of *A Midsummer Night's Dream,* he remarks: "The antithesis between Titania and Bottom is at the heart of comedy." In other words all genuine comedy rests on a detached perception of the dualism in human nature between shrewd asininity and spiritual fatuity, between the limitations of both our lower and our higher selves. By alerting us to these, comedy may serve as "our . . . weapon against the forces of distintegration within human society, and against the germs of anarchy and defeatism in our own minds."[7] When idealisms get so out of hand in a society that individuals refuse to recognize that what they think are their higher selves possess limitations and at the same time tend to abhor or ignore or deny the existence of their lower selves, then comedy begins to lose its appeal and cannot fulfill its aesthetic, moral, psychological, and social functions. In the Caroline period Puritanism and Court Platonism, though as dissimilar in ultimate genesis and temper as it is possible for cultural movements to be, were essentially idealisms out of hand, with the result that many under their sway became either immune or antagonistic to comedy. Neither Puritan zealots nor devotees of *préciosité* were aware of their own spiritual fatuities and the real motives that these often masked, such as the will to power or the will to be let alone in a fashionable fools' paradise. Quipped Peter Hausted of Puritan extremism, after he had forsaken the university stage for the Anglican pulpit: "We have at this houre a Sect of *New Pharises* sprung up, in every branch of description answering the old ones; nay, in many points of Hypocrisie and vaine-glory, going beyond them quite."[8] And Richard Brome, referring to the vogue at Court of the Platonic anti-comedy, observed ironically:

No Time for Comedy?

And such are only good those leaders cry—
And into that beleefe draw on a faction,—
That must despise all sportive, merry wit
Because some such great play had none in it.[9]

Partly responsible for the almost simultaneous growth of Puritan extremism and Court Platonism was the political crisis. This may be described as both revolutionary and counter-revolutionary. Immediately after the accession of Charles in 1625, the Parliament, led by the Commons, increased the opposition that his father had not coped with successfully. The subsidies they voted fell woefully short of his need for funds; various speakers aired their grievances, not the least of which was the influence of his favorite, Buckingham. Charles retaliated by dissolving this Parliament, "to the great grief of all good subjects that loved true religion, their kind, and the commonwealth," as the Puritan diarist, Sir Simonds D'Ewes, put it.[10] The next Parliament went even further. The sermon that Laud preached them, expounding Charles' complete acceptance of the theory of kingship and the relations of church and state held by his father, was not to their liking and received shortly a fiery counterblast in the charges by Sir John Eliot that "those we trust" were bringing disaster upon the nation. Spurred by actions of the Lords, the Commons moved for Buckingham's impeachment. The result was a second dissolution of Parliament in 1626, on which D'Ewes commented thus: "Infinite almost was the sadness of each man's heart, and the dejection of his countenance that truly loved the church or commonwealth."[11] The third Parliament brought the early revolutionary crisis of Charles' reign to its counter-revolutionary turning point. Both Houses joined in a Petition of Right to which Charles equivocally acceded; the Commons then went on to draw up remonstrances so explicit and comprehensive that they seemed to Charles downright seditious. Between Parliamentary sessions one John Felton, a naval lieutenant of the Puritan persuasion obsessed with a personal grudge against Buckingham, read these remonstrances, concluded that he had a mission to assassinate the favorite, and carried out the mission with a dispatch prompting the populace to acclaim him a

David who had delivered England from Goliath.[12] Against the background of this "Enthusiastic" violence the reassembled Parliament split, principally over religion, with the Commons following the leadership of Eliot and John Pym in insisting that the Arminianism fostered by the King and his bishops and striking a *via media* between Popery and Puritanism was a threat to true piety and sound church polity and should be put down by Parliamentary fiat. Enraged at this encroachment on his prerogative, Charles dissolved Parliament a third time. D'Ewes referred to this day in 1629 climactically as "the most gloomy, sad, and dismal day for England that happened in five hundred years last past."[13] His superlative description was not wholly inaccurate. For eleven years Charles was to rule without Parliament. During this period, too, he championed his prerogative courts with their Roman law against the courts where the English common law was administered according to the code Sir Edward Coke had approved.[14] When Charles finally called Parliament again, in 1640, he precipitated the Civil Wars, his own execution, the Commonwealth, and the Protectorate.

It is possible today to view this political crisis as one sequence of episodes in the vast drama of the transition from the medieval feudal order with its baronial localism and Catholic universalism to the order of modern capitalistic democracy with its toleration of diverse faiths. The rising middle classes were the prime movers of this drama, supporting a strong monarchy, an established national Protestant church, and a mercantilist economics, and then modifying each of these instruments as they outlived their usefulness. The drama began with the Wars of the Roses, unfolded its grand second act in the reigns of Henry VIII and Elizabeth, built its confused and ultimately violent third act with the early Stuarts and Cromwell, went into its brilliant, relief-laden fourth act with the Restoration and the bloodless Revolution of 1688, and closed with the compromises and harmonies of the Hanoverians.[15]

Although such a broad view blurs and oversimplifies many details and issues, it has the virtue of underscoring the basic ironies in Charles I's struggle with Parliament and in the relation of this struggle to

Puritanism. Charles acted consistently and thoroughly to implement a theory of kingship and preserve a church establishment that had served the middle classes of the previous century well but that had become in the second quarter of the seventeenth century a menace to the freedom and progress of group enterprise, whether political, religious, or economic. Since the rationale of his own political position was religious, identifying his sovereign will and reason with Providence, his political opponents in Parliament had to encourage a religious view that conceived the operations of Providence somewhat differently. This view they found in Puritanism. Most of its exponents, no matter to what wing of the complex movement they belonged or to what sect they gave adherence, went beyond orthodox Anglicanism in holding that God's wonder-working interference in the processes of nature through acts of special or particular Providence was just as important as his general Providence. They also tended to give more weight to God's revelation of his purposes through Scripture, to be interpreted by properly educated, self-sufficient clergymen, than they did to the divine light in human reason, certes that of kings and bishops. Finally, they were sometimes so ardent in their attitude to God's grace as the source of true virtue in the few that they incurred the charge of "Enthusiasm" they themselves did not scruple to hurl against those exceeding them in the exaltation of the charismatic above the institutional.[16] As David Mathew in his *The Age of Charles I* has so aptly expressed it: "The Puritan feeling was an engine which a political leader could employ to work fresh seams. . . . The Puritan leaven had every quality which would recommend it to a great opposition party in the State." But he also stresses the ironic contretemps that ensued:

> Yet one thing the Parliamentarian leaders could not forsee. They did not realise, for old, accustomed leaders seldom do realise, what spirits they were calling out of the vasty deep. It was beyond their power to imagine the Army and the Independents, who together would compass their destruction.[17]

Caroline Court Platonism had a direct connection with the political crisis in being a mode of escape from it. Three months after his accession, Charles escorted from Dover to London his French bride, Henrietta Maria, the young Bourbon Catholic princess, descendant of the House of Austria, daughter of Marie de' Medici and Henry of Navarre, sister of Louis XIII and sister-in-law of Philip IV of Spain. Gossip about the fashionable salon presided over by the Marquise de Rambouillet—famed as cosmopolitan society's cultural retreat from the sordid world of political intrigue—had englamored her court girlhood. She had read and re-read Honoré d'Urfé's pastoral romance, *Astrée,* wherein the system of etiquette practiced at the salon was elaborately described and dramatized. This system was an aesthetic religion drawing on the Platonism of Renaissance sonnets and pastorals, the medieval courts of love, the Greek romances.[18] It celebrated an operation of Providence neglected by the Stuart theory of kingship and by the Puritans: the creation for each lady and gentleman of a soul-mate or ideal friend of the opposite sex known as "lover" and "mistress" (and often also a friend of the same sex) as the channel of His grace and the revealer of His purposes. It prescribed the ways to find and win and cherish these friends, defined the problems that might arise in such pursuits and relationships, and suggested their appropriate solutions. Henrietta did not grow nostalgic for a retreat comparable to the salon of Rambouillet until the struggle with Parliament, in which her Catholicism and the concessions made to France in her marriage contract were complicating factors, compelled her to feel that England was an alien land. And not until after Charles had dismissed the Parliament of 1629 and embarked on his eleven-year personal rule with the advice of his Council did she achieve such a salon at her own Court, confident that the artificial peace of this absolutist interlude[19] was an atmosphere where she and her valued friends of both sexes might watch and act in plays and read poems and romances all reminiscent of *Astrée,* have their portraits painted by Vandyke, and analyze their personal constancies, rivalries, sacrifices, and visitations of the beatific, with the requisite refined similitudes. The Court performance early in 1633 of Walter Montague's masque, *The Shepheard's Paradise,* with the Queen and her ladies taking roles, was evidence that the salon was well established. The following year, several months before the Court performance of Davenant's *The Triumph of Love,* James Howell wrote to a friend at Paris:

> The Court affords little News at present, but there is a Love call'd Platonic Love, which much sways there of late; it is a Love abstracted from all corporeal gross Impressions and sensual Appetite, but consists in Contemplations and Ideas of the Mind, not in any carnal Fruition. This Love sets the Wits of the Town on work; and they say there will be a Mask shortly of it, whereof Her Majesty and her Maids of Honour will be part.[20]

By 1635 Shackerley Marmion had his Duke of Pisa in *The Antiquary* thus sketch the progress of a poetaster:

> But when he has travell'd, and delibated [had a taste of] the French and the Spanish; can lie a-bed, and expound Astraea, and digest him into compliments; and, when he is up, accost his mistress with what he had read in the morning; now if such a one should rack up his imagination, and give wings to his muse, 'tis credible he should more catch your delicate court-ear, than all your head-scratchers, thumb-biters, lamp-wasters. . . .[21]

To grasp the spirit of Caroline Puritan extremism and the threat it posed to comedy requires some consideration of the early life and work of William Prynne. Of good middle-class stock from the Puritan shire of Somerset and grandson of a member of Commons at the time of the Gunpowder Plot to blow up Parliament, he received his B.A. at Oxford in 1621 and later in the same year entered Lincoln's Inn to study law. Shocked by the revelling of his fellow students and influenced by the militant non-separatist Congregationalism of the chaplain of Lincoln's Inn, Dr. John Preston, Prynne found an outlet for his youthful religiosity, energy, and adventuresomeness in writing reform pamphlets. A series of these between 1627 and 1630 attacking Arminianism, royal absolutism, evidences of Popery in Anglican devotions, the fashion of wearing the hair long, and the custom of drinking healths, brought him before the authorities for censure and got some of his stationer publishers into more serious trouble. Having seen only four plays per-

37

formed but having read more than ten times that many tracts against the stage, Prynne published early in 1633 a monumental 1,006-page treatise in dramatic form entitled *Histrio-Mastix: The Players Scourge, Or, Actors Tragaedie* . . ., on which he had labored nine years. Through the perseverance of Archbishop Laud and the unfortunate but unintentional appearance of the book at a time when the Queen and her ladies were rehearsing their parts for *The Shepheard's Paradise,* Prynne was subjected to several examinations, kept in prison, and finally brought to trial before the Court of Star Chamber. Convicted of libel verging on treason, he had both ears clipped on the pillory, was degraded by Oxford and Lincoln's Inn, suffered disbarment, was fined £5000, had his books and papers sold, and was sentenced to life imprisonment. Serving this sentence in the Tower, he continued to produce pamphlets that were smuggled to the printers. Another series aimed at prelacy brought him again before the Court of Star Chamber with two of his collaborators. The upshot was further pillorying, the complete mangling of his ears, and the branding of one cheek with an S and the other with an L, for Seditious Libeller. On the way back to the Tower, he composed defiant doggerel referring to the S and the L as "Stigmata Laudis." Incarcerated later in Mount Orgueil Castle on the Isle of Jersey, he wrote piously meditative verse dedicated to the wife and daughters of Sir Philip de Carteret, the lieutenant governor. Released after Charles had ended his long personal rule by finally calling Parliament into session, Prynne journeyed from Southampton to London through cheering throngs for a huge torchlight procession beginning at Charing Cross. Commons revoked his various sentences, restored him to his B.A. and to the bar, and decreed other reparations.

So much for Prynne's earlier career. We need not follow him into the years beyond 1641, which surprised, as time usually does, with curiously ironic reversals. From one of the doughtiest spokesmen for the rights of Parliament against the King and his bishops, Prynne was to turn into an unsparing critic of the Independents, the Army, and Cromwell and was to play a decisive role in effecting the restoration of Charles II, whose adviser and pensioner he ultimately became, loaded with such honors as bencher of Lincoln's Inn, Elder Brother of Trinity House, and Keeper of Records in the Tower of London. Not this incredible liberal-conservative is our concern, but only the Prynne thus described in Samuel Butler's epitaph:

> His brain's career was never stopping;
> But pen with rheum of gall still dropping;
> Till hand o'er head brought ear to cropping.[22]

Prynne justifies the *omnium-gatherum* bulk of *Histrio-Mastix* on the ground that the evil he is attempting to combat has outgrown all ordinary proportions:

> Some Play-books since I first undertooke this subject, are growne from Quarto into Folio; which yet beare so good a price and sale, that I cannot but with griefe relate it, they are now . . . new-printed in farre better paper than most Octavo or Quarto Bibles, which hardly finde such vent as they: And can then one Quarto Tractate against Stage-playes be thought too large, when as it must assault such ample Play-house Volumes? Besides, our Quarto-Play-bookes since the first sheetes of this my Treatise came unto the Presse, have come forth in such abundance, and found so many customers, that they almost exceede all number, one studie being scarce able to holde them, and two yeares time too little to peruse them all: And this made this Treatise swell the greater, because these Play-bookes are so multiplied. Againe, I considered with my selfe, that our Players, our Play-haunters are now more in number, more various in judgements, in humours, in apprehensions, than they have beene in former ages; whereupon I thought good to produce more store of different Play-refelling Arguments and Authorities than else I should have done. . . .

Borrowing his classification of dramatic genres from Scaliger and showing some awareness of the fashion among Caroline dramatists to produce hybrid or eclectic plays, he undertakes to establish the following thesis:

That all popular, and common Stage-Playes, whether Comicall, Tragicall, Satyricall, Mimicall, or mixt of either: (especially, as they are now compiled, and personated among us,) are such sinfull, hurtfull, and pernitious Recreations, as are altogether unseemely, and unlawfull unto Christians.[23]

Placing comedy first betrays an animus that soon emerges in the argument. The subject-matter of comedy, as he views it, is of this world in the meanest and most trifling sense. Caroline comedies exceed in licentiousness those of classical antiquity. They are "so many Lectures of Ribaldry"; their themes are "nothing else but the Adulteries, Fornications, Rapes, Love-passions, Meritricious, Unchast, and Amorous practices, of Lascivious Wicked men. . . ." So reprehensible is their subject-matter that

> . . . if the very Stones, and Pillars, which support the Play-house; if the Seates, and Scaffoldes, which adorne it: or the very Theater, and Stage it selfe, had Tongues to speake; they would presently exclaime against it, and reproove it.

What disturbs him as he surveys London is a repetition of the stuff of these comedies, in so far as he knows them. Like Plato in a similar mood and Oscar Wilde in a wholly different one, he is convinced that here is an instance of life imitating art. Just as he is so aesthetically naive that he cannot distinguish between the subject-matter of a play and the attitude of the dramatist toward this subject-matter, neither can he separate causes from effects. The Caroline dramatists are responsible, as he sees it, for the iniquities of Caroline society:

> For alas, whence is all that prodigious desperate dissolutenesse, prophanesse, wickednesse, drunkennesse, impudence, lewdnesse, and disorder; that grosse uncleanesse, that exorbitant obliquity, that stupendious degeneracy in life, apparel, speech, gesture, *haire,* complements, and the intire man? Whence all those severall armies of corruptions, of vices, which infect our Nation? Whence all those severall beastly, diabolicall, audacious, crying, daring sinnes of our *femalized gotish males,* or *mannish females,* who out-stare the very Lawes of God, of Man, of Nature, and send up daily challenges for vengeance to the God of

Heaven; Whence all those common Adulterers, Adulteresses, Whore-masters, Whores, Bawdes, Panders, Ruffians, Rorers, Swearers, Duellers, Cheaters, Fashion-mongers, Fantastiques, Libertines, Scoffers, *haters of God,* of grace, of holinesse; *Despisers and slanders of all religious men;* the Enemies of all modesty and common civility; with such other lawlesse, godlesse persons, who now swarme so thicke of late in the streets of our Metropolis . . . *Are not they all originall from Playes? From Play-houses?*

Finally, Prynne's animus against comedy comes to the fore when he contends that "profuse lascivious laughter" is an "unlawfull Concomitant of Stage-playes. . . ."[24]

It is significant that the best refutation of Prynne's *Histrio-Mastix,* Sir Richard Baker's *Theatrum Redivivum,* which internal evidence shows to have been written sometime between 1633 and 1638, was not published until the early Restoration.[25] Baker ridicules the organization and the length of Prynne's "huge Forest of Confusion," takes him to task for his title on the ground that one of his chief arguments is "wholly imployed upon the defeat of Comedies,"[26] points out that he misunderstands Comedy's relation both to ethics and to actual life,[27] banters him with Democritean gusto on his aspersion of laughter,[28] routs his "seven distinct Squadrons" "of Play-oppugning authorities" by bringing forward a few great champions of another stripe, such as Montaigne,[29] develops the thesis that plays are one of the lesser means to Christian grace, suggests also that they can be defended as "publick benefits" for their many-faceted "delight" alone,[30] and asserts that the kind of Puritan who would "take upon him to be *Censor Morum, in* matters both Civil, and Ecclesiastical" is "another Montanus . . . come amongst us. . . ."[31] The publisher's explanation for the delayed issuance of *Theatrum Redivivum* is that the author feared Puritan disapproval, "knowing very well, that this late World hath been fitter for Bedlam, then for sober, and Rational Discourses," and "if he named a Stage Play, he was sure to meet with a Momus in every corner. . . ."[32] Perhaps this was the case, especially since Sir Richard was one of James I's aging knights domiciled in the debtors' haven

of the Fleet from 1635 to his death in 1645 and eking out an uncertain
livelihood by polymathic labors in the fields of translation, divinity,
and history.[33] Or maybe the true explanation lies in Sir Richard's
essential humaneness. He thought it scarcely sporting to add barbed
persiflage to mutilation.

The temper of Caroline Court Platonism as an influence more favor-
able to romance than comedy may be best defined in the early life and
work of Sir Kenelm Digby.[34] The brutal execution of his quixotic
Catholic father, Sir Everard Digby, as one of the conspirators in the
Gunpowder Plot, overshadowed Kenelm's childhood and youth with
his eccentric mother at the family estate that ironically came to be
known as Gayhurst; to the very end of his career in the early Restoration he is said to have kept close by him the letters his father wrote
from the Tower and to have read them often. Entering Oxford in 1618,
the same year as Prynne, Kenelm had special status as a Catholic and
did not stay for a degree. His student verse contains such couplets
as these:

> But by her face and gesture were expressed
> The lively image of a soul distressed.
>
> . . . . .
>
> Fame, honour, beauty, state, train, blood, and birth
> Are but the fading blossoms of the earth.
>
> . . . . .
>
> Then here I'll sit and sigh my hot love's folly,
> And learn t'affect an holy melancholy.[35]

His grand passion was the beautiful Venetia Stanley, whose mother had
long been dead and whose unhappy father, Sir Edward, sent her to live
temporarily with a relative near Gayhurst. Once they met they knew
they were destined for each other. Venetia rejoined her father at Court
and received attentions from the two Earls of Dorset, Richard and
Edward Sackville. Kenelm, touring Europe, received attentions from
Marie de' Medici, the mother of Queen Henrietta, and joined his uncle,
the first Earl of Bristol, to help with the negotiations for the marriage

of Prince Charles and the Infanta of Spain. Although these negotiations fell through, Kenelm was knighted for his service by James I and made Gentleman to the Privy Council of the Prince. Presently Sir Kenelm was to be a member of the diplomatic mission that arranged for Charles' marriage to Henrietta. Through the high junketings abroad and the personal vicissitudes that accompanied them, Sir Kenelm's devotion to Venetia persisted; she likewise remained spiritually his, even if, as rumor had it, she had many suitors and yielded physically to one or more.[36] At any rate Sir Kenelm and Venetia were secretly married early in 1625. Two years later, while he was winning for England new naval prestige and for himself a new reputation by intrepid privateering in the Mediterranean, he took time out on the island of Milo to write a prose romance about himself and Venetia with fictitious names for persons and places and a style commensurate with his purpose of exalting their mutual fidelities. He gave it the title of *Loose Fantasies;* it was not to be published until two hundred years later, in 1827, under the title of *Private Memoirs* with the omission of certain passages, long known among pornographers as "The Castrations," that one ardent Digby scholar has since made available.[37] Venetia bore Sir Kenelm five children and died in 1633. As in the case of Prynne, there are astonishing *bouleversements* in Sir Kenelm. Converted to Anglicanism in 1630, he was re-converted to Catholicism five years later and struck up a mysterious friendship with Lord Protector Cromwell in the hope of winning toleration for Catholics. In 1640 he edited Ben Jonson's *Works.* Though he was an almost incredibly credulous pursuer of the exotic, he was responsive to the influence of Hobbes and Descartes and a real force in the new science, despite his advocacy of the notorious Powder of Sympathy as a cure-all.[38] Our interest is not in this universal man or cosmopolitan virtuoso but in the lover and celebrant of Venetia.

In the *Private Memoirs* Sir Kenelm appears as Theagenes, indicating the influence on himself of Heliodorus' *Aethiopica, or Theagenes and Chariclea,* while Venetia is called Stelliana. Their story is introduced as "the perfect friendship and noble love of two generous persons, that

43

seemed to be born in this age by ordinance of heaven to teach the world anew what it hath long forgotten, the mystery of loving with honour and constancy, between a man and a woman." Divine Providence brings them together by means of the stars, "the first movers," and then guides them "by a secret working" that includes their "free actions" and ultimately circumvents fortune's "inconstant wheel." From their first meeting in childhood they are possessed by an amorous sobriety that causes them to "mingle serious kisses among their innocent sports." The persistence of their love through "long absence, the austerity of parents, other pretenders, false rumours, and other the greatest difficulties and oppositions" is described by fire imagery that recurs frequently in the narrative.

At a meeting in Corinth (London) before Theagenes' departure for Attica (France), Ionia (Italy), and Egypt (Spain), they exchange metaphysical love tokens, his for her "a diamond ring" signifying "that his heart would prove as hard as that stone in the admittance of any new affection," and hers for him "a lock of her hair . . . the splendour of which . . . seemed as though a stream of the sun's beams had been gathered together and converted into a solid substance." When Theagenes finally returns to Corinth, after the failure of the Egyptian mission, his first glimpse of Stelliana is the experience of "one come suddenly from a dark prison to too great a light," outdazzling the sun itself. Near the end of the romance Theagenes makes a thirty-one page speech to his uncle Aristobolus (the first Earl of Bristol) in defense of his grand spiritual passion. What may be called his fantastic classical romanticism emerges in his contention "that to the end a man may be happy, he ought to permit himself sometimes to be esteemed a fool."[39]

At the outset Digby stresses the tragic seriousness of the conflict in human beings between the higher and the lower self:

> . . . a perpetual civil war; the rational part striving to preserve her dignity and the superiority due to her, as being the nobler substance; and the inferior part, wherein reign the mists and clouds of various and inconstant passions, aspiring to overshadow and dim her brightness, and to range at liberty without any curb. . . .

Much later he has Theagenes' cousin Rogesilius (Robert Digby) urge him to follow Libertinism as more consonant with the activity of a man of honor than is a Platonic attachment to one woman. As the cousin puts it:

> ". . . if humanity be so forcible in you that you must pay some dues to that sex which you receive half your being from, let it be at large, and the main scope thereof your own pleasure; which certainly groweth flat by being confined to one object, and is by variety raised to his greatest height."[40]

Theagenes' reply draws a quite different distinction between these two kinds of love:

> ". . . for satiety and repentance, they are qualities not incident to spiritual actions, as I understand the fruition and joy begotten by this noble love to be for the most part; but accompanieth inseparably that gross and material enjoying which you recommend to me to extinguish or to mitigate my divine flame."[41]

A recurrent theme of the romance is the struggle of the Platonic lovers to resist the Libertine advances of others. Ursatius (probably one of the Earls of Dorset)[42] actually abducts Stelliana with the help of the bawdish governess, Faustina, who in one of "The Castrations" asserts that maids are prone to become quickly fond of their ravishers,[43] and Stelliana has to escape from the lodge where he has immured her by tying her bedsheets together to let herself down from the window and using her garters to drop over a wall from an arbor. Even Mardontius (probably the other Earl of Dorset), who rescues her from a real wolf in the wood near the lodge, proves later on to have wolfish tendencies that have to be discouraged.[44] Theagenes, in order to elude the "loose and unchaste desires" of the aging Marie de' Medici, who "felt at the first sight of him a secret love,"[45] has to quit Attica and cause to be circulated the report of his death.

Also, Platonic lovers must guard against their own Libertinism. When Theagenes is restored to Stelliana after his long tour abroad, "her excessive beauty and gracefulness did so win upon his senses" that "he attempted her to consent to his passion, and prosecuted his suit with all the vehemence and subtlety that an earnest and well ex-

45

perienced lover could use, without mention of any provision to her honour." For this loss of control and insult to her virtue, "she banished him from her presence." When she eventually readmits him, "their manner of living, each towards other, confuted the opinion of those who hold that the laws of a high and divine friendship cannot be observed where a woman hath a part."[46] A few pages further, however, there is a lengthy description of how Theagenes climbs into bed with her, gloats over her complete and glorious nudity, awakens her with his onset at rape, and is brought back to his proper Platonism only by the "grave and settled manner" of her reproof and the "sense-bereaving music" of her singing.[47]

Enter such conventional themes of Platonic romance as the rival friends and love versus honor when Theagenes self-sacrificingly but vainly urges upon Stelliana the suit of one Clericus and when, after finally marrying her himself, he leaves her temporarily for the privateering expedition that is to refute any who may charge him with "uxorious humour." On this expedition "he got a glorious victory, and gave testimony to the world, that a discreet and stayed valour is not to be resisted in what it undertaketh, although at the first sight it may seem to attempt things with much disadvantage."[48] The atmosphere thus maintained is simply too rarefied, too far moonwards, for the comic spirit to breathe. Somewhat the same atmosphere prevails in many of the masques, heroic plays, and narrative poems admired at Queen Henrietta's Court.[49]

Whenever we are tempted, however, to regard any period as no time for comedy, we should remember S. N. Behrman's play *No Time for Comedy,* written toward the end of the 1930's. Behrman had apparently concluded that the Spanish Civil War and the threat posed to men of good will by the twin tyrannies of Fascism and Communism meant a lean season for the art he had so deftly practiced. In his play he undertook to allegorize this personal conviction and predicament by presenting his hero, a New York playwright named Gaylord Esterbrook, nicknamed Gay, in throes of being lured from his actress wife Linda by Amanda Smith, a wealthy married woman with a mission. Linda is obviously the comic spirit; Amanda, described as "a Lorelei with an intellectual patter," is the spirit of ideology, the muse of propaganda. Under the spell of her humorless idealism, Gay writes a tragic drama of the Spanish Civil War and is on the point of joining the Loyalists in the role of the artist turned man of action. Linda, however, is not to be defeated, no matter how unpropitious the climate of opinion and events may be to her philosophy. She saves him from lugubrious infidelity and restores him to sanity with this shrewd comment on his and Amanda's brain-child:

> But even if it were everything you wanted it to be I still shouldn't be impressed. I am not impressed by the dead. Your hero says to the girl that in Spain he learned how to die and now he will practice what he has learned. . . . That does not impress me— that he knows how to die. Millions of people know how to die— Stoics and fanatics—the insensitive and the robots. In any case it is an art that sooner or later Nature impresses on all of us. No, the difficult thing, the admirable thing is to live. That requires ingenuity, that requires skill, that requires imagination—that is the index of civilization—the ability to live, not the ability to die. Don't spin for me fantasias of death. Imagine for me variations of life. . . .[50]

Behrman, in the very act of dramatizing his departure from Comedy, her inappropriateness to the ideological pressures of the day, had to re-instate her, to use her in exposing irrationality, to acknowledge her timeless and invincible appeal and function. Perhaps in the Caroline period, despite Puritan extremism and Court Platonism, the comic spirit was not to be gainsaid. Their very excesses, even, it may be argued, required her occasional ministrations. And other phases of Caroline society threw down gages, as it were, that her mettle forced her to take up.

The spirit of intolerance, for example, rather than being exorcised by the Puritan plea for toleration of reform within and sectarianism without the Anglican church, grew and flourished in both public and private life as sometimes an expression and at other times a partial

47

consequence of too much politico-religious or ethico-sexual zeal. Richard Brathwait, best known for his popular conduct books, *The English Gentleman* (1630) and *The English Gentlewoman* (1631), contributed ably to the literature of charactery or "characterisme," as he calls it, in *Whimzies: Or, A New Cast of Characters* (1631). Since he seeks to avoid ambiguity, embellishment, and subjectivism in this kind of writing[51] and believes in moderation as the fundamental virtue,[52] he may be used as a fairly reliable witness. Three of his sketches suggest that unwillingness to live and let live, a human failing at all times and everywhere, was especially noticeable in Caroline England in the attitude toward public entertainment and in family relations. Of "A Zealous Brother," Brathwait says: "No season through all the yeere accounts hee more subject to abbomination than *Bartholomew* faire. . . . The very *Booths* are *Brothells* of iniquity, and distinguished by the stampe of the *Beast*," and "His *devotion* consists rather in elevation of the eye, than bending of the knee." Of "A Xantippean," he observes:

> She makes such a pattring with her lips, as if she were *possest;* and so shee is with the *spirit of contention*. She is *wormewood* in *bed,* and a *Chafing-dish* at *boord*. Shee cannot possibly take *cold,* for shee is ever in a *heat*.

Of "A Jealous Neighbour," he quips: "He hath solemnly vou'd, never to take journey when either the Signe is in Aries, Taurus, or Capricorne," and "he trifles out his time in the discovery of his owne shame."[53] Another observant moralist, John Stephens, in his *New Essayes and Characters* (1631), gives this advice to fathers: "Indeede mistrust makes children disobedient. . . . It is more available then, to governe by liberalitie, not base compulsion. . . ."[54] William Gouge, in his *Of Domesticall Duties* (1622, 1626, and 1634), one of the most elaborate and systematically organized conduct books of the period, is particularly emphatic in his warning to both husbands and wives to abstain from jealousy:

> Above all they must take heed of rash and unjust jealousie, which is the bane of marriage, and greatest cause of discontent that can

48

be given betwixt man and wife. Jealous persons are ready to picke quarrels, and to seeke occasions of discord: they will take every word, looke, action, and motion, in the worse part, and so take offence where none is given. When jealousie is once kindled, it is as a flaming fire that can hardly be put out. It maketh the partie whom it possesseth implacable.[55]

The acquisitive spirit, another universal human failing, with the many evils that usually accompany it, took a new lease on life, according to the best modern scholarship in economics and sociology, during the period when the transition from medieval feudalism to modern capitalism was in its mercantilist stage.[56] Since Caroline England came at the very middle of this stage, it saw no slackening but rather a full garner of all those expressions of the acquisitive spirit known to the Elizabethan-Jacobean world. Probably writing in 1641, on the eve of the Civil Wars, Henry Peacham, author of *The Compleat Gentleman* (1622), well summarized the situation in his *The Worth of a Penny, or a Caution to Keep Money:*

> Whosoever wanteth money is ever subject to contempt and scorn in the world, let him be furnished with never so good gifts, either of body or of mind. . . . In these days we may say with the wise man: My son, better it is to die than to be poor, for now money is the world's god, and the card which the devil turns up trump to win the set withall. . . . *Pecunia omnia obediunt:* hence it is so admired that millions venture both souls and bodies for the possession of it.[57]

In the years just before Charles I's accession, three memorable events underscored the tyranny of Pecunia. Lord Chancellor Bacon was fined, imprisoned, and deprived of high office for taking bribes. Sir Francis Mitchell and Sir Giles Mompesson were charged and found guilty of abusing the patents or monopolies for alehouses and inns respectively that the King had granted them.[58] Between 1620 and 1624 the country was in the throes of a great depression, whose effects have thus been sketched:

> Markets and fairs were sparsely attended, prices for cattle and wool were low, weavers and agricultural labourers were out of

work. There was necessarily a great increase in pauperism; and, as the crisis developed, there were "mutinies" of the unemployed. At Bath, for instance, the clothiers were "much decayed," and many of the weavers were being supported by the city. In Gloucester, by 1622, the trade was described as "growing worse and worse." The local authorities were unable to relieve "the infinite number" of those out of work. Many of these "were in case to starve as their faces did manifest, and they so far oppressed those parts, wherein they lived, that the abler sort of people there were not able longer to maintain the same." Cloth-makers, who kept their looms running, only paid the weavers ls. a week in 1622; and, even under these conditions, the work was carried on at a loss, since in some districts cloth was "almost valueless." Bankruptcies were multiplying. . . .[59]

The feverish activities of joint stock-companies and other private enterprise groups became so common that Roger Williams in his *The Bloudy Tenent of Persecution,* published in London in 1644, could use them as a precedent to argue that the fervent dissensions of religious sects pursuing salvation were harmless to the unity of the well-ordered commonwealth:

> The church, or company of worshippers, whether true or false, is like unto a body or college of physicians in a city, like unto a corporation, society, or company of East India or Turkey merchants, or any other society or company in London; which companies may hold their courts, keep their records, hold disputations, and in matters concerning their society may dissent, divide, break into schisms and factions, sue and implead each other at the law, yea, wholly break up and dissolve into pieces and nothing, and yet the peace of the city not be in the least measure impaired or disturbed. . . .[60]

The usurer thrived, hit off thus by another writer of charactery, Wye Salstonstall, in his *Picturae Loquentes* (1631):

> . . . he's one that makes haste to be rich, and therefore cannot be innocent. Like thieves he undoes men by binding them. And lastly his estate is raised out of the ruin of whole families, which first sends him in ill getting it, and afterward his son in ill spending it, both to the devil; and there I leave them.[61]

The gamester found his victims in ordinaries; Brathwait says of him: "Hee remembers God more in *Oaths* than in *Orisons,*" and "The Ordinarie is his Oratorie, where hee preyes upon the Countrey-gull to feede himselfe."[62] The well-staffed brothel was another means of getting rich. For example, on the Bankside, within sight of the Globe, the Hope, and the Swan theaters, a Mrs. Holland operated a brothel known as "Holland's Leaguer" that apparently prospered.[63] Nicholas Goodman, in his pamphlet of 1632 describing it, remarks:

> But *Lust* is a *Gangrene,* & having once poisoned a member, never leaves spreading till the whole body be confounded, She hath now broken one linke in the golden chaine of *Chastity,* and she cares not though all the rest be molten with confusion; hence it com's that she entertaines more devils, variety is pleasant, one ship yelds small custome, great *Navies* fil large treasures, & her revenues came in with such full Tydes, that false Pleasure made her beleeve there would never come ebbing.[64]

Alchemists, astrologers, projectors, monopolists, news-mongers, fortune-hunters in marriage, and other rogues continued to ply their schemes for gain.[65] If we follow closely the diary of Sir Humphrey Mildmay, a Royalist gentleman who after July 3, 1633, at the age of forty-one, began recording his experiences in London, we get some sense of how the acquisitive spirit of the age affected the daily vices, follies, and drolleries of one individual. His favorite spots were the Royal Exchange in Cornhill and the New Exchange in the Strand. He squandered money on "the wanton nurse at Mrs. Langborne's," "two bawds," and a "shee friend," and in excessive drinking with such boon companions as Captain Cranley and John Skepham. He involved himself in frequent lawsuits, bestowing the epithets "knave" and "rascal" on his opponents. A connoisseur of proceedings at the criminal courts and of executions at Tyburn and Gray's Inn Lane end, he felt compassion for cutpurses along with husband poisoners, ordinary murderers, and ravishers.[66]

The spirit of affectation, another universal human failing widespread in the Elizabethan-Jacobean world, was even more alive in Caroline

England. Yeomen climbed into the country gentry; this gentry mingled with the wealthier citizens of the country towns; London set the standard in fashions, manners, prices; and the Court constituted a coterie for rich townspeople to imitate.[67] Charles I, like his father, "created peerages wholesale." In fact, one of the expressions of the acquisitive spirit was the selling of peerages; it was charged against Buckingham in his impeachment "that he frightened a West Country gentleman into paying him £10,000 for a barony." Godfrey Davies, in his *The Early Stuarts,* dissents somewhat from Pym's denunciation of this practice:

> Selling peerages had one indirect advantage: it prevented the house of lords from being based solely on blue blood or real estate and, by opening a place for the *nouveau riche,* gave the middle classes representation.[68]

Such social stratification permitting and even encouraging a limited mobility had the effect of inspiring individuals in all walks of life to appear other than they were, to ape the ways of gentlemen and gentlewomen.

The conduct books sought to improve their conception of these ways. Brathwait, for example, draws this portrait of the true gentleman:

> . . . a Man himselfe, without the addition of either Taylor, Millener, Seamster or Haberdasher. . . . A Crest displayes his house, but his owne actions expresse himselfe. . . . *Education* hee holds a *second Nature;* which (such innate seeds of goodness are sowne in him) ever improves him, seldome or never depraves him. *Learning* he holds not only an additament, but ornament to Gentry. . . . He eyes the *Court* with a vertuous and noble contemplation; and disvalues him most, whose *sense* consists in *sent.* . . . For honest pleasures, he is neither so *Stoicall* as wholly to contemne them, nor so *Epicureall* as too sensually to affect them. . . . A true and generous Moderation of his affections, hath begot in him an absolute command and conquest of himselfe.[69]

In his companion sketch of the true gentlewoman he emphasizes comely rather than gaudy apparel, "loving modesty" in behavior, admission only of the kind of compliment not affected by the age, and such qualities as decency, "estimation," fancy, gentility, and honour.[70] While providing patterns for both sexes, however, he is careful to point out that these diverge considerably from the prevailing actuality.

There are too many pseudo and would-be gentlemen about. Among these he includes "our *Ordinary Gentlemen*" who "leave their beds, to put on their cloathes formally, repaire to an *Ordinary,* and see a *Play* daily. These can finde time enough for *Recreation,* but not a minutes space for *Devotion*." He also cites "many of our younger brood of gentry":

> . . . either for want of Education in Learning, or their owne neglect of Learning, [they] have no sooner attained to the strength of making their fist a Pearch for a *Hawke,* but by the helpe of some bookes of faulconry, whereby they are instructed in the words of Art, they will run division upon discourse of this pleasure: whereas, if at any time they be interrupted by occasion of some other conference, these *High-flyers* are presently to be *mewed* up, for they are taken from their Element.[71]

Elsewhere, he says of the tavern ruffian: "Hee hath ranked himselfe with a troope of shallow uncivile Shallops . . . whose chiefest valour consists in braves, scru'd faces, desperate mouchato's, new-minted Oaths"; and of the traveller: ". . . to accomodate himselfe all the better for this giddy age wherein hee lives, hee culls out some humorous Observance or other from every Countrey, to make his fruitless freight more valued, himselfe more admired, and his returne more accepted." He thus expands the latter portrait:

> He can moulde himself to all conditions, fashions & religions. But in all these three hee returnes for most part, far worse than before he went forth. In the *first* he ha's learn'd to be loose & lascivious; in the *second,* phantastically humorous; in the *third,* strangely superstitious.[72]

Amongst this plethora of false wits, it is difficult for the true gentleman to find worthy friends and acquaintants, such "as are neither Timists

nor Timonists, Fawners nor Frowners." Men everywhere have become
pretenders furthering their own ends:

> In the *Court* we shall find smooth and sweet-sented *friends*, who
> make friendship a complement, and vow themselves ours in
> Protests, Congres, and Salutes: but whereto tend they, but to
> winde us in, and so become engaged for them? . . . Too precious
> are these mens *Acquaintance*, and too heavie their engagements;
> let us therefore turne from them, and travell towards the *Cittie*.
> And what shall we finde there, but many dangerous and subtill
> *friends*. . . . We are therefore to seeke further, and descend to the
> *Countrey*, where we likest to finde them. Yet see, the generall
> infection of the Age![73]

Women, according to Brathwait, are not much better. The spirit of
affectation has corrupted them as well, in the same three social worlds:

> Fashion is now ever under saile: the Invention ever teeming;
> Phantasticke Wits ever breeding. More time spent how to *abuse*
> time, and corrupt licentious youth, than how to address employ-
> ment for the one, or to rectifie the distempers of the other. Take
> a survey of all degrees, and tell me what uniformity you finde in
> this particular. And to make instance in three severall places (for
> to these all others may have proper relation) take a more precise
> and punctuall perusall of *City, Court,* and *Countrey,* and returne
> me a briefe of your Survey. In the *first,* you shall finde many grave
> Matrons, modest Maids, devout Widdowes; but are these all?
> No; with these you shall finde a strangely mixt generation. Some
> affecting nothing more than what is most novell and phantasticke;
> Others envying what they disdainfully see in others, which
> fashion rather that they will misse, they will not sticke to set their
> honour at sale: All, or most, true Biantines, carrying all their
> wealth about them. For the *second,* you shall find, amongst many
> other plants of promising growth and excellent proficience, sundry
> sweet-sented sprigs of Cynnamon, whose rinde is worth all the
> body. No discourse can rellish their formall palate, but fashion;
> if *Eves* Kirtle should be now showne them, how they would geere
> their Grandam? For the *last,* though it be long ere they creepe
> into forme, having once attain'd it, they can take upon them as
> unbeseeming a State in a Countrey Pew, as if they were Ladies for

that yeare, and had beene bred in the Art of mincing since their childhood.

Perhaps his most memorable comment on feminine affectation is this one:

> See our compleatest *Fashionmongers,* how much they tyre them-
> selves with their attiring, how they trouble themselves with their
> trimming! It seemes wonderfull to me, that they are not wholly
> crushed, with that onerous burthen with which they are pressed.
> What a shop of guga trifles hang upon one backe? Here the
> remainder of a greater worke, the reliques of an ancient Mannor
> converted to a pearle Chaine. There the moity of an ill-husbanded
> demaine reduced to a Carknet. Long traines must sweepe away
> long acres: the Epidemicall vanity of this age doth exact it; and
> shee is held least worthy affecting, that doth least affect it.[74]

Other contemporary writers support Brathwait in his didacticism and add vivid details to his survey of types and manners. John Stephens, for example, has these quite definite notions about the true gentleman, whom he calls "A Complete Man":

> His religion, learning, and behaviour, hold a particular cor-
> respondence: He commands the latter, whilst himselfe and both
> be commanded by the first. . . . He seemes willingly to seeke
> acquaintance with vice and with temptation, meaning to allure it,
> til, without suspition, he may soone disrobe and disarme it. . . .

Commenting on "My Mistresse," he is uncertain whether she is a true or a pseudo lady: she is *"a Magicke glasse:* in which you may discerne vanities of the *world,* her selfe, and other *women.* She is a most intricate female text. . . ." The pseudo gentleman or wit appears under the label, "A Ubiquitary":

> Talke of Academies and hee rels you Court-newes: search into the
> estate of a question, and he tels you what new booke is extant. . . .
> In his behaviour he would seeme French, Italian, Spanish, or any
> thing, so he may seeme un-vulgar; accounting it barbarous not to
> contemne his owne nation, or the common good, because he loves
> to bee more valued by seeming singularly pretious. . . .

The would-be gentleman or wit is called "A weake-brain'd Gull." For him, "a round oath is valour enough, a foolish Dittie Art enough, and good fellowshippe honesty enough." "He studies a new fashion by the six months together, and reades *Albertus Magnus,* or *Aristotles Problems* in English, with admiration"; "fooles of his owne fashion praise him, for a *witty Gentleman,* or a *gentlemanly Fellow.*"[75]

A witness from the country, Edmund Cobbes, in his collection of sermons, *Mundanum Speculum, or, The Worldlings Looking Glasse* (1630), takes occasion to use the topic of "pride in apparell" as springboard for a garrulous plunge into general social criticism:

> But I may spare my labour to say much in this licentious age of this point; because men and women are fallen into such an excesse of bravery, whereby all respect of order and degree is neglected; for whereas Christ restrained gorgious apparell to Kings Pallaces, now it is grown so common, that we may see it in every house almost; which comes to passe because everie one is so farre fallen in love with himselfe, either for his person, qualities, or apparell, which are so excellent in their owne eyes, that a poore mans wife will bee as fine as a gentlemans, and in all places we shall see pride ruffle in Rustickes, for every one will be in the fashion how ever they come by it; the servant can hardly bee knowne from the Master, and the maide from the Mistres, nor scarce any mans estate can be distinguished by his apparell, but plaine Coridon that hath no more wit then to know the price of Satten, and Silkes, and Taffeties, and other toyes, to make him foole-fine, cannot longer be content to hold the plough, and to be one of these good Common-wealths-men which keepe good hospitality; and spend their wealth moderately, doing good in the places where they dwell, but being advanced in wealth by the death of his miserable father, must instantly bee dubbed gentleman, and purchase Armes though it be at a deare rate, and be a smoaky gallant in his youth, though hee begge his bread in his age, and thinke hee is no-body unlesse he bee out of the fashion, and can swagger, and brave it out, sweare himselfe into smoake, with pure refined oathes, and fustian protestations, and take Tobacco with a whiffe, and so lash out that riotously, which his father got miserly, but hee is now a gentleman, therefore hee will not take it as he hath done, nor will hee bee clad any longer

in good cloath, but will creepe into acquaintance with Sattens,
Velvets, and Plush, too high and costly for his meane conditions.
And country maides that have but thirty or forty shillings a yeare,
and a few base shifts, must be trick't and trim'd up like a Maid-
Mayrian in a Morris dance; sometime her Ruffes are pinned up
to her eares, and sometime they hang over her shoulders like a
windmill sayle fluttering about her eares.

If Cobbes is to be accepted as a reliable witness, the spirit of affectation
has played havoc not only with the classes and the sexes but also with
the age-groups. Even old men have become problems in this changing
and immoral time:

> Old age is honourable if it be found in the wayes of righteous-
> nesse; but if old men be found in the wayes of sinne, ignorance,
> and prophanenesse, oh how dishonorable are those gray hayres!
> what, an old man a swearer! an old man a Drunkard! an old
> man a Gamester! an old man a Lyar! an old man a Whore-
> master! an old man an ignorant man! oh what a shame is this!
> . . . It is said of Ephraim, that gray hayres were upon him, yet
> he knew it not; he had markes of death upon his face, and hayre,
> yet would still be young; and what was said of Ephraim may
> justly bee said of many old men in our dayes. . . .[76]

One curious working of the spirit of affectation was that Court
Platonism and the Libertinism it sought to restrain were both reflected
on the citizen and yeoman level, where Puritanism had already done
much to promote an idealistic single standard of sexual morality. If
some citizens' and yeomen's wives and daughters bartered their virtue
to dress fashionably and pass themselves off as grand ladies, thus
furthering the Libertinism that the double standard of sexual morality
assumed men were prone to before marriage and must be indulged in
then and even later, other women of these classes observed in their
conduct a strict chastity that they also exacted of their husbands and
suitors, and were sometimes as resourceful as the Stellianas of romance
in thwarting the amorous designs of Ursatiuses, Mardontiuses, and
even Theageneses of their own walk of life and superior social circles.
This is the phenomenon that Brathwait has in mind when he contrasts

the grave, modest, and devout with "a strangely mixt generation," the "plants of promising growth" with the "sprigs of Cynnamon." It also accounts for Stephens' ambiguity in the portrayal of "My Mistresse." In other words, the new woman was emergent, who was content no longer to be the mere pawn of man's possessiveness and sexuality but who cultivated a wit capable of resisting and punishing his Libertine advances, manipulating them to get herself a husband, or so curing them as to deter and diminish concupiscence and foster "the ends of mariage."[77] Mathew Griffith, in his *Bethel: Or, A forme for families* (1634), thus defined the former:

> Then know that this *concupiscence* is the *fire* of hell, whose fuell is *gluttony,* whose *flame* is *pride,* whose *sparkes* are *evill* communications, whose *smoke* is *infamy,* whose *ashes* are *uncleannesse.* It is the *bodies tempest,* the *Soules bawd,* the *shipwrack* of *chastity,* the *cancker-worme* of *good purposes, reason's leaprosie, earth's burthen, the mother* of *shame,* and the *shame* of the *mother.*[78]

William Gouge, in defining "the ends of mariage" in his *Of Domesti-call Duties,* listed as one of them "that men might avoid fornication . . . and possesse their vessels in holinesse and honour," praised marriage "as an haven to such as are in jeopardy of their salvation through the gusts of temptations to lust," and admitted that "of all the children of *Adam* that ever were, not one to a million of those that have come to ripenesse of yeares have beene true *Eunuches* all their life time."[79]

Confronted by the spirit of intolerance, the acquisitive spirit, the spirit of affectation, and this curious new liveliness in the relations between the sexes on the level of ordinary life, the Sons of Ben and their fellow dramatists could not very well abstain from writing comedy. For all these aspects of Caroline England were a definite challenge to an art concerned with the antithesis between Titania and Bottom, exploiting both the shrewd asininities and spiritual fatuities of human nature, laughing its audiences toward the sane society and the sane self. Even though potent forces were astir to relegate Thalia to the pillory or the closet, there was still time for her in the halls and on the boards.

CHAPTER
TWO

Thalia's Double Image

*A*lert to Thalia's danger, two of the Sons
of Ben held up full-length images of her to dispel doubts of her
sovereign virtues. In Thomas Randolph's *The Muses' Looking Glass,*
first performed at Cambridge, shown in London in 1630 as *The Entertainment,* and published under its present title in 1638,[1] she is an
erudite gay beadle with a mirror. In Richard Brome's *The Antipodes,*
composed in 1637 and first acted at the Salisbury Court playhouse in
1638,[2] she is a rollicking hoyden from a cloud-cuckoo topsy-turvydom.
As comedies primarily about the art of comedy, each presenting a
crowded, many-actioned play within a play, these are unique in the
drama of the period[3] and deserve detailed comparative study for their
richly schematic craft and live literary theory.

The basic situations of these two plays are similar: a comedy, introduced, presided over, and occasionally explicated by a master of
ceremonies, is enacted before spectators whose reactions are likewise
dramatized as a principal theme. Indebtedness for this basic situation
to Elizabethan, Jacobean, and earlier Caroline plays employing ex-

positors on the stage, or containing a play within a play, is obvious and need not be labored. Jonson's *Every Man Out of His Humour* (1599), Beaumont's *The Knight of the Burning Pestle* (1607), Massinger's *The Roman Actor* (1626), and Ford's *The Lover's Melancholy* (1628) are the closest analogues and most probable sources.[4] Randolph and Brome differ notably, however, both from their predecessors and from each other, in the nature of their fictitious spectators and masters of ceremonies and in the substance of each inset performance looked at as a whole. As for the theories they are seeking to convey about the art of comedy, these are unlike but complementary and go quite beyond Jonson or any other earlier English dramatist in speculative fullness and thoroughness of demonstration.

The chief spectators of Randolph's *The Muses' Looking Glass* are two Puritan extremists violently prejudiced against playhouses and plays. Both are shop-keepers and artisans, such as resided in Black-friars.[5] One is Bird, a feather-man, whose ware consists of feathers of his own making. The other is Mistress Flowerdew, the wife of a haberdasher, and her ware consists of pins and looking-glasses. From the player Roscius, who is to be master of ceremonies, they have received orders for their respective wares and are delivering these in person. Only in pursuit of their "callings" would it be probable they would ever enter the playhouse.

Approaching it, they discuss theaters in such a way as to reveal Randolph's understanding of the theological premises behind the Puritan extremist's opposition to drama and the stage. To Mistress Flowerdew, plays are "works of vanity" and playgoers are "the wicked throng" and "the lewd reprobate," in other words, the damned, who have no infusion of God's grace. To Bird, theaters are "shops of Satan." Just as Prynne at the beginning of *Histrio-Mastix* was to associate increase in playbooks and playgoers with increase in the time's iniquity, so Bird and Mistress Flowerdew agree that the boom in playhouses is a manifestation of the persistent flourishing of "bad

works." They further agree that the tendency of one theater to beget
another is a consequence of theaters having become more obscene and
that this multiplying process is an evil comparable to "flat fornication."
Mistress Flowerdew's remark—

> Iniquity aboundeth, though pure zeal
> Teach, preach, huff, puff and snuff at it,
> Still it aboundeth. . . .—

is an unconscious admission of the futility of fanatical reform. Her
inability to draw such an inference from the fact she is citing serves to
characterize the Puritan mind as invulnerable to discouragement in the
armor of its assurance. Her further remark—

> . . . Had we seen a church,
> A new-built church, erected north and south,
> It had been something worth the wondering at.—

is Randolph's way of suggesting that the Puritan's imperturbability
before what he regards as the lethargy of human goodness rests on
moral cynicism, the assumption that evil is predestined to have more
vitality. When Bird says that "good works are done," and Mistress
Flowerdew replies,

> I say no works are good;
> Good works are merely popish and apocryphal,

Randolph underscores his point that the Puritans are moral cynics and
at the same time stresses their ultimate dependence on God's grace and
Scripture as the way to virtue.

To both Bird and Mistress Flowerdew he attributes the kind of
aesthetic naiveté that is unable to distinguish between the subject-matter
and the dramatist's attitude toward that subject-matter. Their remarks
shows that Randolph thought of this naiveté as due to inexperience of
the theater and to such literalism of mind as children exhibit when
they mistake fiction for fact, the world of make-believe for the world
of actuality. For example, Bird says to Mistress Flowerdew:

The Sons of Ben

> . . . I have heard
> That in a tragedy—I think they call it,
> They make no more of killing one another
> Than you sell pins.

And Mistress Flowerdew replies:

> Or you sell feathers, brother;
> But are they not hang'd for't?

Bird's real animus, however, like Prynne's, is against comedy. He contends that the comedies of the period abuse ordinary respectable folk like himself and Mistress Flowerdew, that these folk cannot carry on any of their usual activities, such as lending money, or trading in "false wares," or keeping their wives better dressed than some, "but our ghosts must walk upon their stages." Mistress Flowerdew's reply to this speech—

> Is not this flat conjuring
> To make our ghosts to walk ere we be dead?—

emphasizes Puritan literalism and superstition to the point of caricature. Bird then proceeds to condemn comedy on the ground that its subject-matter is worldly and also comic actors because they perform their roles for gain:

> That's nothing, Mistress Flowerdew: they will play
> The knave, the fool, the devil and all, for money.

Whereupon Mistress Flowerdew falls back on the premises of Puritan theology to express her amazed indignation:

> Impiety! O, that men endu'd with reason
> Should have no more grace in them!

Bird and Mistress Flowerdew are also unable to distinguish between causes and effects. They are convinced, as was Prynne, that the sins of society are traceable to plays and playhouses. This point, however, they have not had the wit to think out for themselves. Mistress Flowerdew repeats it from a sermon she has heard:

62

Thalia's Double Image

> I have heard our vicar
> Call playhouses the colleges of transgression,
> Wherein the seven deadly sins are studied.

And Bird replies:

> Why, then, the city will, in time, be made
> An university of iniquity.

After Mistress Flowerdew has quoted "a zealous prayer" she "heard a brother make concerning playhouses," the substance of which is that all should be destroyed, she becomes suddenly aware of the discrepancy between what she has been saying and her present errand:

> Indeed it something pricks my conscience
> I come to sell 'em pins and looking glasses.

For her scruples, Bird has a ready answer:

> 'Tis fit that we, which are sincere professors,
> Should gain by infidels.

Thus Randolph directs his satire against the kind of rationalization by which the spirit of intolerance compromises with the acquisitive spirit.[6]

After Bird and Mistress Flowerdew have delivered their wares to Roscius, they try to convert him. Losing patience, he castigates them for their own pluming of folly and decking of vainglory through the trades they follow. To educate them, he insists they remain to see the play and offers to expound its purport. They justify their consent on the ground that here is a new temptation against which they should show the force of their zeal and their contemptuous defiance of Satan and "his engines."[7] As the play progresses, their emotions ebb and flow. Alternately angered by its subject-matter, and mollified by Roscius' learned commentary, they eventually undergo a drastic change in their conception of comedy. As Bird, speaking for both himself and Mistress Flowerdew, expresses it:

> Hereafter I will visit comedies,
> And see them oft; they are good exercises!
> I'll teach devotion now a milder temper;

63

Not that it shall lose any of her heat
Or purity, but henceforth shall be such
As shall burn bright, although not blaze so much.[8]

The chief spectators of Brome's *The Antipodes* consist of a country family, the Joylesses, and three hangers-on of the wealthy Lord Letoy, who acts as master of ceremonies at his fine London house. The Joylesses, as their name indicates, are a sad lot. Old Joylesse is so insanely jealous of his young wife, Diana, that he is a prime example of the spirit of intolerance in domestic relations. Joylesse's son, Peregrine, is a would-be wit who has been driven out of what wits he had by too much reading of travel literature—too much Mandeville. In consequence he has never had sexual relations with his wife, Martha, to whom he has been married for three years. So long a period of sexual deprivation, not even titillated by attentions that can be described as Platonic, has put Martha into what Robert Burton, in *The Anatomy of Melancholy* (1621), called a "love-melancholy":[9] she is indeed, to use one of Digby's youthful lines, "the lively image of a soul distressed."[10] Letoy's hangers-on consist of Dr. Hughball, who is interested in curing Peregrine; Blaze, an expert on heraldry and genealogy, who emblazons coats of arms or ensigns armorial; and Blaze's wife, Barbara. Diana Joylesse and Barbara Blaze are two entirely different types of women. Whereas Diana, despite her husband's jealously, is fundamentally virtuous and anxious to cure him without sacrificing her chastity, Barbara turned sexual rebel under Blaze's constant suspicions, bore two bastards, has by now reduced him to the despicable complacency of a wittol, and continues to multiply his antlers, with Libertine Dr. Hughball as her latest partner in concupiscence.[11] Lord Letoy has been touched, as his name implies, with the spirit of affectation. He keeps actor-servants and writes and produces plays and masques to be fashionable. He has also employed Blaze to provide him with a sufficiently ancient lineage and all the bearings that go with it.[12] Yet, though labeled "Phantasticke," he is not merely a pseudo; his delight in good plays and his shrewd craftsman's views of acting are probably Brome's own.[13] Furthermore he has an overruling design to cure Joylesse's jealousy for the sake of Diana, who is actually his own long put-by daughter; carries this design out with considerable skill; and, in explaining his motives, reveals moral wisdom learned from bitter experience years ago.[14]

The central problem of the play, however, is the cure of Peregrine's demented romanticism so that he can fullfill his obligations as a husband and thus in turn cure Martha's quite different type of melancholy. It is to cure him that Letoy has his actor-servants perform the play-within-the-play. When Dr. Hughball tells Peregrine about its Mandevillian setting as if it were an actuality rather than make-believe, Peregrine is moved to moonstruck laughter and cannot hear enough about so delightful a place. Arrived at Letoy's and believing he is really in another and golden London, he is ready to agree with Byplay, Letoy's servant, that the only virtue is here.[15] But as the comic scenes unfold, his reactions wax from perturbation to violence. He wanders into the tiring room, plays Don Quixote with the monsters and puppets stored there, imagines that he is King of the play's world by right of conquest, and sets out

> . . . to governe
> With purpose to reduce the manners
> Of this country to his owne. . . .

At one point he cries,

> Can men and women be so contrary
> In all that we hold proper to each sex?

and indulges in this rueful reflection:

> 'Twill aske long time and study to reduce
> Their manners to our government.[16]

At another point he exclaims: "Will you make me mad?" Finally he denounces the laws of this ideal land as "Abhominable, horrid!" and threatens to hang all his subjects. When his wife is presented to him as one of them, he will perform the long-postponed consummation of his nuptials only after he is assured that she is not one

65

. . . of that serpentine generation
That stings oft times to death, as Mandeville writes.

As Diana points out to Joylesse, the doctor's use of Letoy's play

. . . has shifted your sonnes knowne disease
Of madnesse into folly, and has wrought him
As farre short of a competent reason as
He was of late beyond it. . . .[17]

But she further explains that this has been a necessary step in his complete cure, and this cure is presently accomplished. Letoy's comedy can take much of the credit. Its ingenuities have brought Peregrine back to reality and ultimately to Martha, as surely as those of Roscius' play have overcome the prejudices of Bird and Mistress Flowerdew. In other words, two diverse idealisms flagrantly out of hand, one pock-marked by intolerance and the other spawned by affectation, have yielded respectively to Thalia the beadle and Thalia the hoyden.

I stress the beadle quality of Randolph's final image of Thalia in *The Muses' Looking Glass* because the play Roscius presents and expounds is a "comicall satyre"—the term Jonson invented to describe some of his best early comedies—[18] rather than comedy in the usual sense. It has too much "porch" in its preliminary matter. Its first pre-prolog skit, involving business with a couple of Mistress Flowerdew's looking-glasses between Roscius and a "Deformed Fellow," is a refutation of the Puritan extremist's view of the relationship between comedy and actuality.[19] The second pre-prolog skit is a brilliant hodge-podge portraying the Muses of Comedy and Tragedy in debate, then their attendants—"brother beadle" Satire and "manlike-monkey Mime"—exchanging defenses, followed by a dance of the Seven Deadly Sins, and ending with Roscius' prolog. It is noteworthy that Satire is the "beadle" and is an attendant on Tragedy rather than Thalia. But since Thalia and Tragedy declare a truce and agree, in Tragedy's words, to "join whips together" "that vice may bleed," it is to be understood that Satire, Tragedy's attendant, who is directed by Mime

66

to prepare the masque of the Sins, is very much involved in the spirit of what is to follow.[20] This is borne out by Roscius' prolog, which says of the author and the play-within-the-play proper, employing the customary apologetic self-depreciation:

> . . . he brings you
> No plot at all, but a mere Olla Podrida,
> A medley of ill-plac'd and worse-penn'd humours.
> His desire was in single scenes to show
> How comedy presents each single vice
> Ridiculous; whose number, as their character,
> He borrows from the man to whom he owes
> All the poor skill he has, great Aristotle.[21]

The intention here announced is carried out with a vengeance. The *Nicomachean Ethics* is translated into *picturae loquentes,* or speaking pictures, by the device of having the excesses and deficiencies that represent deviations from Aristotle's golden mean virtues appear in pairs in most of the scenes. This means twenty-four personified vices[22] in more than a dozen scenes, with Roscius pointing up the contrast each pair entails. Since many of these so-called vices are also follies, the resulting "comicall satyre" goes considerably beyond ethical allegory and has a full social dimension, with recurrent vivid reference to even the lighter aspects of contemporary life. The effect is that of a dramatized book of charactery by Overbury or Earle, Brathwait or Salstonstall or Stephens, although most of the vices or follies have Greek names derived from Aristotle's words for them.

Colax or Flattery is contrasted with Dyscolus or Quarrelsomeness in the opening scene. As Roscius explains:

> The first that we present are the extremes of a virtue necessary in our conversation, called Comitas or courtesy, which, as all other virtues, hath her deviations from the mean. The one Colax, that to seem over-courteous, falls into a servile flattery; the other (as fools fall into the contraries which they shun) is Dyscolus who, hating to be a slavish parasite, grows into peevishness and impertinent distaste.[23]

The Sons of Ben

Colax is a voluble hanger-on of the elderly eccentric Dyscolus. In order
to win the esteem of Dyscolus, he flatters him in divers ways, but every
bit of flattery merely succeeds in affecting Dyscolus à rebours. The
contrast is similar to the one Brathwait draws between Timists and
Timonists.

Randolph violates Aristotle's order in treating Flattery and Quarrelsomeness at the outset,[24] but he is justified by considerations of dramatic
technique. Colax remains on the stage and flatters each of the other
characters introduced, making each believe that his particular vice or
folly is a virtue. In praising every character embodying an excess, he
decries the corresponding deficiency, and vice versa. He thus serves as
a kind of supplementary expositor to Roscius, with the important difference that he is a participant in the scenes rather than an outsider looking on. This use of Colax in *The Muses' Looking Glass* is probably
derived from Jonson's use of Macilente or Envy in *Every Man Out of
His Humour,* but in ingenuity and irony surpasses it.[25]

The presentation of the remaining eleven pairs of characters does not
require detailed analysis. With Roscius introducing them and Colax
flattering each in turn, they file across the stage in scene after scene,
constituting a pageant of ironic dichotomies, a classical morality play
anticipating modern vaudeville. Aphobus or Foolhardiness frightens
with his "tall" talk the quavering Deilus, who is Cowardice, both deviations from the virtue Fortitude or Courage.[26] One is reminded of
Brathwait's tavern ruffian and Stephens' "weake-brain'd Gull." Acolastus or Licentiousness expounds his desire to experience all manner of
sensuous delights, much to the disgust of Anaisthetus or Insensibility,
the former representing the excess and the latter the deficiency of the
virtue Temperance.[27] Thus an insatiable Libertine grossly in thrall to
the acquisitive spirit, like Jonson's Sir Epicure Mammon in *The Alchemist,*[28] might shock an ascetic or an anchorite. The excess of Prodigality
and the deficiency of Illiberality—deviations from the virtue Liberality—are contrasted in an argument between an old miser Aneleuth-
erus and his spendthrift son Asotus.[29] Here are Cobbes' "plaine
Coridon" and his "miserable father" as well as several of Jonson's

68

characters.[30] The excess Vulgarity versus the deficiency Meanness, both deviations from the virtue Magnificence, are hit off in the characters of Banausus, a statesman with an exhibitionist flair for lavish and unnecessary charities, and Microprepes, a churchwarden who insists on an absurdly rigorous economy in the administration of church affairs. Both have value as commentaries on the curious interplay of the spirit of affectation and the acquisitive spirit. The extremes of the virtue Magnanimity or Highmindedness contradict one another in the persons of Chaunus, a carpenter whose desire to be a privy-councillor ridicules the excess Vanity, and Micropsychus, whose inferiority complex about the performance of his duties in the relatively minor and undemanding office of constable castigates the deficiency Littlemindedness. The excess Passionateness and the deficiency Impassivity, both extremes of Meekness or Gentleness or Mansuetude, react against each other as Orgylus heaps profuse and insulting billingsgate on Aorgus, who simply refuses to show anger. The relation of the excess Boastfulness to the deficiency Irony as deviations from the virtue Truth is exemplified in the exaggerated claims to valor and learning made by Alazon versus the self-depreciation of the slyly contemptuous Eiron. The excess Ambition versus the deficiency Lack of Ambition, deviations from a virtue that Aristotle fails to name, along with the excess Bashfulness versus the deficiency Shamelessness, deviations from the virtue Modesty, are exploited respectively in a group of four characters linked together in two scenes: Philotimia, a pseudo lady who prides herself on her dress and toilet; Luparius, her husband, who has so little social ambition that he prefers to be an abominable sloven; Kataplectus, a timid scholar who becomes tongue-tied when he attempts to pay adulterous court to Philotimia; and the bawd Anaiskyntia, Kataplectus' aunt, who had procured him to satisfy Philotimia's Libertinism.[31]

Randolph's one important departure from the list of excesses, deficiences, and virtues in the *Nicomachean Ethics* occurs when he substitutes two whimsical justices, Nimis and Nihil, with their clerks Plus and Parum, representing extreme deviations from true justice,[32] for characters who might have illustrated envy and malice, the respective excess and deficiency for the virtue righteous indignation. And this departure, it is worth noting, is justified by Aristotle's further exposition of his list and his admission elsewhere that envy and malice do not fit very well into his ethical schema.[33]

The last pair of characters are Agroicus, or Clownishness, and Bomolochus, or Scurrility, the former the deficiency and the latter the excess of the virtue wittiness or urbanity. Here are the old lack-witted wiseacre from the country and the city scandal-monger. They are given separate scenes[34] so that Flattery, after gagging Scurrility, can announce his own reformation and thus prepare for the closing masque, wherein Golden Mediocrity herself introduces a dance of eleven Virtues, Modesty and Aristotle's unnamed virtue being merged into one masquer.[35]

The dialogue between Roscius and Bird about this dance of the Virtues deserves quotation:

> *Bird.* I hope there be no cardinal-virtues there!
> *Ros.* There be not.
> *Bird.* Then I'll stay. I hate a virtue
> That will be made a cardinal: cardinal-virtues,
> Next to pope-virtues, are most impious.
> Bishop-virtues are unwarrantable.
> I hate a virtue in a morrice-dance.
> I will allow of none but deacon-virtues
> Or elder virtues.
> *Ros.* These are moral virtues.

But in the end it is this dance of truly humanistic "moral virtues" that wins out over mere "deacon-virtues." As Mistress Flowerdew puts it:

> Most blessed looking-glass,
> That didst instruct my blinded eyes to-day!
> I might have gone to hell the narrow way![36]

To revert now to *The Antipodes,* I stress the hoyden quality of Brome's final image of Thalia because the substance of Letoy's play-within-the-play, unlike Roscius', is primarily farcical, including satire, of course, but turning its whip into a stuffed baton and applying this buttockwise in a spirit of pure anticry. It is as if Randolph's "manlike-monkey Mime" had taken charge of both her mistress, Thalia, and "brother beadle" Satire. The setting of Letoy's play is a strange city in a never-never land where things go completely by contraries to the way they happen in contemporary London. In other words, the inhabitants of the Antipodes behave precisely as the folk of dreams are popularly supposed to do.

It is likely that Brome had read about such a country in Josa Acosta's *Natural and Moral History of the Indies,* published in translation in London in 1604. Lucian's *Vera Historia, The Travels of Sir John Mandeville,* Jonson's masque *News from the New World Discovered in the Moon,* and a scene attributed to Heywood in *The Late Lancashire Witches* had perhaps supplied him with fruitful suggestions.[37] But the main source was probably Jonson's *Bartholomew Fair,* in the first performance of which in 1614 Brome may have been a bit player.[38] He knew things did not go at Jonson's Fair absolutely by contraries to actual life, but its world *was* one of fast-crowding incongruities and grotesqueries, with the madman Trouble-all demanding of everybody, "Have you a warrant for what you do?"[39] Here was the notion of existence as a fantastic higgledy-piggledydom,[40] and all Brome had to do was to turn this into a consistent topsy-turvydom, substituting Peregrine for Trouble-all. Randolph's *The Muses' Looking Glass* doubtless gave him the idea of a stricter scheme of scenes combining repetition and variety. The underlying concept of Letoy's scenes is the fact of incongruity rather than the need for moderation, and the emerging theme of the whole is that in Utopia they are even madder than we are here rather than that for every virtue to achieve, there are two vices to avoid.

How the idea of topsy-turvydom subordinates satire to farce or blurs satiric point or bypasses satire altogether becomes apparent upon analysis. Consider the first scene, where two sergeants flee from a gentleman who begs them to arrest him for debt. When he overtakes them, they crave his pardon, saying:

71

But sooner shall the charter of the city
Be forfeited then varlets like ourselves
Shall wrong a gentlemans peace.

If this is satire, it is rather difficult to define its object—the manners of sergeants, or the laxity of law enforcement, or the constant harassment of gentlemen for petty misdemeanors, or the contempt gentlemen have for sergeants, or the tendency of gentlemen to put off paying what they owe.

Consider the second and third scenes. In the first of these appears a gentleman who has taken a mercer's wares as an inducement to lie with the mercer's wife, then refused to lie with her out of the scruple that he will be wronging his own wife, and now is in danger of being haled into court by the mercer for not committing adultery. The gentleman's wife reproaches him for not living up to his bargain with the mercer. Their conversation reveals that in the Antipodes husbands bring portions to their wives, the wives make jointures, old wives allow their young husbands to cohabit with young mistresses, and old husbands approve their young wives taking young lovers. In the second of these scenes a pregnant waiting-woman desires her gentleman-seducer to marry her, and his wife insists that he shall do so.[41] This sequence is charged with overtones of satirical mockery at the relations of the sexes and the classes, but the farcical idea of topsy-turvydom is uppermost, and our laughter is at a rapid cumulative perception of sheer incongruities.

In another scene, where a lawyer and a poet appear, the lawyer refuses fees for championing the poet's cause, aldermen are represented as lovers of poetry, and the poet is strait-laced in conduct and speech, praises the City's clemency, and writes more than he talks. In still another scene, where a captain converses with his lawyer, the captain tells him again how he has been beaten by a coachman and is being dunned "against all humane reason" not to pay his bill by a feather-maker, whereupon the lawyer decides that, rather than proceed to trial, the best solution is for the coachman to beat the feathermaker until the latter will take the captain's money. Then, in a third scene, a woman prize-fighter threatens to beat a lawyer for refusing to take a fee.[42] Although poets and lawyers are satirized here, the main purpose is to carry out the idea of topsy-turvydom with respect to the characteristic habits of professions and types, the upshot being a doubling of farcical effect.

In three later scenes, all connected, an old woman who is fond of bear-baiting is reproved by a young woman who is a Puritan; then a young gentleman, accompanied by an old servingman whom he calls his boy, is accosted by the young Puritan, who admits that her blood rebels against her spirit at the sight of so dainty a masculine morsel. After the gentleman rebuffs her advances, she kicks both him and his servant, and then is so skillful at misrepresentation that a constable is on the point of arresting both the innocent males when Peregrine intervenes to see that justice is done.[43] This playlet has some value as wide-glancing satire against Puritanism, Libertinism, the new woman, and changing relations of the age-groups, but such implications are certainly subordinated to the gamut of reversed probabilities.

In another trio of scenes, two courtiers conduct themselves in the manner of a carman and a waterman, exchanging kicks in the posteriors, boxes on the ears, and other buffetings. After one courtier has knocked down the other, a third courtier attempts to pacify them by showing a ballad, which the victorious courtier lacks the learning to read. Then a carman and a waterman talk the stilted language of compliment employed by courtiers.[44] Here is certainly satire aimed at the dregs and froth of contemporary society, but it is again keyed to emphasis on incongruities for their own sake.

Another scene, where a statesman confers with several projectors, castigates a major contemporary manifestation of the acquisitive spirit but makes less of the latter than of the projects as devices to multiply the citation of topsy-turvities. One project, for example, is

> . . . for keeping of tame owles in cities
> To kill up rats and mice, whereby all cats
> May be destroyed, as an especiall meanes
> To prevent witch-craft and contagion.

Another project proposes charity for criminals who can no longer carry on their profession and jailing for persons who are robbed.[45] In other words, the Swift of *Gulliver's Travels* and the Butler of *Erewhon* are here, but in a context that prognosticates Samuel Foote, J. R. Planché, and W. S. Gilbert.[46]

With particular reference to Letoy's farcical extravaganza, Swinburne praised *The Antipodes* for "the logic of the burlesque, its topsy-turvy coherence, its preposterous harmony, its incongruous congruity of contradictions."[47] So abundant and bewildering are the latter that it is little wonder Peregrine is jolted from his traveler's madness into the imperial folly of wanting to restore everything in cloud-cuckooland to the familiar London pattern. At least this is moving in the direction of the adjustment to reality that Dr. Hughball feels is essential to sanity. To quote Diana again:

> As a man
> Infected by some fowle disease is drawne
> By physicke into an anatomy
> Before flesh fit for health can grow to reare him,
> So is a mad-man made a foole before
> Art can take hold of him to wind him up
> Into his proper center, or the medium
> From which he flew beyond himselfe.[48]

It remains now to contrast what Randolph and Brome are trying to say, in this creative, indirect, and complex fashion, about three basic problems of comedy: its end, its subject-matter, and its artistic method.

For Randolph, the end of comedy is primarily moral education; it is a form of delightful teaching; it strives toward the correction of typical vices and follies through laughter and with reference to ethical and social standards clearly defined, rational, and humanistic; and it ultimately effects this correction in the individual spectator by a catharsis quite different from that of tragedy. As Thalia explains to her sister Muse in the course of their debate:

> You move with fear; I work as much with shame—
> A thing more powerful in a generous breast.

74

Who sees an eating parasite abus'd;
A covetous bawd laugh'd at; an ignorant gull
Cheated; a glorious soldier knock'd and baffl'd:
A crafty servant whipp'd; a niggard churl
Hoarding up dicing-moneys for his son;
A spruce, fantastic courtier, a mad roarer,
A jealous tradesman, an o'erweening lady,
A corrupt lawyer—rightly personated;
But (if he have a blush) will blush, and shame
As well to act those follies as to own them.[49]

For Brome, the end of comedy is primarily psychological therapy. Delightful teaching and the correction of vice and folly are not ruled out but are less important than restoring to intellectual and emotional stability minds out of balance through passions, fixations, deprivations, and the like—the many varieties of Renaissance "melancholy." To set right the lost or distorted or merely disturbed sense of reality in such minds is best accomplished by engrossing them in a world more incongruously out of balance than they are; this engrossment will carry them, if they are stark mad, only this side or folly-wards of sanity; if they are more normal, they will have a catharsis wherein their own troubles and disorders are forgotten in the belly-shaking mirth at the omnipotence and ubiquity of imperfection. In a masque at the close of *The Antipodes,* Discord and her "faction" of Folly, Jealousy, Melancholy, and Madness are "confounded" by Harmony and her four great deities—Mercury or Wit to put down Folly, Cupid or Love to cast out Jealousy, Bacchus or Wine to liquidate Melancholy, and Health to overcome Madness.[50] This masque allegorizes what happens in the individual spectator's consciousness as the catharsis of comedy completes itself.

For Randolph, the subject-matter of comedy, to fulfill his conception of its end, must be principally characters of two kinds—those embodying vices and follies and those defining the standards with reference to which their correction is to be carried out. In the contention between Satire and Mime early in *The Muses' Looking Glass,* the latter defends "apish imitation" against the "proud whip, with all his firks and jerks"

75

of the former.[51] Mime's case is the better stated of the two—an indication that Randolph thinks the impersonation of vices and follies in a play should take precedence over their rhetorical excoriation by spokesmen of the dramatist's own normative notions. All this means, of course, an oversimplified fictive humanity, a dramatis personae in each of whom an excess or deficiency or virtue is his *raison d'être,* apparent in most of his speeches and actions. Yet, in so far as possible, such abstract constructs must be brought out of the domain of allegory and enriched with recognizable particularity for the sake of stage illusion with its potent appeal to the mind through the sight. Since the ratio of vice and folly to virtue is so uneven—a two-to-one proposition in Aristotle—it follows that the "world" of comedy, its visible scene, will be primarily sordid or ugly or deformed, but this is necessary if comedy is to accomplish its corrective end. As Roscius puts it:

> They abuse our scene
> And say we live by vice. Indeed, 'tis true
> As the physicians by diseases do,
> Only to cure them.
>
> .   .   .   .   .
>
> Boldly, I dare say,
> There has been more by us in some one play
> Laugh'd into wit and virtue, than hath been
> By twenty tedious lectures drawn from sin
> And foppish humours; hence the cause doth rise,
> Men are not won by th' ears so well as eyes.[52]

For Brome, however, with his somewhat different end in view, situations are more important than characters as comedy's subject-matter. The principle of the comic situation is incongruity, the more the merrier and the quicker the cure to take effect on the mind in discord. Characters, of course, are necessary, and they may exemplify vice and folly in abundance, but they exist to bring out the principle in the situation rather than to implement a system of ethics or a program of social reform.

The artistic method of comedy, for Randolph—inescapably implied in his view of its end and its subject-matter—must be realistic in the sense of reproducing as faithfully as possible the specific typical forms that vice or folly assumes in the actual world of the audience. In the first preliminary skit of the play-within-the-play, Roscius proceeds to demonstrate this all-important thesis in Randolph's theory in order to refute the Puritan notion that comedy is responsible for the sins and abuses of Caroline society. A "Deformed Fellow" comes upon the stage, peers into one of Mistress Flowerdew's looking-glasses, and recoils before the monster therein revealed. Then Roscius asks him to look again. This time the "Deformed Fellow" beholds the reflection, not only of himself, but of Roscius as well, and avers that he sees "An angel and a devil." This is Roscius' cue to make two important points concerning comedy. In the first place,

> 'Tis not the glass, but thy deformity,
> That makes this ugly shape: if they be fair,
> That view the glass, such the reflections are.
> This serves the body: the soul sees her face
> In comedy, and has no other glass.[53]

This is equivalent to saying that just as physical deformity and physical beauty are reflected in a looking-glass precisely as they are in actuality, so moral or spiritual ugliness and moral or spiritual proportion are portrayed in comedy exactly as they exist in life itself. As it would be foolish for one to condemn a looking-glass for giving him back his true appearance, so it is foolish to condemn the art-form of comedy for adumbrating evil as it actually is. One thinks of Stendhal's defense of the modern realistic novel:

> Ah, Sir, a novel is a mirror carried along a high road. At one moment it reflects to your vision the azure skies, at another the mire of the puddles at your feet. And the man who carries this mirror in his pack will be accused by you of being immoral! His mirror shews the mire, and you blame the mirror! Rather blame that high road upon which the puddle lies, still more the inspector of roads who allows the water to gather and the puddle to form.[54]

In the second place, it is only by seeing ourselves as we really are, in the way that comedy by its realism makes possible, that we can preserve what is fair in us and correct what is unclean. Roscius phrases part of this contention so as to justify comedy to the theologically minded:

> And yet, methinks, if 'twere not for this glass,
> Wherein the form of man beholds his grace,
> We could not find another way to see
> How near our shapes approach divinity.

Addressing himself to the women in the audience, he elaborates:

> Ladies, let they who will your glass deride,
> And say it is an instrument of pride:
> I will commend you for it; there you see,
> If you be fair, how truly fair you be:
> Where, finding beauteous faces, I do know
> You'll have the greater care to keep them so.

He then attempts to clarify the whole argument by an appropriate example. "A country slut"—though such, he adds, exist in the city as well as in the country—"kept her hands clean" because she could see them as they were, but having no looking-glass, she neglected to wash her face until it became

> . . . as nasty as the stall
> Of a fishmonger, or an usurer's hall,
> Daub'd o'er with dirt: one might have dar'd to say
> She was a true piece of Promethean clay,
> Not yet inform'd; and then her unkemb'd hair
> Dress'd up with cobwebs, made her haglike stare.

But one day she caught a glimpse of her face and hair in the pail of water she carried and was so ashamed that she used the water forthwith and "wash'd her filth away."

> So comedies, as poets do intend them,
> Serve first to show our faults, and then to mend them.[55]

78

The fact that the mirror of comedy reflects the soul in the body, the spirit in its incarnation, the idea in its form, keeps it realistic in the Aristotelian sense rather than making it naturalistic in the modern scientific sense or reportorial according to journalistic standards.

For Brome, the artistic method of comedy is best described as "extra-realistic." The comic writer is not confined to the kind of verisimilitude suggested by the image of the mirror. Burton, in *The Anatomy of Melancholy,* explaining how to rectify "perturbations of the mind," points out that occasionally "some feigned lie, strange news, witty device, artificial invention" may serve the purpose.[56] This is the conception that Brome supports. The comic writer is free to copy life or distort it or frolic in pure fantasy, and all in the same play. His illusory world must hang together, with "words and action married," even if it is "the world turn'd upside down,"[57] but it is consistency to its own logic that matters and not fidelity to the world with which the audience is familiar.

It should not be inferred that either Randolph or Brome follows strictly, in all his other comedies, the theories respectively set forth in *The Muses' Looking Glass* and *The Antipodes.* But it can be inferred that these theories define the poles between which the comic practice of the Caroline Sons of Ben as a group tends to oscillate. They are drawn now toward Thalia the beadle and now toward Thalia the hoyden, and often this attraction is simultaneous. The beadle theory is the more traditional, the more in harmony with the commonplaces of classical and Renaissance criticism, the more consonant with the combined heritage of Roman comedy and Aristophanes. That Randolph, whose background was Cambridge, should have provided its fullest formulation is not surprising. The hoyden theory belongs primarily to the tradition of the popular stage, is more in harmony with Renaissance notions about psychology and medicine, and yet has a striking affinity, in the freedom of its extra-realism, with Aristophanes' Old Comedy. That Brome, a professional playwright of the popular theaters, who had learned his craft the hard way, should have come forward with the most challenging adumbration of this theory, is only appropriate. Randolph's theory, as has been said, is that of "comicall satyre" or satirical comedy; Brome's is that of farce, with philosophic and satiric overtones, wide-glancing. In the light of the poles these theories represent, the use the Sons of Ben made of Jonson and other "fathers" can be understood as an eclecticism that, although it often failed to come off well and occasionally seems a decadent confusion, was something more than mere inept imitation of major by minor writers, without benefit of reflection on aesthetic principles.

CHAPTER
THREE

More Than One Father

*I*n Balzac's *Cousin Bette,* Valérie Marneffe, the wife of an unscrupulous clerk in the Ministry of War, tells her husband and each of her four lovers—a Polish count and sculptor, a wealthy perfumer, a titled Brazilian millionaire, and the baron who heads the ministry—that he is to be a father. "Thanks to successful strategy, based on the vanity and self-love of man in the condition of lover," observes Balzac, "Valérie sat down to dinner surrounded by four joyful, animated, fascinated men, each feeling that she adored him alone, while Marneffe called them all, under his breath . . ., including himself in the category, 'the five fathers of the church.' "[1] The Caroline Sons of Ben had two advantages over the coming addition to the Marneffe menage. There was no doubt they were the offspring of Jonson, and they really did have more than one father.

Chapman and Marston, Jonson's colleagues in the development of "humour comedy" and his collaborators in *Eastward Ho,* have minor claims. The earlier masters of "citizen comedy," Dekker, Heywood, Middleton, and Massinger, must be included. And, finally, Beaumont and Fletcher and Shirley, architects of a comedy of witty amorous intrigue that brought Shakespeare's Benedick and Beatrice, Orlando and Rosalind into the high life of London, are also involved in the complex paternity.

In 1638, the year following Jonson's death, many of his Sons in poetry and drama joined in issuing a volume of memorial verse, the *Jonsonus Virbius*. Some of the contributions contain suggestive statements as to why the majority of Caroline writers of comedy chose him as their chief father. One reason is that he was able, above all other dramatists, "to recreate for his age the image of man"—to use Allen Tate's now famous phrase—[2] and at the same time to present this image in terms of his age's actual life with the result that this life, continuing into the Caroline period, bore striking correspondences to the world of his plays and proved their comic truth, their mirror-like fidelity. Such is the substance of the following lines by William Cartwright:

> Where shall we find a Muse like *thine*, that can
> So well present and shew *man* unto *man*,
> That each one finds his *twin*, and thinks *thy Art*
> Extends not to the *gestures*, but the *heart?*
> Where one so shewing *life* to *life*, that *we*
> Think *thou* taughtst *Custome*, and not *Custome thee?*
> *Manners*, that were themes to *thy* Scenes still *flow*
> In the same *streame*, and are their *comments* now. . . .[3]

Another reason is that Jonson's truthful image of man achieved the catharsis of "comicall satyre" and yet was sufficiently various to include humours in at least three senses, one of them certainly hospitable to farce. Falkland refers to

> . . . th' *Ethicke Lectures* of his *Comedies,*
> Where the Spectators act, and the sham'd age
> Blusheth to meet her follies on the stage;
> Where each man finds some *Light* he never sought,
> And leaves behind some vanitie he brought. . . .[4]

And Edmund Waller classifies the humours as biases of nature, stamps of custom, and the accrued distortions of personal habits:

More Than One Father

Thou not alone those various inclinations,
Which *Nature* gives to *Ages, Sexes, Nations,*
Hast traced with thy All-resembling *Pen,*
But all that custome hath impos'd on *Men,*
Or ill-got Habits, which distort them so,
That scarce the Brother can the Brother know,
Is represented to the wondring Eyes,
Of all that see or read thy Comedies.[5]

A third reason is that Jonson was a source for principles of craft, the Solon of the English theater, "who," as James Clayton puts it, "first reform'd our *Stage* with justest Lawes."[6] In examining Jonson's fatherhood to his Sons in comedy, there is perhaps no better strategy than simply to explore each of these reasons further.

In recreating for his age the image of man and making this image live in contemporary terms, Jonson did not neglect the spirit of intolerance, both in its domestic and its public manifestations, nor its antidote, the spirit of tolerance. Perhaps his most memorable treatment of domestic intolerance is in *Every Man in His Humour,* first performed with an Italian setting and Italianate dramatis personae and then turned into a comedy about London,[7] symbolic of his desire to bring home to his audience his insights into universal comic truth concerning mankind. The humour characters showing one or another form of intolerance in family relations are the elder Knowell, guilty of such an excessive paternal solicitude toward his son that he tries to check up too closely on his personal life and gets himself, with the aid of the tricky servant Brainworm, into a most embarrassing predicament; the jealous husband Kitely, who goes to fantastic lengths to prove himself cuckolded by his wholly virtuous wife; and the cross-grained Downright, who demonstrates his lack of breeding and self-control in his violent efforts to deprive his younger half-brother Well-bred of his household right to entertain with reasonable discretion his friends and acquaintances.[8]

The characters most memorably embodying public intolerance are the two representatives of Puritan extremism in *The Alchemist,*

Tribulation Wholesome and Ananais, the first possessed by an inordinate will to power and the other by a perfervid literalism;[9] their fellow-traveller of *Bartholomew Fair*, Rabbi Zeal-of-the-Land Busy, rampaging reformer, arch-hypocrite, and would-be martyr,[10] and the half-crazed Justice Overdo, who, in trying to put down such "enormities" as the consumption of ale, the smoking of tobacco, and the singing of ballads, gets himself into the stocks, mistakes an incorrigible cutpurse for a good man at heart, and lets his own wife fall into the hands of a brothel-keeper.[11]

The tolerance Overdo eventually achieves near the end of the play—a resolution to correct rather than destroy, to instruct rather than suppress—[12] is best shown earlier in Justice Clement of *Every Man in His Humour*. Clement is a whimsical eccentric, but also a wise student of human nature. When the various humour characters appear before him for final judgment, he diagnoses each vice and folly shrewdly and prescribes the punishment that will effect a cure.[13] In giving us such norm characters as Clement, Jonson meets the second demand Allen Tate makes of the responsible writer—that "he must propagate standards by which other men may test that image [of man], and distinguish the false from the true."[14]

Against the acquisitive spirit and its attendant evils in their contemporary manifestations, Jonson also launched a frontal attack.[15] Again he tends to move from the abstract or universal human vice to the kind of concrete examples of it best known to his audience. In *Every Man Out of His Humour* the grasping countryman Sordido, who hoards corn in anticipation of a ruined harvest and consequent enormous profit and then tries to hang himself when he finds he has been merely a dupe of the almanac, is concrete enough, but it is also clear that, in creating him, Jonson had in mind Aristotle's treatment of excess and deficiency in the *Nicomachean Ethics* as definitely as did Randolph later in *The Muses' Looking Glass*. Sordido, saved from his suicidal noose, starts giving his money away; extremes, in short, meet; illiberality is metamorphosed into its opposite, prodigality.[16]

The carrion-feeding legacy-seekers of *Volpone*—Corbaccio the raven,

Corvino the crow, and Voltore the vulture—belong to Venice rather than to London, and body forth, not an Aristotelian vice or folly, but the deadly sin of greed; and their other basenesses as well as those of their rogue-exploiters, Volpone the fox and Mosca the fly, serve to illustrate the traditional truism that money is the root of all evil, or, as Jonson prefers to phrase it, "one baseness still accompanies another."[17] All doubtless had their meaner parallels in fortune-hunters and rogues of Jacobean London, but their monstrosity lifts them into a world apart, as if they had been drawn with one eye on the villain-protagonists of tragedy.

In *The Alchemist* Sir Epicure Mammon is brought into striking juxtaposition with the intolerant Puritans, Tribulation Wholesome and Ananias, and this certainly indicates Jonson was thinking of him with reference to Aristotle's licentiousness—the excess—in contrast to the deficiency insensibility, as the meeting extremes of the virtue temperance. But Sir Epicure, as well as the Puritans, becomes far more concrete than that—the crackbrained Renaissance voluptuary whose basic drive for wealth has in train such allied sins and vices and follies as lust, gluttony, hypocrisy, ambition, and credulity. His mind is a lumber room of the cabalistic lore of the age, his conversation a patter of its "vulgar errors."[18] The rogues Subtle, Dol Common, and Captain Face are also nearer home than Volpone and Mosca. The process of concretizing the acquisitive spirit in contemporary terms continues in the shady underworldlings of *Bartholomew Fair* and in the projectors of *The Devil is an Ass* as well as their prize victim, Fabian Fitzdottrel.[19]

Both *The Staple of News* and *The Magnetic Lady* are complex comedies about the acquisitive spirit. In the first it displays itself inversely, so to speak, in the misuse of money by a prodigal with an illiberal guardian in an attempt to live to the hilt according to the wild gallantry of the day; but in the second, acquisition is the most positive motive of the plots and counter-plots centering about a rich widow and a false and a true heiress. Such situations were certainly familiar ones in Jonson's time, but, for some reason, probably his failing creative powers, the old abstractionism returned to play fast and loose with the

85

impetus towards the concrete. The result is that *The Staple of News* has something of the unintentional effect of Aristotle travestied,[20] and that *The Magnetic Lady,* by reason of its over-involved metaphor of moth, magnet, loadstone, needle, compass, and treasure in a well,[21] turns into an extended comic "metaphysical" conceit that fails to come off.[22]

In holding up a standard to reveal the falseness of the acquisitive spirit, Jonson experimented with a variety of character-types and again had to wrestle with the problem of concretizing his universal. In *Every Man Out of His Humour* he leant too heavily on Aristotle. Asper, who remains majestically outside the action as a symbol of the virtue righteous indignation, is forced in the play itself to assume the guise of Macilente, who represents envy—the excess—and whose function is constantly being taken over by Carlo Buffone, a personification of the deficiency malice.[23] In *Volpone* Bonario and Celia are an undeveloped hero and heroine who serve a bit melodramatically as romantic rebuffs to evil, and to lust particularly, rather than real-life embodiments of the anti-acquisitive spirit. It is in Eustace Manly of *The Devil is an Ass* and Pennyboy Canter of *The Staple of News* that Jonson comes through with prototypes, respectively, of solid English honesty and integrity and shrewdly perceptive parental liberality acceptable as credible counterblasts to the unscrupulous, the miserly, and the spendthrift. The trouble with Manly, however, is that he is too much like the Mr. Friendly Morals of later sentimental comedy, reforming the witty Libertine Wittipol so that he can help in the thwarting of the projectors.[24] And the trouble with Pennyboy Canter is that his farcical drollery is too much of a distraction from his Aristotelian virtue.[25]

It was in his critique of the spirit of affectation, however, that Jonson was to be most successful in breaking away from mere abstractionism and in evolving brilliant and believable norm characters. The concretizing process is noticeable early in this phase of his comedy. Evidence of it occurs in one of the stylistic revisions of the first *Every Man in His Humour.* The Italian Piso thus defines "humour" as it applies to social pretenders: ". . . it is a monster bred in a man by selfe love, and affectation, and fed by folly."[26] This definition approaches the spirit of affectation from an abstract, ethico-psychological perspective, emphasizing its narcissistic egotism. The English Cash, however, in the second version, has a different definition: "It is a gentleman-like monster, bred, in the speciall gallantrie of our time, by affectation; and fed by folly."[27] This is to see social pretenders in concrete terms of the manners of the age, as stamped by custom, as victims of the "other-direction" that, even though David Riesman thinks of it as a primarily modern phenomenon, has competed with "tradition-direction" and "self-direction" at all times and everywhere.[28]

In play after play Jonson presented a stratification of characters with "the humour of gentilitie"[29] that reflected the actual stratification in Jacobean and Caroline society. Dominating his microcosm of pretension is the pseudo lady of the Court or the town *beau monde* or a coterie of such pseudo ladies. The best examples are Saviolina of *Every Man Out of His Humour;* Moria, Philautia, Phantaste, and Argurion of *Cynthia's Revels;* Lady Politick Would-Be of *Volpone;* the Ladies Collegiates of *Epicoene;* and Ladies Tailbush and Eitherside of *The Devil is an Ass.* Just below them and usually much taken in by their assumed sophistication are the pseudo wits of the same milieu. Fastidious Brisk, of *Every Man Out of His Humour,* for example, looks up to Saviolina.[30] Anaides, Hedon, and Amorphus are his corresponding types in *Cynthia's Revels.* Sir Politick Would-Be, in *Volpone,* tries to rival his wife in modish "inside knowledge." Sir John Daw and Sir Amorous La-Foole are hangers-on of the Ladies Collegiates in *Epicoene.* Bobadill and Matthew of *Every Man in His Humour* have no pseudo lady to pay court to, but the latter with his poetaster's melancholy and ill-digested scraps of erudition is impressed by the former's military braggadocio.[31] The Jeerers of *The Staple of News,* the Roarers of *The New Inn,* and Sir Diaphanous Silkworm of *The Magnetic Lady* are later, more fantastic portraits of the type. Below the pseudo-wit because admiring him for a true gentleman are the would-be wits from the town citizenry or from the country. The country would-be is best illustrated by Stephen of *Every Man in His Humour;* Sogliardo and Fungoso of *Every Man Out of His Humour,* and Kastril of *The Alchemist;* the town would-be by Asotus of *Cynthia's Revels,* Dapper of *The Alchemist,* Plutarchus of *The Devil is an Ass,* and Pennyboy Junior of *The Staple of News.* Alongside this type should be placed the social-climbing citizen couple or husband or wife or widow, an older man and woman obsessed with the necessity of making a social splurge, of moving in what they regard as the most fashionable set. Amusing instances are Deliro and Fallace of *Every Man Out of His Humour,* the Downfalls of *Cynthia's Revels,* the Otters of *Epicoene,* Dame Pliant of *Bartholomew Fair,* and Fitzdottrel of *The Devil is an Ass.*

The norm characters that Jonson devised to put these pretenders in proper critical perspective range from a gentleman of balanced integrity like Crites of *Cynthia's Revels,*[32] to an unpretentious ironic traveller like Peregrine of *Volpone,*[33] to mercurial, genuinely witty gallants like Ed Knowell and Wellbred in *Every Man in His Humour,* Truewit, Clerimont, and Dauphine of *Epicoene,* and Wittipol of *The Devil is an Ass.* In *Epicoene* he even introduced an elderly eccentric Morose, the embodiment of social aversion, and a page dressed up as a witty woman to provide further machinery to put social pretenders in a ridiculous light.[34] In *The New Inn,* a comedy anticipating the vogue of Court Platonism, he aligned a Libertine against a Platonist, permitting each to state his credo as a way of defining the complete gentleman, but being more critical of the Platonist as tending toward affectation.[35]

The contrast of norm characters with those illustrating sin or vice or folly guaranteed that Jonson's comedies worked the kind of catharsis in his audience that Randolph describes in *The Muses' Looking Glass.* But Jonson himself seemed worried over one drawback in his earlier "comicall satyres." The norm characters had to talk too much to provoke the shame that was the basic emotional ingredient in the catharsis. There were too many scenes primarily expository or documentary, didactic or reportorial, included for the purpose of defining the vices and follies and giving them a convincing realistic setting. In consequence, action suffered, movement lagged, suspense was lost. So Jonson experimented with devices to get more action, to speed it up, to keep his audience guessing about its outcome. The result was that the rogue-exploiters and the wit-intriguers,[36] characters with considerable importance for plot but less for the ethical and social "spire of meaning," to use Galsworthy's phrase,[37] began to attract him. He managed to employ rogue-exploiters with no great diminution of satirical relevance in *Volpone* and to blend the wit-intriguer with the truewit in *Epicoene* so that the critique of affectation did not falter;[38] but in *The Alchemist, Bartholomew Fair, The Devil is an Ass, The Staple of News,* and *The Magnetic Lady* the element of intrigue for its own sake gradually increases to the point that satire is weakened and some of the effects of philosophic farce supplant it. In *Bartholomew Fair* this is a positive gain; the integrated view of man and the world that emerges is a more profound and valuable achievement than the correction of specific vices and follies, although these are not omitted from the motley extravaganza.[39] But in the plays after *Bartholomew Fair* a kind of chaos of fantastic incongruities in a pattern of complicated intrigue supervenes, and meaning suffers. From Thalia the beadle Jonson has definitely turned to Thalia the hoyden, and she has got somewhat out of hand.

This brings us to the three kinds of humour characters in Jonson's comedies. Those with biases of nature might best be treated from an ethico-psychological perspective for purposes of soberly corrective satire, a comedy of humanistic instruction. Those with traits imposed on them by an attempt to follow custom, to keep up with the mode, were admirable material for lighter social satire, for a comedy of wit or manners. But those with distorting ill-got habits tended to be mere drolls or eccentrics, not particularly significant for the implementation of ethical or social philosophy, but excellent to diversify a fast-moving plot, to pack a situation with laughs rising to a crescendo. In Jonson's later comedies these capricious humours predominate; even char-

89

acters intended to satirize vices or follies partake of their fantasticality; and the upshot is that the hoyden, instead of collaborating with the beadle, drives her out. What remains is a decadent comedy of farcical intrigue, a throwback to Roman comedy at its most mechanical and to Aristophanes' Old Comedy and traditional popular comedy at their most exaggerated and disorderly.[40]

Of the many principles or laws of craft that Jonson impressed on his Sons, none was more challenging than that pertaining to dramatic unity. He rejected the common misconception that such unity was exclusive, involving one line of action unbroken or unrelated to other actions. Instead he called unambiguously for a unity of inclusion, in which many actions are drawn in one direction and merged, as they develop, into a whole. Here is his acceptance of the principle in *Timber, or Discoveries,* in a translation from Heinsius:

> One is considerable two waies: either, as it is only separate, and by it self: or as being compos'd of many parts, it beginnes to be one, as those parts grow, or are wrought together. That it should be one the first way alone, and by it self, no man that hath tasted letters ever would say, especially having required before a just Magnitude, and equall Proportion of the parts in themselves. Neither of which can possibly bee, if the Action be single and separate, not compos'd of parts, which laid together in themselves, with an equall and fitting proportion, tend to the same end; which thing out of Antiquitie it selfe, hath deceiv'd many; and more this Day it doth deceive.[41]

To even a casual spectator or reader of his own comedies, it was obvious that he practiced this principle consistently, blending in a single play actions involving either two or all three of his varieties of humour characters and the different modes of comic effect associated with them and using them to pursue all the maleficent spirits deserving comic exorcism in the contemporary world. To students with artistic insight, it was also apparent that he showed great resourcefulness in inventing ways to hold each many-actioned play together, from the employment of such an intriguing Plautine servant as Brainworm in

More Than One Father

Every Man in His Humour to the provision of a symbolic setting as in *Bartholomew Fair* or the manipulation of the supernatural in *The Devil is an Ass*. Certainly this view of unity was an invitation to eclectic experimentation, with all the diverse materials of life itself, and not merely with situations and characters, devices and themes from his own ample repertoire but also from those of his talented collaborators and colleagues and rival masters.

Of Jonson's collaborators, Chapman has the distinction of anticipating by one year, in his *An Humorous Day's Mirth* of 1597, much of Jonson's initial achievement in *Every Man in His Humour* and some aspects even of his later canon. In a French setting, Lemot, a young gallant and a kind of Timist, assisted by two others of his type, Colinet and Castalian, is contrasted with the melancholy Dowsecer, more of a Timonist or Jaques, as the agents of satire. Prototypes of domestic intolerance, the jealous Count Labervele and Countess Moren, and the unduly solicitous father, Old Foyes, appear alongside a pseudo wit and a would-be wit, Labesha and Blanuel. Count Labervele's wife, Florilla, is a Puritan whose hypocrisy is more fully presented than the vices of any of the other characters.[42] The structure is a loose series of scenes with expository character sketches occurring in the dialog and with one striking documentary or reportorial scene at an ordinary.[43] A final scene containing disposals of lots and a masque draws the many actions toward one end, with the King having some faint resemblance in function to Jonson's Clement.

Already apparent here, however, is an interest in intrigue for its own sake, executed by a clever wit-intriguer and reducing some of the characters intended for satire to the more farcical status of drolls or eccentrics. These tendencies were to persist in Chapman's later comedies. Rinaldo of *All Fools*, Lodovico of *May Day*, and Tharsalio of *The Widow's Tears* display Lemot's skill at stratagems. The intrigue in the first of these is borrowed directly from Terence; in the second from Italian *commedia erudita*, itself indebted to Roman New Comedy;

and in the third from Petronius' *Satyricon*.[44] *Sir Giles Goosecap* and
Monsieur D'Olive have main plots whose intrigue is of the type found
in romantic comedy.[45] As for the satirized humour characters, they
certainly parallel some of those in Jonson but tend uniformly toward
the shadowy and distorted creatures of ill-got habits. This generalization applies to such characters in *All Fools* as the Terentian father,
Gostanzo, the jealous cuckold, Cornelio, the pseudo-wits, Dariotto
and Valerio, to the chief humours of *May Day:* the old man turned
lecherous gallant, Lorenzo, the braggart soldier, Quintiliano, and his
gull, Innocentio;[46] to the three pseudo wits of *Sir Giles Goosecap,* Sir
Giles himself, Sir Cuthbert Rudesby, and Foulweather;[47] and to the
pseudo wits of *The Widow's Tears:* Rebus, Hiarbos, and Psorabeus.
Only in the title character of *Monsieur D'Olive,* fully drawn from
contemporary life,[48] does Chapman give us a newly created knight
comparable as a study in the spirit of affectation to Jonson's Fastidious
Brisk of *Every Man Out of His Humour,* or some of the courtiers of
Cynthia's Revels, and the likelihood is that he was partly inspired by
Brisk.[49]

One of Chapman's minor successes that links him with Marston is
his transformation of the wit-intriguer of *The Widow's Tears,* Tharsalio, into a spokesman of Libertine philosophy more cynical and
hedonistic than that entertained by the truewits and wit-intriguers of
Epicoene.[50] Jonson, later, in Wittipol of *The Devil is an Ass* and Lord
Beaufort of *The New Inn,* was to follow this lead, although being
careful—as already pointed out—to convert Wittipol to Manly's moral-
ism and to balance Lord Beaufort's ideas with the Platonism of Lovel.

As one of the best satirists of his time, Marston, the second of Jonson's
collaborators, was well equipped to rival him as a writer of "comicall
satyres," and made several attempts to do so between 1600 and 1604.[51]
In none of these is the element of intrigue sufficiently under control,
but in most of them the satiric impulse is more powerful than in Chapman. Somber ethical and social satire aimed at the corruptions of an
imaginary Genoese court in *The Malcontent* goes beyond *Cynthia's*

Revels to anticipate some of the semi-tragic, semi-melodramatic effects
of *Volpone*. In *Jack Drum's Entertainment* a stratified world of social
pretenders comparable to Jonson's emerges—a young pseudo lady,
Camelia; two pseudo wits, Puffe and Monsieur John fo' de King; and
a country would-be wit, John Ellis. *What You Will*, with its setting
in Venice, has a full-length portrait of a pseudo wit in the Frenchman
Laverdure, with his "civet scent of perfumed words."[52] In *The Fawn*
the theme is Court gallantry, and what interests Marston most is the
affectation of amorous prowess, the many varieties of what may be
called pseudo Libertinism. Sir Amoroso Debile-Dosso, who is always
taking aphrodisiacs for his hopeless impotence; Nymphadoro, whose
satyriasis sends him drooling after every woman he sees; Herod Frap-
patore, described as one of those who are "forgers of love-letters, false
braggarts of ladies' favours, and vain boasters of counterfeit tokens";
and Granuffo, a philandering nincompoop who can only "abuse ladies
with counterfeit faces, courting by signs, and seeming wise only by
silence"[53]—these are the erotic cargo of a new Ship of Fools.[54]

In his conception of norm characters Marston departed radically from
Jonson by scorning the golden mean of righteous indignation embodied
in Asper or the gentleman of balanced integrity represented by Crites.
Malevole in *The Malcontent* is closer to Macilente than to Asper. And
in *What You Will* Marston fully defines the stance he prefers in a norm
character by upholding Pietro Aretino's genuine Libertinism, with its
hedonistic, skeptical *Weltanschauung*, in the views of Quadratus, the
four-square wit, as opposed to the Aristotelianism of the academic
humanist, Lampatho Doria.[55] In his only comedy that subordinates
satire to farcical intrigue, *The Dutch Courtesan*, Marston contrasts the
Libertine philosophies of a young gallant, Freevill, and a witty woman,
Crispinella, with the sobrieties of an idealist, Malheureux, who is a
curious amalgam of Puritan and Platonist.[56] Marston's intellectualiza-
tion of his chief comic protagonists and his use in *The Dutch Courtesan*
of a notorious brothel as a background for the play of ideas[57] must
have endowed him with considerable appeal for Caroline readers, to

whom Puritanism, Court Platonism, and Mrs. Holland's Leaguer were live issues. Evidence of such appeal is the publication of a folio of his plays in 1633.[58]

The stratification of society, in Jonson's comic world, was viewed primarily with reference to social affectation and the kinds of false wit and lack of wit that this involved, judged from a standard of genuine wit. Not of his world, at least in the earlier comedies—or present only in hints, incidental touches, and minor characters—was a broad sense of the middle classes and their sexes and age-groups in ferment, with a dynamic give-and-take for money and love going on between members of the *nouveau-riche* and the lower *bourgeoisie* as well as between young people on the make and older folk on the loose or holding fast to what they had or trying to maintain the proprieties. The distinction of Middleton, Dekker, Heywood and Massinger was to dramatize this give-and-take amongst the strata of the town citizenry and the country yeomanry with both reportorial veracity and a genius for farcical intrigue and without worrying overmuch about norm characters, particularly humanistic ones.

In six comedies between 1604 and 1611,[59] Middleton managed to present this give-and-take, these inter-strata dynamics, with an ironic impartiality, laughing both at the social climbing of the lower middle classes and the false pretensions of the upper and subjecting both young and old, male and female to derision for being so bedevilled by the mixed motivations of the acquisitive spirit, the spirit of affectation, and their natural sexual urges.[60]

In *A Trick to Catch the Old One* the laughter is primarily at lower middle-class social climbing and miserliness. A down-at-heel city gallant, Witgood, is the young man on the make. By passing off his country mistress as a wealthy widow, he recovers his mortgaged estate from a usurer Uncle Lucre, marries the niece of another usurer Hoard, and exposes the social aspirations not only of Hoard but also of two city would-be wits, Moneylove and Freedom.

In *A Mad World, My Masters* several clever intrigues are in train.

94

One is steered by Follywit, another city gallant, with the aid of two rogue companions, against his *nouveau-riche* grandsire, Sir Bounteous Progress. A second is carried on by the pseudo Libertine Sir Penitent Brothel to cuckold a citizen. A third is engineered by the courtesan, Gullman, who is kept by Sir Bounteous and in league with Sir Penitent, to gull the two pseudo wits Inesse and Possibility and finally the clever Follywit himself.

In *Michaelmas Term* a woolen-draper, Quomodo, cheats a young country gentleman, Master Easy, out of his estate in order to rise socially[61] and then plays dead to see what his family will do with his new wealth. His socially ambitious wife pursues Easy and provides him with information that enables him to get back the estate he has been swindled out of. At the same time the pseudo wit Andrew Lethe, son of a country "tooth-drawer," pretends he has a place at court, will not acknowledge his own mother, Mrs. Gruel, condescends to a trio of young citizens, Rearage, Salewood, and Cockstone, and attempts to play the rake with three women. The young citizens expose him; a judge forces him to marry a country girl he has seduced; and he is renounced by his own mother.

In *Your Five Gallants* the young upper middle-class wit, Fitsgrave, by out-maneuvering and exposing the pretensions of five lower middle-class pretenders to gentility, wins the orphan-heiress Katherine, while Mistress Newcut, in the absence at sea of her merchant husband, plays the wanton at a bawdy house under the illusion that the middle-class clientele there are gentlemen.[62]

The focus shifts in *The Family of Love* to the uproarious predicaments that two pseudo courtiers, Lipsalve and Gudgeon, get themselves into trying to be Libertines. They are no match for a young citizen suitor, a doctor who is a member of a Libertine religious sect, "The Family of Love," and an apothecary who disguises himself to have sexual relations with his own wife, one of the more active members of "The Family."

A Chaste Maid in Cheapside derides the morality and the pretensions of two middle-class families and a *nouveau-riche* Libertine. Sir Walter

Whorehound keeps Mistress Allwit, who has several bastards by him—one born during the play. Her husband connives at the infamous arrangement because it permits him to live like a gentleman. The goldsmith Yellowhammer and his wife have social aspirations for their son Tim and their daughter Moll. Home from Cambridge, Tim is an absurd geyser of Latin and logic, but his simplicity and bawdiness remain unmistakably of the town rather than the gown.[63]

What is most impressive in Middleton is the communication of derision through farcical intrigue. In so far as derision is a satiric effect,[64] this amounts to a satisfying collaboration between the beadle and the hoyden. On the other hand, the absence of clearly defined ethical and social standards tends to rob the derision of ultimate meaning, character is less important than situation, and incongruity becomes the essential fact about existence, as the title *A Mad World, My Masters* so plainly announces.[65]

Occasional intimation of the sterling goodness and sound sense of the ordinary citizen enters into Middleton's derisive, well-made comedies. This is a bourgeois sentimentalism or democratic prejudice that Jonson generally avoided, except for Manly in *The Devil is an Ass,* but that Dekker and Heywood made the most of in three comedies between 1604 and 1607.[66] Dekker's *Westward Ho* presents a trio of citizens' wives, Judith Honeysuckle, Clare Tenterhook, and Mabel Wafer, whose engagement of a tutor to improve their manners and knowledge of the world is not held against them as evidence of their false wit or possession by the spirit of affectation. This tutor, for the sake of the intrigue, turns out to be a horn-mad husband bent on getting other citizens into the condition of the forehead that he imagines to be his own. Seemingly on the way to an immorality comparable to that of the Ladies Collegiates in Jonson's later *Epicoene,* Dekker's witty wives surprise us, their tutor, the pseudo Libertines who have them in tow, and their cheating but jealous husbands by revealing themselves as chaste agents of reformation. Here is the new woman, challenging the double standard of sexual morality on the level of ordinary life. In a sub-plot the tutor joins with his really virtuous wife in reforming the

Libertinism of an Earl, further stressing the value of an idealistic single standard.

In *Northward Ho* Dekker shows a staunch citizen husband, Mayberry, turning the tables completely and uproariously on two Libertine pseudo gentlemen, Greenshield and Featherstone, who, having tried unsuccessfully to seduce his wife, attempt to prove to him that they have. In a sub-plot a city strumpet, by setting herself up as a virtuous pseudo lady, gulls three citizens less astute than Mayberry.

Heywood, in *The Wise Woman of Hogsdon,* concentrates on the exposure and reformation of a pseudo Libertine, Young Chartley, who seduces a country Luce, thinks he is secretly married to a city Luce, and then would desert his supposed wife, with whom he has not yet had sexual relations, in order to win a socially more desirable Grace. He thus expresses his change of heart at the end:

> O covetous man! I see
> I sought to engross what now sufficeth three,
> Yet each one wife enough.[67]

This is not a conversion to the doctrine of one woman of Court Platonism but to the kind of common-sense economy in emotional entanglements and sexual obligations that was its moral parallel on the citizen level.

It remained for Massinger, in two important comedies of the late Jacobean, early Caroline period, to demonstrate how "citizen comedy" might be combined with Jonson's more genuinely satirical comedy.[68] In *A New Way to Pay Old Debts* he borrowed his intrigue from that of Middleton's Witgood in *A Trick to Catch the Old One,*[69] but indicted the acquisitive spirit by drawing his villain, Sir Giles Overreach, directly from the actual Sir Giles Mompesson, the monopolist, and Marrall—Overreach's man—from Mompesson's clerk.[70] At the same time he portrayed them with obvious reference to Jonson's Volpone and Mosca and possibly to the projector Meercraft and his aide, Everill, in *The Devil is an Ass.*[71] In *The City Madam* he borrowed his intrigue from that of Middleton's Quomodo in *Michaelmas Term* and Gullman in *A Mad World, My Masters,*[72] but in his central humour character, Luke Frugal—possessed by the spirit of intolerance and the acquisitive spirit—he fused the characters of Jonson's Tribulation Wholesome and Sir Epicure Mammon in *The Alchemist.*[73] In censuring the social pretensions of Lady Frugal and her daughters, after the supposed demise of Sir John Frugal, Massinger made use of Luke and another expositor, Lord Lacy, in the tradition of Jonson's Macilente, Asper, and Crites.[74] Finally, in the character of the astrologer Stargaze, he levied on Jonson's rogue-exploiter, Subtle, of *The Alchemist.*[75] By such eclecticism Massinger achieved powerful effects, both comedies moving with the speed of Middleton's and having his broad sense of the middle-class milieu, yet maintaining a satiric rigor superior to mere derision.

Absent from Jonson's comedy was the witty woman as a match for his truewits and as a norm character to implement the castigation of his pseudo wits and would-bes. He may have ignored her because he thought of himself as leading a revolt against romantic comedy and of her as one of its stock characters.[76] His nearest approach to her is in *Epicoene,* where the page, disguised as a silent woman to lure Morose into marriage, becomes the talkative woman after marriage, and talks with considerable sophistication. Since the audience does not know the page's identity until the end of the play, his performance is indistinguishable from the witty woman's, especially in his dealings with the play's social pretenders. The most effective use the witty woman can be put to in comedy, however—as a seeming recalcitrant to passion testing the sincerity of her suitor—was not possible in *Epicoene.*

It was this use of her that Beaumont and Fletcher explored in four comedies between 1605 and 1614. They borrowed her, of course, from Shakespeare, and preserved the dramatic irony of the inner conflict between wit and emotion that her duel with her suitor usually involved. But they portrayed her in a milieu more closely approximating upper-class English life than does the milieu of *Much Ado About Nothing* or *As You Like It.* Furthermore, they treated her assumed recalcitrance to passion as a strategy—and her tricks against her suitor as tactics—

made necessary by the double standard of sexual morality. Since men under that standard claimed a license that true love deplored, she would put her man out of his humour of variety, his penchant for the chase, and the arrogance that went with it, before she committed herself to the true love she really felt for him. His reaction to her strategy and tactics was, of course, to devise his own, calculated to bring her to commitment before she intended and thus to ultimate acknowledgement of his masculine superiority. Here was a dynamic pattern of intrigue to lend speed and suspense to comedy. And into this pattern the satiric exhibition of humour characters, especially of pseudo wits and would-be wits and old men on the loose, might be easily fitted by making them rivals to the truewit in the pursuit of the witty woman.

In *Wit at Several Weapons* Beaumont and Fletcher developed this pattern in Cunningham's courtship of the unnamed Niece of Sir Perfidious Oldcraft and fitted into it the absurdities of the pseudo wit Sir Gregory Fop and the would-be Pompey Doodle. In *The Scornful Lady* the unnamed titular character deflates the ardors of the Elder Loveless because he has been indiscreet in boasting of her infatuation for him, and he retaliates by a ruse provoking her jealousy to undo her scorn. At the same time his younger brother, with three pseudo wits as hangers-on, competes with an old usurer to overcome a wealthy young widow's pretended disinclination to matrimony. In *The Wild-Goose Chase* three young French rakes, Mirabel, Pinac, and Belleur, having sown their wild oats in Italy, meet their matches in three witty maidens of their own country, Oriana, Lillia-Bianca, and Rosalura, who want to be won, but not too easily. Finally, in *Wit Without Money,* a widow, Lady Heartwell, and her virgin sister Isabella, both wealthy and witty, fall in love with two penniless wits, Valentine and Francisco, but must be sure they are being courted not merely for their money. While they are testing out their men, in discussion more than by stratagem,[77] the men themselves are not without resource. The love-game is diversified by the attitudinizing of three pseudo wits pursuing Lady Heartwell—Fountain, Bellamore, and Harebrain.

The comic eclecticism achieved here—Jonson's satire of the spirit of affectation in a pattern of amorous intrigue between wit and witty woman—appealed to Shirley, who carried it even further in several of the best comedies of the Caroline period. He also incorporated in most of them sub-plots based on the more sentimental type of citizen comedy, perhaps convinced that he had Jonson's warrant for this in *The Devil is an Ass*. So attentive was he to Jonson's principle of the many-actioned whole and means to achieve its unity of inclusion that these comedies, despite their complexity of themes, crowded casts of characters, and diversity of situations, are anything but chaotic.

The first of them, *Love Tricks,* is the least successful hybrid, for Shirley here resorted to Elizabethan romantic fiction for a main plot composed of three courtships,[78] with only one—that between Antonio and Hilaria—having effects reminiscent of Beaumont and Fletcher. The Jonsonian element is chiefly present in a long, semi-expository satirical interlude describing "The School of Complement."[79] Over this academy of fashion, the suitor Gasparo presides like another Well-bred, Truewit, Crites, or Wittipol. His students are a motley crew of townsfolk and countryfolk, all smitten with "the humour of gentilitie."

In *The Witty Fair One* Shirley found his stride, devising two amorous intrigues to speed the action. That of Aimwell to win Violetta, despite her uncle's care and the rivalry of the pseudo wits Sir Nicholas Treedle and his Tutor, is partly borrowed from Beaumont and Fletcher's *Wit at Several Weapons*.[80] The attempt of the rake Fowler to seduce Violetta's cousin, Penelope, and Penelope's counter-attack to reform him and snare him in wedlock constitute an interesting blend of Beaumont and Fletcher and sentimental citizen comedy.[81] Finally, Aimwell and Fowler are provided with two friends, Clare and Manly, who respectively recall Jonson's Truewit and Manly and perform their normative functions.

Hyde Park has three amorous intrigues. The main one—that of Fairfield and Carol—is pure Beaumont and Fletcher, drawn directly from *The Scornful Lady* and enriched with dialog comparable to that in *Wit Without Money*. The remaining two owe something to citizen comedy, one involving the reformation of an aristocratic Libertine and the other the return of a supposed widow's "dead" husband to claim her from her suitor.[82] At the outset of the play, three of the wits converse so as to create a *beau monde* atmosphere like that of *Epicoene*.[83] They are contrasted with two pseudo wits, Venture and Rider, who are Fairfield's rivals for Carol's favor. In the third and fourth acts, intrigue is relegated to the background while the chief characters promenade at the races in Hyde Park and along the shrubbery-protected walks. These scenes are brilliantly documentary in a style that looks both back to Jonson and ahead to Etherege.[84]

The Lady of Pleasure of the mid 1630's is Shirley's greatest: in Caroline comedy it ranks as *The Way of the World*. It is dominated by a strikingly witty woman, Celestina, who has a philosophy of pleasure consonant with virtue. Hers is an admirable intellectual Libertinism. Subordinated to her in an elaborate stratification are Lady Aretina Bornwell, a pseudo lady of the country gentry who is a lady of pleasure by being an adultress; four pseudo wits of the town *beau monde*—Kickshaw, Littleworth, Scentlove, and Haircut; and Master Frederick Bornwell, Aretina's nephew, a country would-be who has been to the university. This essentially Jonsonian stratification of social pretenders is modified by a domestic triangle sub-plot involving Aretina and ending in her reformation, as in citizen comedy. Celestina has two friends, Mariana and Isabella, to whom she expounds her ideas, echoing Montaigne, as did Marston's Crispinella.[85] Lord A., a disciple of the new Court Platonism, solicits Celestina to become his "mistress" and meets with a chiding rebuff for an invitation to dalliance disguised as a *précieuse* "friendship."

Of the several supplementary fathers of the Sons of Ben, Shirley showed the Sons how to revive Jonson with the most bizarre transmutations. Having both Massinger's and much of Shirley's work before them, they were provided with practical guidance to illuminate and extend their dichotomous theory. They could see clearly some of the possible eclecticisms open to them and most of the problems involved in adapting a rich heritage of craft to meet the many-faceted challenge of the time. At least four comic styles were appropriate for them. They

101

might, like Chapman, put on the learned sock, and do classical adaptations invaded by Jonson's English realism. Or they might don either the plain sentimental sock or the stuffed sock of satiric farce by combining Jonson with citizen comedy. Or they might ease into the brighter sophisticated sock by joining Jonson to Marston and Beaumont and Fletcher.

CHAPTER
FOUR

The Learned Sock

$\mathcal{N}$ever was "Jonson's learned sock" more "on," in Milton's words, than in the induction to *Every Man Out of His Humour*. Asper, preparing to assume in the play itself the envious role of Macilente, has just left the stage to his two friends, the critics Mitis and Cordatus. When Mitis asks, "You have seene his play, Cordatus? pray you, how is't?" the latter points out that it is to a certain degree an exotic attempt to revive the unique spirit of Aristophanes and hence, although it has been greatly to his own liking, is something of a gamble so far as the audience is concerned. His answer is as follows:

> Faith sir, I must refraine to judge, only this, I can say of it, 'tis strange, and of a particular kind by it selfe, somewhat like *Vetus Comoedia:* a worke that hath bounteously pleased me, how it will answere the generall expectation, I know not.

When Mitis goes on to ask, "Does he observe all the lawes of *Comedie* in it?" and explains that he means those rules usually regarded as classical, such as "the equall division of it into *Acts,* and *Scenes,*

103

according to the *Terentian* manner," the "true number of Actors," "the furnishing of the *Scene* with GREX, or CHORUS," and respect for the unity of time—"that the whole Argument fall within compasse of a dayes businesse"—, Cordatus replies that "these are too nice observations" and that he can discern no necessity for the comic writer to follow them to the letter. He then launches into a short lecture on how the moderns should create with reference to the ancients, based on his knowledge of the evolution of Greek and Roman comedy:

> If those lawes you speake of, had beene delivered us, *ab initio,* and in their present vertue and perfection, there had beene some reason for obeying their powers: but 'tis extant, that that which we call Comoedia, was at first nothing but a simple, and continued *Song,* sung by one only person, till SUSARIO invented a second, after him EPICHARMUS a third; PHORMUS, and CHIONIDES devised to have foure Actors, with a *Prologue* and *Chorus;* to which CRATINUS (long after) added a fift, and sixt; EUPOLIS more; ARISTOPHANES more than they: every man in the dignitie of his spirit and judgement, supplyed something. And (though that in him this kinde of *Poeme* appeared absolute, and fully perfected) yet how is the face of it chang'd since, in MENANDER, PHILEMON, CECILIUS, PLAUTUS, and the rest; who have utterly excluded the *Chorus,* altered the property of the persons, their names, and natures, and augmented it with all liberty, according to the elegance and disposition of those times wherein they wrote? I see not then, but we should enjoy the same licence, or free power, to illustrate and heighten our invention as they did; and not bee tyed to those strict and regular formes, which the nicenesse of a few (who are nothing but forme) would thrust upon us.[1]

Here is a sound, enlightened, liberal view of the problem that T. S. Eliot has called "tradition and the individual talent."[2] Cordatus recognizes that the individual talent must create from tradition but holds that, since tradition itself is a growth or a process of accreting originality, the truest following of it is the free rather than the slavish, the experimental rather than the literalistic. It was in this way that Asper-Jonson had revived Aristophanes. It was in this way that Jonson and

104

any who chose to be his Sons should work when drawing on any phase of the classical heritage—Old or Middle or New Comedy. Even in adaptations of Greek or Roman plays, fidelity to the original was not the main desideratum. The adaptation, rather than a mere exercise in the resurrection of the dead, should be a virtuoso performance in grafting the living on the still alive.

This was in 1599. A generation later, the prestige of the classics was still high as the very basis of the tradition that the comic writer must carry on. But Jonson's prescription for freedom in the process was taken for granted, even if this freedom was to be shown chiefly in an intelligent eclecticism. Richard Brathwait, in his *The English Gentleman* of 1630, approves of playgoing as one of the proper recreations of a gentleman, if not over-indulged in. As he puts it:

> There is another *Recreation* used by Gentlemen, but especially in this Citie; which used with Moderation, is not altogether to be disallowed; and it is repairing to *Stage-playes* where, as they shal see much Lightnesse, so they may heare something worthy of more serious attention.

A few pages further on, he shows his preference for comedies which are definitely eclectic and whose eclecticism should be predominantly classical, levying from each of the great Greek and Roman practitioners of the craft the virtue that was eminently his: ". . . Comedies should breath nothing but *Terences* art, *Cecilius* gravity, *Menanders* sweetnesse, *Aristophanes* conceit, and *Plautus* wit. . . ."[3]

The Son of Ben to whom Aristophanes' "conceit" appealed so strongly that he attempted imitation and even adaptation was Thomas Randolph. The imitation was done first, at least one skit and possibly two. The skit we can be sure of as his was *Aristippus; or, The Joviall Philosopher,* probably performed at Cambridge sometime between the beginning of the academic year in October 1625, and the November of the following year. Its popularity was immense, since it was printed seven times between 1630 and 1635.[4] The other skit, *The Drinking Academy,* extant in manuscript, has been attributed to Randolph by four of the most competent scholars of the period, but this attribution has been challenged by another and accepted only as a fairly strong probability by the most distinguished authority.[5] Its date is uncertain also, but the best guess places it alongside *Aristippus* in 1626.[6] The adaptation—and it is more that than a translation—is *Hey for Honesty, Down with Knavery,* based on *Plutus,* and there are unsolved problems relating to both its date and authorship. The likelihood is that Randolph wrote the original version of it sometime between 1626 and 1628. The only text we have, however, is one published in 1651, about seventeen years after Randolph's death, and "augmented" by an unknown friend of Randolph's, "F.J.," thought to be a minor fellow dramatist, Francis Jaques. It is practically impossible to determine the full extent of his augmentations or their date, but most of them were probably made between 1648 and 1649.[7] Despite the uncertainties here involved, I will treat all three plays as substantially Randolph's, and on this assumption will develop positions as to his use of Aristophanes that, although stated as if they were fully warranted by the evidence, must of course be regarded as tentative.

The typical Old Comedy, as represented by most of the surviving plays of Aristophanes, has a linear action in which the scenes are as episodic as in modern Expressionist drama. Conflict is oversimplified and without ensuing complications. Two antagonists or groups of antagonists are introduced; the impending trouble between them is prepared for; they clash; the victory of one or their mutual reconciliation follows; the consequences thereof are revealed. Fantastic allegory may be central or incidental, but is nearly always present. Personal satire may figure in the treatment of both major and minor characters. Physical incongruity (including violence), grotesque exaggeration, caricature, and bawdry are employed. At the same time, wide-glancing satire, both topical and universal, abounds. Usually the basic conflict, the fulcrum behind the contending characters, is one of ideas. The author's position in such an ideological melee may be clarified through an expositor or mouthpiece character.[8]

The Clouds is fairly typical. The opening scene indicates that the old

106

Athenian, Strepsiades, is to be engaged in a three-fold conflict—with the creditors of his spoiled son Phidippides; with Phidippides himself, who refuses to go to the Academy of Socrates and learn sophistry to get out of paying his debts; and with the Academy's Sophists, since the father must go in his son's place. On arriving there, he is met by a disciple, who explains to him some of the bizarre activities in progress under Socrates' direction, and shortly he has a chance to observe the pupils and their master. Socrates lectures him, learns his object in coming to the Academy, and undertakes his instruction. Fantastic allegory enters in the Chorus of Women Clouds. Physical incongruity, accompanied by some violence and by grotesque exaggeration, caricature, and bawdry, figures in Strepsiades' instruction, and certainly the personal satire directed at Socrates as the chief of the Sophists is sufficiently obvious and malicious. Once it is decided that the father is no fit pupil but must bring his son, the conflict between Strepsiades and Phidippides reaches a crux, with the father temporarily victorious. The introduction of Phidippides' instructors permits Aristophanes to state through Dicaeus his own humanistic conception of discipline as opposed to the Sophists' discipline expounded by Adicus. After Phidippides has been thoroughly exposed to the latter, he provides his father with ammunition to make the worse appear the better cause. The result is that Strepsiades puts to rout two of the creditors and their witnesses. Now, however, victory boomerangs. Phidippides is so skilled in the new learning that he can justify beating his own father and mother. Appalled at this consequence of sophistry, Strepsiades decides that the Academy must go and successfully implements his decision in a climactic scene of farcical, satirical, allegorical violence. Wide-glancing satire at Athenian science, philosophy, justice, sports, and delinquency, at human greed, hypocrisy, selfishness, and ingratitude enters into the dialog. The basic modern issue between essentialist and progressive education is apparent behind all of Strepsiades' imbroglios.

Both *Aristippus* and *The Drinking Academy* are based on *The Clouds*. The first introduces a young student of logic, Simplicius, who takes his difficulties with "possibilities and incompossibilities" to the great philosopher Aristippus, whose academy is the Dolphin Tavern. The second shows the old usurer Worldly, metamorphosed from an illiberal to a prodigal father, following dotingly and emulously his son Knowlittle's education at the academy of gallantry presided over by Chavalero Whiffe. Although starting with these basically similar situations, the two plays diverge radically from each other in their manipulation of the pattern of Old Comedy and the effects that usually go with it.

Allegory is central in *Aristippus* in that this jovial philosopher is an incarnation of the spirit of sack. He thus praises it:

> But sack is the life, soul, and spirits of a man—the fire which Prometheus stole, not from Jove's kitchen, but his wine-cellar, to increase the native heat and radical moisture, without which we are but drowsy dust or dead clay.

In passages lively with incidental satire, he argues that it is the foundation of military discipline in the garrisons, where the soldiers are "trained up to the mustering of pewter pots daily: learning to contemn death by accustoming to be dead-drunk"; that it is as potent as the philosopher's stone in effecting transmutations, since the young heir who is sedulous in its study usually changes his estate into *"aurum potabile"* and is thus made "more capable of divine meditation" by "being purged and freed from so much earth"; and finally that it is the best means to the promotion of the peculiar kind of lightheadedness on which depend "all intelligence, intellect, and understanding." "No wine, no philosophy," concludes Aristippus, *"In vino veritas. . . ."* Aristippus is the most Falstaffian character in English comedy since Falstaff, as is plain from his explanation of how sack got its name— ". . . it may justly seem to have taken the name of sack from sacking of cities"—and from one of his scholars' reasons for not going to bed until dawn: "Why, a pox of the morning, what have we to do with the sober time of the day?"[9]

The main conflict of the skit is between Aristippus and Wild-man, apostle of the malt heresy of beer. The trouble between them is forecast when Wild-man comes to the tavern denouncing Aristippus' "red-nosed philosophy" and threatening varieties of dire revenge. In their first clash, Aristippus wins, commanding his scholars to "Kick him out of the presence: his company will metamorphose us to balderdash." Wild-man, however, is capable of equally effective violence and returns with two brewers to rout the scholars who have kicked him out of the tavern and to clobber their master into insensibility. Now follows the reconciliation. Wild-man takes a drink of sack, is impressed by its authority, regrets that he has broken the pate of its philosopher, and stands anxiously by while a garrulous, boastful, much-travelled, and therefore mendacious barber-surgeon, Signior de Medico Campo, prepares to revive Aristippus. After all his exhibition of medical lore, Campo ends by prescribing sack. Whereupon Aristippus recovers with this observation: "I am newly come back from hell, and have seen so many of my acquaintance there, that I wonder whose art hath restored me to life again." Wild-man thus addresses him:

> O reverend philosopher and alchemy of understanding, thou very sack of sciences, thou noble Spaniard, thou Catholic Monarch of Wines, Archduke of Canary, Emperor of the Sacred Sherry, pardon me, pardon my rudeness; and I will foreswear that Dutch heresy of English beer, and the witchcraft of Middleton's water; I'll turn myself into a gown, and be a professed disciple of Aristippus.

Although Randolph in his "Praeludium" conventionally abjures personal satire—"Let's have no one particular man traduc'd"—,[10] we know from the manuscript of the skit that the "vaine glorious Quacksalve" Medico de Campo was a thrust at "Dick Litchfield a Barber Surgeon in Cambridge" and that Wild-man was a caricature aimed at "Buttler of Trinitie Coll. in Cambridge, & one that keeps a Tipling house."[11]

Where *Aristippus* falls short as an Aristophanic imitation is in the grounding of its farce and fantasy in a real conflict of ideas. Such a conflict is certainly suggested. When Wild-man is introduced, he is referred to as "The University Ramist" and as "a zealous brother," whereas he himself speaks of "Aristippus his Arminianism."[12] When

Randolph was a student at Cambridge, Ramist logic was well established there as one of the bulwarks of Puritan theology. Sir William Temple, a fellow and tutor of logic at King's College, Cambridge, in the 1580's, had propagandized for it; his last work, *A Logicall Analysis of Twenty Select Psalmes,* published in 1605, applied the system to theology. George Downame, one of whose sermons against Arminianism Laud was to suppress in 1631, delivered a Ramist commentary at Cambridge, published in 1610. Alexander Richardson, tutor at Queen's College, Cambridge, was a popular lecturer on Ramus, his notes being circulated in manuscript amongst Puritan students before their publication in 1629. In the very year *Aristippus* was performed, an alumnus of Cambridge, Anthony Wotton, who had become a leading Puritan divine, published his translation of Ramus' *Dialecticae* under the title, *The Art of Logick. . . . Gathered out of Aristotle and set in due forme. . . .*[13] Since Ramus, in the words of one modern scholar, was guilty of a "confusion and corruption of logic, rhetoric, and poetic,"[14] he was anathema to a true Aristotelian, and no Cambridge student of the 1620's surpassed Randolph in his devotion to Aristotle. As he wrote of his student days in an eclog to Ben Jonson:

> When I contented liv'd by Cham's fair streams,
> Without desire to see the prouder Thames,
> I had no flock to care for, but could sit
> Under a willow covert, and repeat
> Those deep and learned lays, on every part
> Grounded on judgment, subtlety, and art,
> That the great tutor to the greatest king,
> The shepherd of Stagira us'd to sing—
> The shepherd of Stagira, that unfolds
> All Nature's closet, shows whate'er it holds;
> The matter, form, sense, motion, place, and measure
> Of everything contain'd in her vast treasure.[15]

Furthermore, as a good Anglican very much opposed to the Puritans, all of Randolph's sympathies were with Arminianism. One of his spokesmen in a poem about the Cotswold Games thus ironically observes:

110

The Learned Sock

Some melancholy swains about have gone
To teach all zeal their own complexion:
Choler they will admit sometimes, I see,
But phlegm and sanguine no religions be.[16]

He obviously had both his Aristotelian anti-Ramism and his Arminian-ism in mind when he pitted Aristippus and his wine of truth against Wild-man and his Dutch heresy of English beer, but the allusions remain merely incidental and the real issues involved are not developed in the dialog. Thus *Aristippus,* which might have had considerable value as a satiric commentary on the Cambridge climate of opinion, fails to rise above the level of a clever college farce concerning the respective merits of two forms assumed by that deity whom Thomas Lovell Beddoes was so memorably to apostrophize as "Lord Alcohol."[17]

The Drinking Academy begins in a manner that Aristophanes would have applauded. Simple, the servant of the would-be gallant, Know-little, enters "with a pipe in one hand and a candle in the other spewing." He informs us of his master's progress under Chavalero Whiffe:

my young master Knowlittle hath past his accidence of drinking and is now in his quarreling grammer whilst I like a blocke head stay yet in the A B C of tobaco.

When Knowlittle's doting father Worldly comes to check on his progress, Whiffe indicates that the pedagogy has so far been phe-nomenally efficacious:

Sir yo se the effects of my skil that in a moments space was able by my chimistrie to extract so compleat a gentleman out (as I may say almost) of a dung hill. he is now the Phoenix of the age who was latly alumpe of Pesantry the gallants adore him and happy is he who can pay homage to his potent toe. wher ere he goes honer waits upon him and fortune follows him with propetious wings.

Thus carefully prepared for, Knowlittle appears and in a succession of scenes demonstrates his knowledge of "quarreling grammer" and the "accidence of drinking," to the accompaniment of his tutor's flattery

111

and his father's admiration. It is in the higher learning of courtship, however, that he most brilliantly acquits himself. He is to pay his addresses to a Madam Pecunia, Lady Inconstantia Fortune's eldest daughter, and with this end in view, Whiffe, as Simple informs us, "hath put all his braines in a presse to sqees out new frases and poetical annagrams." With Worldly playing the role of Pecunia, Knowlittle sonorously rehearses his conned rigmarole of gimcrack adjectives and mixed metaphors. Pecunia, of course, is an allegorical figure representing money. She never appears as a character because what action remains is devoted to the conflict foreshadowed by the introduction of Knowlittle's rival, the cheater Timothy Shirke, and his gang, the cutpurse Tom Nimmer and the highwayman Jack Bidstand. They lure Whiffe, Knowlittle, Worldly, and Simple to a supposed meeting with Pecunia among ruins on the outskirts of the city, frighten them by appearing in the disguises of Plutus, the Devil, and Madam Pecunia's ghost, leave them stripped of their clothes and wandering in the woods, and then depart to help themselves to Worldly's coffers, "where Pecunia lies." Their final destination is

> . . . the taverne where wee'l make
> Her grave and all here present ther invite
> To morne with us in wine both red and white.[18]

What has happened in this skit is that Aristophanic "conceit" has had to yield to Jonsonian humours, either drawn directly from his plays or from those of his colleagues and rivals. The relationship between Knowlittle and Whiffe is that between the country would-be Sogliardo and the town rogue, Cavalier Shift, alias Whiffe, in *Every Man Out of His Humour*. The relationship between Worldly and his son is based on that between Canter Father Pennyboy and prodigal Pennyboy Junior in *The Staple of News*. The three rogues are reminiscent of those in *Bartholomew Fair*. The old usurer in Beaumont and Fletcher's *The Scornful Lady* as well as the "School of Complement" in Shirley's *Love Tricks* may have figured in the complex eclecticism.[19] Satire on the acquisitive spirit and the spirit of affectation with some concrete

112

reference to contemporary life is carried out in an action that becomes increasingly more farcical. No real conflict of ideas is even suggested. Amusing scoundrels have merely won a fantastic victory over a motley quartet of gulls—two social pretenders illustrating Aristotelian vice and folly, a more respectable fellow scoundrel, and a droll nincompoop of a servant.

The *Plutus* of Aristophanes is one of his plays belonging to Middle rather than to Old Comedy.[20] The period of Middle Comedy was from 404 to 338 B.C. The form was transitional, a modification of Old Comedy in the direction of the New Comedy of Menander. Mythological burlesque, a minor characteristic of Old Comedy, became in Middle Comedy a major emphasis. Wealth and poverty and death were its dominant themes or motifs. Personal satire diminished and disappeared; satire on sycophants and women increased. The slave emerged as one of the important characters. Dream-fulfillment, providing an escape from the depressing atmosphere of an economic order unbalanced by luxury, shaped the action. Clear-cut conflict faded into ensuing complications, with the exploitation of stock characters serving as interruption and diversion. The Chorus and the vital clash of ideas frayed into vestiges or withered quite away.

Plutus takes us into an unlikely dream world where Wealth bestows his favors only on the good and the just. Chremylus, an old yeoman anxious about his son's future, is told by the oracle of Apollo to follow and take home the first person he meets. With his querulous slave, Cario, he follows a dirty blind man who turns out to be Plutus, the God of Wealth. Jupiter made him blind so that his distribution of riches would be indiscriminate. He is dirty because he has just come from a miser's house. A Chorus of Chremylus' poor tenants, a down-at-heel but honest neighbor, Blepsidemus, and the old hag Poverty, who has been residing with Chremylus, react variously to the new-found Wealth. Despite Poverty's defense of herself as a bringer of blessings in disguise, Chremylus and Blepsidemus go through with their plan of taking Plutus to the temple of Aesculapius in the hope of restoring his sight. With Cario describing how the cure was accom-

113

plished, Plutus returns with perfect vision and sets about a redistribution of wealth to those who deserve it. Dicaeus, a just man once in rags, appears in expensive new apparel. Sycophantes, a parasite and informer, is stripped of his finery. An old nymphomaniac who has been keeping a gigolo with her money must face his scorn and the prospect of losing him. Even the gods are upset. Mercury and the high-priest of Jupiter complain they are no longer raking in sacrifices, since wealth is being equally spread. At the close of the play, Plutus, now the scrupulous servant of virtue, is to be worshipped in Jupiter's place.

Randolph's *Hey for Honesty, Down with Knavery* is twice as long as *Plutus*. All Aristophanes' characters are retained, but half of them appear under different names. There are about a dozen new characters and six and a half new scenes. Even where the characters, incidents, and dialog of the original are being followed, Randolph translates everything into English terms. Chremylus, for example, thus explains his reason for seeking out the oracle:

> . . . I repaired to Delphos to ask counsel of Apollo, because I saw myself almost arrived at Gravesend, to know if I should bring up my son suitable to the thriving trades of this age we live in, namely, to be a sequestrator, or pettifogger, or informer, or flatterer, or belonging to knights o' th' post, or a committee-man's clerk, or some such excellent rascal, clothing himself from top to toe in knavery, without a welt or gard of goodness about him. For I see, as the times go now, such thriving education will be the richest portion I can leave him.[21]

One of the exchanges between Plutus and Chremylus' servant, who has become Carion in Randolph's version, goes as follows:

> Plutus: . . . I am Plutus, the rich god of wealth: my father was Pinchback Truepenny, the rich usurer of Islington; my mother, Mistress Silverside, an alderman's widow. I was born in Golden Lane, christened at the Mint in the Tower; Banks the conjuror and old Hobson the carrier were my godfathers.
> Carion: As sure as he can be, this Plutus, god of wealth, is a pure Welshman, born with his pedigree in his mouth, he speaks

it so naturally. I'll lay my life he was begot and bred in the silver-mine that Middleton found in Wales.[22]

Chremylus thus stresses money's power: "It is most certain, money is the Catholic empress of the world, her commands are obeyed from Spain to the Indes."[23] The Chorus of tenants is turned into four English yokels, Scrape-all, Stiff, Clodpole, and Lackland; and a parson, Dull-pate, and a curate, Clip-Latin, add to the farcical realism. Poverty, who appears as Penia-Penniless, is not content merely to debate her case but leads a mob resembling Falstaff's troops and suggesting the episodes of violence that marked the great depression of the early 1620's.[24] The informer Sycophantes, rechristened Never-Good, is referred to as bringing a Puritan to the pillory "With Prynne and Burton" and "conspiring with/Sir Giles Mompesson in the persecution/Of innocent tapsters." The old nymphomaniac, renamed Anus, and her gigolo, Neanias, become most repulsively alive as illustrations of the decadent concupiscence and irresponsible gallantry inveighed against by such critics of Caroline manners as Mathew Griffith and Edmund Cobbes. Says Anus:

> Half putrified, I walk up and down like the picture of death's head in a charnel-house. But see, yonder's my gamester, my cock o' th' game: he's marching to some banquet or other: 'tis Shrove Tuesday with him, but Lent with me. O grief, to be bound from flesh!

Whereupon Neanias reels drunkenly across the stage singing the following ditty:

> *I'll kiss the old hag no more,*
> *She has no moisture in her:*
> *If ever I lie with a lass ere I die,*
> *It shall be a youthful sinner.*
>
> *Give me a lass that is young:*
> *I ask no greater blessing.*
> *I'll ne'er lie again with fourscore-and-ten,*
> *A carcase not worth the pressing.*

115

The Sons of Ben

I will not embrace her again
To set the town on a scoffing:
I'll never make more Death's widow a whore
And cuckold the innocent coffin.

When Mercury appears, he impersonates a whole gallery of contemporary characters—a vagrant, a braggart soldier, a gipsy pickpocket, a porter, a merchant, a fool, a juggler, and a poet. And he is followed by a large group of complaining money-grabbers drawn from the life—an attorney, a tinker, a miller, a tailor, a shoemaker, and others.

Perhaps Randolph's most startling transformation of his source is his satire on Puritanism and Catholicism as religions subservient to the acquisitive spirit. As an antagonist to the informer Never-Good, he introduces an entirely new character, the Puritan extremist Ananais Goggle, a combination of Jonson's Tribulation Wholesome and Ananais of *The Alchemist*. Goggle thus states to Carion his will to wealth:

> I come to Plutus' conventicle now,
> 'Tis he can cure my troubles; he brings joy
> To the fraternity of Amsterdam,
> To the Geneva brotherhood, and the saints,
> Whose pure devotions feed on Banbury cakes:
> He can restore my wealth, give me abundance
> Of holy gold and silver purified. . . .

For the high-priest of Jupiter, Randolph or perhaps the "augmenter" substitutes a vicious caricature of the Pope, who cries out to Parson Dull-pate:

> O, I am dead with hunger! A saucy hunger,
> With heresy as bad as Arianism,
> Knaws on my sacred guts.

He elaborates his dilemma as follows:

> . . . since Plutus hath received his eyes,
> Indulgences are grown cheap and at no price:
> An absolution for a rape made now

116

Is nothing worth.
Give me but one poor crust before I faint,
And I will canonise thee for a saint.

For a leg of mutton, the Pope promises remission of all Dull-pate's
sins, no matter what they are. Amazed, Dull-pate queries, ". . . though
I should ravish nuns/Under the altar?" "Tis a venial sin," replies the
Pope. "Or kill a king?" asks Dull-pate. "Tis meritorious," says the
Pope. Then Dull-pate calls on his powers of invention:

> Cuckold my father, whore my natural mother,
> Grant the supremacy of the secular powers,
> Be drunk at mass, strip all the feminine saints
> Into their smocks, laugh at a friar's bald crown,
> Piss in the pix, deny your mysteries,
> Outlie your legend, get Pope Joan with child,
> Eat flesh in Lent, slit off my confessor's ears:
> Or any sin, as great as your own holiness
> Or any of your predecessors acted?

The Pope sticks to his original proposition: "A leg of mutton wipes
all sins away. . . ."[25]

At the end of Randolph's adaptation, the marriage of Plutus to fair
Mistress Honesty serves to underscore with allegory the ethical theme
stated earlier by the just man, Dicaeus:

> As the mad world goes now, who could believe
> But purblind fate and chance did hold the sceptre
> Of human actions? Who beholds the miseries
> Of honest mortals, and compares their fortunes
> With the unsatiable pleasures of gross epicures,
> Whose bursting bags are glutted with the spoils
> Of wretched orphans—who (I say) sees this,
> But would almost turn atheist, and forswear
> All heaven, all gods, all divine providence?
> But if to Plutus we his eyes restore,
> Good men shall grow in wealth, and knaves grow poor.[26]

All this is in keeping with the spirit of Aristophanes and even goes
him one better in ethical rigor with a Jonsonian smack. The mysterious

117

F.J. was aware of these points when he penned his preface, which is worth quoting entire:

This is a pleasant comedy, though some may judge it satirical. 'Tis the more like Aristophanes the father: besides, if it be biting, 'tis a biting age we live in. Then biting for biting. Again, Tom Randal, the adopted son of Ben Jonson, being the translator hereof, followed his father's steps; they both of them loved sack and harmless mirth, and here they show it; and I (that know myself) am not averse from it neither. This I thought good to acquaint thee with. Farewell.[27]

New Comedy, perfected in Greece by Menander and passed on to the Roman masters, Plautus and Terence, for somewhat divergent modes of imitation,[28] was "well-made" in an almost Scribean sense that neither Old nor Middle Comedy had been. Its distinguishing feature was intrigue, with more complex conflict and with ensuing complications often intricately tangled. The ubiquitous slave of Middle Comedy came to the fore as an arch executor of stratagems, usually in the interests of his young master. The thematic range was narrowed toward domestic and love relationships—father and children, husband and wife, lover and sweetheart, frequently in pairs. Disguise, mistaken identity, exchanged and long-lost children, rival friends of brothers and sisters, obstacles to love, and money problems—these took over as the standard gambits. Flattering parasites, grasping merchants, gossipy courtesans, braggart soldiers, and similar stock characters furnished farcical merriment, with some satiric overtones. Underlying the happy endings with their recognitions, restorations, and marriages was a standardized romantic justice, atoning in the domain of stage illusion for the actual atrocities of war, slavery, institutionalized lust, and inconstant fortune. Realism replaced fantasy and allegory, but it was superficial and highly conventionalized rather than normatively analytical or empirically documentary.[29]

The way of the Sons of Ben with New Comedy—with that mixture of "*Terences* art, *Cecilius* gravity, *Menanders* sweetnesse . . . *Plautus* wit" described by Brathwait—may best be observed in Randolph's *The*

The Learned Sock

Jealous Lovers and Brome's *The New Academy.* The first of these was the more successful of two comedies performed for King Charles and Queen Henrietta on the occasion of their visit to Cambridge in March 1632. Its less liked competitor, Peter Hausted's *The Rival Friends,* to be discussed in a later chapter, was acted by the men of Queen's College on March 19, three days before *The Jealous Lovers* was put on by the men of Trinity. Involvement of university officials in the matter of priority of performance, the suicide of one of them later, a brawl between visiting gentlemen over a lady's being jostled in the "great preasse of people" at one of the performances and an outbreak of poetical "flyting" from the student factions supporting Randolph and Hausted—all these events made *The Jealous Lovers* famous among Randolph's plays.[30] Brome's *The New Academy, or The New Exchange,* first published in 1659, had no comparable reputation, if indeed any at all, since nothing definite is known of its performance or date of composition. Its use of material resembling the "School of Complement" in Shirley's *Love Tricks* has led to *The New Academy's* being dated between 1625 and 1628, but since *Love Tricks* was not available in published form until 1631 and *The New Academy* has a main plot strikingly like that of *The Jealous Lovers,* there is ground for thinking that Brome's play belongs to the 1630's and that he wrote it—probably after July 1635—to reap on the popular stage some of the success Randolph had won at the university.[31]

With its setting in Thebes and many of its dramatis personae named after characters in Roman comedies, especially Plautus',[32] *The Jealous Lovers* unfolds the complicated love story of a pair of sons and a pair of daughters whose identities have become confused. Tyndarus is the son of Demetrius; Pamphilus the son of Chermylus. Chremylus' daughter is Techmessa; Demetrius' daughter is Evadne. The two fathers have exchanged offspring, with the result that Evadne and Techmessa both pass for the daughters of Chremylus and that Tyndarus and Pamphilus are both considered the sons of Demetrius. Demetrius, to save the sons from being drafted as food for the Minotaur,[33] has taken them to Athens. Both daughters believe they are

119

sisters; both sons, believing they are brothers, return to Thebes, where each unwittingly courts his sister. When their true identities are revealed at the close of the play, they merely switch sweethearts. Their love-relationships, besides having this surprising outcome, are complicated by Techmessa's jealousy of Pamphilus and by Tyndarus' jealousy of Evadne as well as the intrigues of Chremylus' wife Dipsas, who is obsessed with malicious envy of her adopted daughter, Evadne. Ballio, a parasite, serves as chief intriguer, at one time for Dipsas, at another for the jealous lovers, and in the end for himself.

This complex intrigue pattern borrowed from Roman New Comedy is invaded by Jonsonian imitation in two ways. Randolph studies the respective jealousies of Tyndarus and Techmessa with much of the psychological detail and ethical nuance that Jonson devotes to Kitely in *Every Man in His Humour*.[34] He also introduces a prodigal, Asotus, who is modeled after Knowlittle in *The Drinking Academy,* and develops him into a full-length study in the spirit of affectation. Ballio, the intriguing parasite, is his Chavalero Whiffe. Simo, his father, is a miser turned into a doting lecher, and thus an improvement upon Worldly of *The Drinking Academy* as an example of an Aristotelian extreme becoming its opposite. A quartet of pseudo wits, two Bobadills bragging of their valor and two Matthews with poetical pretensions, admire Asotus in the latter stages of his progress. Coached in drinking, gourmandizing, dicing, and wenching, he makes a fool of himself in testing Evadne's chastity at Tyndarus' jealous instigation and in boasting later with a stolen ring that he has possessed her, but he shines to better advantage with his courtesan, Phryne, even though she regards him as "a poor mushroom."[35]

However, Randolph makes Asotus something more than a "mushroom" in an adaptation of the graveyard scene in *Hamlet*.[36] He and his courtesan and his pseudo wit admirers confer wtih a sexton, supposed to have coffined the bodies of Tyndarus and Techmessa, who have faked suicide to try the fidelity of their respective loves. The pseudo wits cannot believe that either a soldier or a poet, once dead, rests valorless or verseless. Sexton, speaking satirically, but at the same time with a mournful insight into the transience of human life that rises to prose poetry, undertakes to disillusion each pair in turn:

> This was a captain's skull, one that carried a storm in his countenance and a tempest in his tongue; the great bugbear of the city, that threw drawers down the stairs as familiarly as quart-pots; and had a pension from the barber chirugeons for breaking of pates: a fellow that had ruined the noses of more bawds and panders than the disease belonging to the trade; and yet I remember, when he went to burial, another corse took the wall of him, and the bandog ne'er grumbled.

> This was a poetical noddle. O, the sweet lines, choice language, eloquent figures, besides the jests, half-jests, quarter-jests, and quibbles that have come out o' these chaps that yawn so! He has not now so much as a new-coined compliment to procure him a supper. The best friend he has may walk by him now, and yet have ne'er a jeer put upon him. His mistress had a little dog deceased the other day, and all the wit in this noddle could not pump out an elegy to bewail it. He has been my tenant these seven years, and in all that while I never heard him rail against the times, or complain of the neglect of learning. Melpomene and the rest of the Muses have a good time on't that he is dead; for while he lived, he ne'er left calling upon 'em. He was buried (as most of the tribe) at the charge of the parish, and is happier dead than alive; for he has now as much money as the best in the company, and yet has left off the poetical way of begging, called borrowing.

Phryne, curious to know the fate of courtesans after death, questions Sexton thus:

> Pray, sir, how does Death
> Deal with the ladies? Is he so unmannerly
> As not to make distinction of degrees?

Sexton's reply is in the same mood of *de contemptu mundi*:

> Death is a blunt villain, madam; he makes no distinction betwixt Joan and my lady. This was the prime madam in Thebes, the general mistress, the only adored beauty. Little would you think there were a couple of ears in these two auger-holes: or that this

121

pit had been arched over with a handsome nose, that had been
at the charges to maintain half a dozen of several silver arches to
uphold the bridge. It had been a mighty favour once to have
kissed these lips that grin so. This mouth out of all the madam's
boxes cannot now be furnished with a set of teeth. She was the
coyest, [most][37] overcurious dame in all the city: her chamber-
maid's misplacing of a hair was as much as her place came to.
O, if that lady now could but behold this physnomy of hers in a
looking-glass, what a monster would she imagine herself! Will
all her perukes, tires, and dresses; with her chargeable teeth, with
her ceruse and pomatum, and the benefit of her painter and
doctor, make this idol up again?

> Paint, ladies, while you live, and plaister fair;
> But when the house is fallen, 'tis past repair.

Phryne opposes Sexton with the philosophy of *carpe diem:*

> No matter, my Asotus: let Death do
> His pleasure then; we'll do our pleasures now.
> Each minute that is lost is past recall.
> This is the time allotted for our sports,
> 'Twere sin to pass it. While our lips are soft,
> And our embraces warm, we'll twine and kiss.
> When we shall be such things as these, let worms
> Crawl through our eyes, and eat our noses off;
> It is no matter—while we lived, we lived.

Asotus is fully equal to her gallant wit before the threat of mortal
doom. He caps her Libertine defiance of death by a neatly turned
one of his own:

> And when we die, we die. We will be both embalm'd,
> In precious unguents to delight our sense,
> And in our grave we'll buss and hug, and dally,
> As we do here: for death can nothing be
> To him that after death shall lie with thee.[38]

After these speeches of Phryne and Asotus, it seems but poetical justice
that they should be married; and, in this case at least, the wedding of
would-be and strumpet, involving still further flouting of Sexton and
his gloom, does not strike us as satirical. In other words, Asotus, in the

dénouement, loses his function as a Jonsonian would-be and becomes a semi-romantic symbol of exuberant gayety.

Jonson's two most Plautine comedies, *The Case is Altered* (before 1598) and *A Tale of a Tub* (1633),[39] move the intrigue patterns homeward from Milan to Finsbury Hundred, from conventionalized to downright linsey-woolsey romance and realism. The same generalization applies to Brome's *The New Academy* when compared to Randolph's *The Jealous Lovers.* Philip is the son of a London merchant, Matchil; Galliard, the son of a French tradesman, Lafoy. Joyce is Matchil's daughter; Grabriella is Lafoy's. For the advantages of a foreign education, Matchil has sent his son Philip to France to be reared by Lafoy, and Lafoy has sent his daughter Gabriella to England to be reared by Matchil. The two daughters are aware they are not sisters, as are the two sons that they are not brothers. But the daughters, falling into the hands of Matchil's villainous half-brother Strigood, serve as hostesses at his academy of fashion ultimately intended to be a high-class brothel; and the sons, coming to London in disguise, visit the academy, with the result that each marries his own sister. Before incest occurs, however, they discover their wives' identities and agree to trade.

Even more than in *The Jealous Lovers, The New Academy*'s Plautine intrigue pattern serves as a framework for imitation of Jonson and his rivals. Matchil's experience with his second wife, Rachel Maudlin, formerly his housemaid and many years his junior, recalls Morose's experience with his supposed silent woman in *Epicoene.*[40] Demure, quiet, and obedient as a servant, Rachel turns shrewish as a wife, asserts her freedom as a new woman, takes a young pseudo wit as her Platonic servant, proposes to use him and his friend to cuckold her husband, and at Strigood's academy blossoms into a prize pseudo lady. Poor Matchil, who lacks Morose's vigorous aversion to society, has to compromise with her whims, agreeing to suffer her mastery in private if she will make a show of obeying him in public. They become variations of the social-climbing citizen couple of Jonson's comedy. As Rachel profits from her lessons at the academy, Matchil at least

123

has the consolation that she is growing less of a virago, however flourishing the condition of his forehead.

Brome derides the spirit of affectation in other characters at the academy, although each is so much of an eccentric that their total effect is more farcical than satirical. Lady Nestlecock, instead of being as effective a pseudo lady as Lady Politick Would-Be of *Volpone* or either of the members of the Eitherside-Tailbush coterie in *The Devil is an Ass,* is a fantoddish shrew of a widow. Nehemiah, her son, instead of being a would-be as credible and carefully delineated as Jonson's Stephen or Sogliardo or Asotus, is a grotesquely clownish moron, spoiled by his mother's foolish pride in his half-witted facility at pointless repartee and by the indulgence of his servant-tutor Ephraim. Nehemiah's sweetheart, Blithe Tripshot, rather than being a striking female would-be, is a bouncing pert trull, scarcely out of the toy age. Her widower uncle, Sir Swithin Whimlby, who in Jonson's hands might have been an impressive pseudo wit, a Fastidious Brisk or Sir Amorous La-Foole grown older but no wiser, alternately weeps for his dead wife and cackles over Lady Nestlecock, whom he proposes to make his second wife. On the stage together with Matchil's apprentice Cash, arrayed in what he takes to be fashionable attire, they are an entourage out of Bedlam.[41]

Not content with these bewildering modifications of the well-made Roman New Comedy, Brome levied on the sentimental citizen comedy of Dekker.[42] His Valentine Askal would play the Casanova with citizens' wives and to this end has formed a wide acquaintance among merchants, such as Matchil and another named Rafe Camelion. Askal's friend Erasmus is skeptical of his amorous prowess, but Askal seeks to convince him by showing him Mrs. Hannah Camelion, whom he designates as a "present probability." He does not at first boast of having lain with her, but merely points out the fact that "I lay with, drink, and weare her money." He then explains how she made the first advances to him, seemingly struck by his good looks, how he informed her of his lodging, how she invited him to dinner, and how she has given him a total of thirty pounds out of her husband's profits.

To demonstrate what an impression he has made on her, he asks Erasmus to step aside while he accosts her. Lightly dismissing her concern that another gentleman should be aware of their conversation, he invites her to amorous dalliance:

> . . . Come, be wise,
> Thy husband's a dull ducking Gamester. And
> Kennels his water-dog in *Turnbull*-street.
> We'll answer his delights with better sport.
>
> When shall we walk to *Totnam?* or crosse o're
> The water, or take Coach to *Kensington*
> Or *Padington;* or to some one or other
> O' the' City out-leaps for an afternoon,
> And hear the Cuckow sing to th' purpose? when?

Although she does not consent to the assignation he suggests, she does present him with ten more pounds. Returning to Erasmus, Askal ostentatiously counts out the money, and, although he does not specifically say that she has consented to lie with him, implies as much. Erasmus, shocked by his immorality, reproaches him as follows:

> Yet thou hast the conscience
> To work a mans estate out of his hands
> By his wives frailty, even to break his back.

To which Askal replies:

> 'Tis rather to be fear'd she may break mine.
> She's a tight, strong dock't Tit.

Erasmus laments: "O Tradesman, why do you marry?" Askal has a ready answer: "Why? To make Tradeswomen/For Gentlemen that want money and commodity." Whereupon Erasmus makes the following resolve to himself:

> But I shall put you off
> O' one of your sweet courses, or at least
> I'le strain a point of friendship to be satisfied
> Touching this woman, 'twil be worth discovery.

125

Erasmus' resolve is well-founded, for Hannah is not what she seems. She has, to be sure, full reason to cuckold her husband Rafe, for he is nauseatingly uxorious, calls her repeatedly by such names as "My Cock, my Nansie Cock, my Cocksie Nansie." Furthermore, he suggestively insists on leaving his menage at the appearance of "one of the Blades" and keeps reiterating that he cannot be made jealous. However, Hannah is virtuous, and, more than that, Askal is in reality her half-brother and her father has sent her a hundred pounds with specific instructions to seek out Askal and give him the money to pay his debts. Carefully foreshadowing this latter fact by having Hannah receive a mysterious letter near the beginning of the play, but concealing the full revelation from his audience as a means of surprise, Brome succeeds in achieving an ironic exposé of the amorous pretensions of Askal and, incidentally, in putting the uxorious Rafe out of his humour. Erasmus, playing the role of intriguing benefactor, undertakes to disillusion Rafe and hides him where he can eavesdrop his wife and Askal. Rafe, thinking himself a cuckold from Askal's insistence on more money and sneering aspersion of Hannah's virtue, is transformed from uxorious obsequiousness into jealous moroseness. Whereupon Hannah reveals the truth by displaying the contents of her father's letter. Turning to the crestfallen Askal, Erasmus contemptuously remarks: "Now, Val, your brags to make men think you lay with her."[43]

In his essay on Jonson, T. S. Eliot has posed the following problem: "We want to know at what point the comedy of humours passes into a work of art, and why Jonson is not Brome."[44] The answer to the latter half of the problem is not far to seek in the case of *The New Academy*. Eclecticism has simply been carried too far; the many actions fail to grow toward one end; inclusion has achieved not unity but incongruous chaos.[45]

Incongruity and chaos, however, have their comic values—the theoretical point that Brome wrote *The Antipodes* to demonstrate. Furthermore, in turning back to classical comedy and trying to adapt it to their native heritage of craft, Randolph and Brome were experimenting in accord with the precept and example of their primary "father," learning useful lessons in technique, and teaching their brother Sons both what to do and what not to do. For Brome and others, the learned sock was less comfortable than the sentimental or the stuffed socks, as the next two chapters should make clear.

CHAPTER
FIVE

The Sentimental Sock

$\mathcal{T}$he sources of sentimentalism in early seventeenth century literature are difficult to trace. The facile exaltation of the heart above the head as an ideological and aesthetic motif in fiction and drama portraying contemporary life arose out of the complex conflict of attitudes now associated with the Renaissance and the Counter-Renaissance.[1]

One source was the modification of humanism by Christian religious thought. The concept of grace, variously interpreted by Catholics, Anglicans, Puritans, and the Enthusiastic sects, tended to undermine the notion that the unaided intellect through knowledge and self-discipline could achieve a lasting and dependable virtue. Such virtue was incomplete without the mysterious inflowing of the divine spirit into the individual soul. So long as this inflowing was restricted to God's chosen few and could not be induced save by unremitting ardor and even then only by God's sovereign permission, Christian grace remained as aristocratic as humanistic reason, and their collaboration encouraged a lofty Christian sentiment rather than sentimentalism,

128

with its tendency to subordinate reason to feeling as the basis of practical morality. But inevitably the inflowing was universalized, the ardor eased, the permission assumed to be bargainable. Thus viewed, grace became indistinguishable from good nature, of which good deeds and works were both a consequence and proof. It was no longer an aristocratic principle but a kind of people's commodity, the manna of heaven in the common life.[2]

A second source was the multiplication of meanings for the term "nature." So long as nature was identified with reason and art, humanism, even though modified by Christian religious thought, maintained its ascendancy as a literary force. But as nature came to mean the works of God as opposed to those of men—to man's reason and art as embodied in social organization, institutions, traditions, customs, and artifacts—cultural primitivism challenged the man of letters, forcing him to re-examine his concepts of both the good life and the good society. Such re-examination sometimes led him to the conviction that the good life was the life where one followed his own impulses rather than the accepted conventions of conduct, that the good society was some version of the pastoral, of simple nomadry in the out-of-doors, free from the cares and corruptions of so-called "civilization."[3]

Perhaps a third source was the unconscious will of some men and women of the rising middle classes to impose their new emotional orientation toward grace, the good life, and the good society on the dominant code governing relations between the sexes. This code—the double standard—divided women into the virtuous and the wanton, the elect to marriage and the damned to whoredom, while it tacitly encouraged philandering by men before marriage, on the ground that the sowing of their wild oats was a necessary educational prelude to their ultimate connubial responsibilities. Toward post-marital amorous adventure, the code showed some lenience in the case of husbands, none for wives. Cuckoldry and unwed motherwood were looked at more cynically than seriously as the deserved punishments, respectively, of men unfit to be husbands and women too stupid to become wives. The double standard, in its assumptions as to the sexually elect, was basically aristocratic. In the premium it placed on intellectual judgment as the *sina qua non,* after physical appeal, of success in sexual relations, its rationale was to some extent humanistic, despite its obvious in-humanities. These were what made the code objectionable, proof of civilization's corruption, one of the traditions and customs that must be drastically reformed. Chastity in both men and women before marriage and strict mutual fidelity of husbands and their wives—in short, the idealistic single standard of sexual morality—was the only practical basis for the good sexual life and the decent society. Literature must teach this code, by precept and example, as one of its ethical and social responsibilities.

Jonson, deeply grounded in classical humanism, keenly alert to trends in the thought of his time, creatively responsive to the best impulses of the middle class from which he came, and committed to the ethical and social responsibilities of the drama, could not avoid succumbing somewhere in his work to sentimentalism. He knew, of course, that its temper was unsuited to comedy, that its facile exaltation of the heart above the head was more appropriate to romance and tragedy, that, even there, sentiment was preferable to sentimentalism. But vice and folly had to be combatted at all costs, and the public should not be entirely denied what it wanted in the way of moral perspectives. Even in the ideal gentleman, Crites, of *Cynthia's Revels,* there is evidence that Jonson's humanism was strongly veined with Christian sentiment. Mercury's description of Crites is as follows:

> A creature of a most perfect and divine temper. One, in whom the humours and elements are peaceably met, without emulation of precedencie: he is neyther to[o] phantastikely melancholy, too slowly phlegmaticke, too lightly sanguine, or too rashly cholericke, but in all, so composde & order'd, as it is cleare, *Nature* went about some ful worke, she did more than make a man, when she made him. His discourse is like his behaviour, uncommon, but not unpleasing: hee is prodigall of neyther. Hee strives rather to bee that which men call judicious, then to bee thought so: and is so truly learned, that he affects not to shew it. Hee will thinke, and speak his thought, both freely: but as distant from depraving

another mans merit, as proclaiming his owne. For his valour, tis such, that he dares as little to offer an injurie, as receive one. In summe, he hath a most ingenuous and sweet spirit, a sharp and season'd wit, a straight judgment, and a strong mind. *Fortune* could never breake him, nor make him lesse. He counts it his pleasure, to despise pleasures, and is more delighted with good deeds, then goods. It is a competencie to him that hee can bee vertuous. He doth neyther covet, nor feare; he hath too much reason to doe eyther: and that commends all things to him.[4]

It is noteworthy that this "character" begins with emphasis on Crites' "divine temper" and stresses, toward the end, his delight with "good deeds." Later, of course, Jonson was to create Truewit to take the place of Crites as a norm character, and Truewit is a fluent spokesman of Libertine philosophy.[5] But it is also noteworthy that Truewit is not shown putting his Libertinism into practice. When Jonson did reach the point, in *The Devil is an Ass,* where he found it necessary to create in Wittipol a Truewit who attempts seduction, his own moral sense— and his sense of his audience's moral sense—demanded that Wittipol be properly chastened and that a genuine "man of feeling," a true sentimentalist, should preform the service. As pointed out in Chapter Three, the result was Eustace Manly, the bourgeois Crites. With Manly's good nature, impulsive rather than merely judicious virtue, and advocacy of the idealistic single standard of sexual morality as earnest that Jonson was broad enough to entertain in comedy other didactic perspectives than those of Asper or Truewit, the Sons of Ben had ample warrant to pull on the sentimental sock with its complex warp and woof and still think of themselves as carrying on the Jonsonian tradition. The two Sons who did it best were Brome and Thomas Nabbes.

Nabbes' *Tottenham Court,* probably performed in 1633 and first published in 1638, was his second attempt at comedy.[6] It has a framework plot that suggests Shakespeare's *As You Like It* in reverse on a lower social level and in a realistic milieu. Into this plot, also, certain reminiscences of Roman New Comedy obviously enter. The country gentlewoman, Bellamie, accidentally becoming separated from the down-at-heel gentleman, Worthgood, with whom she is eloping, requests a milkmaid, Cicely, to help her get to London. Cicely leads her to a hostelry in Tottenham Court, and they exchange clothes and places, with Cicely playing the mistress and Bellamie her servant. Cicely desires in her new role to test the sincerity of a courtier, Frank, who has professed honorable love to her after an unsuccessful series of attempts at seduction. She therefore poses as a high-class courtesan and as a result attracts not only Frank, but several other young men to the hostelry, including Sam, Bellamie's brother, a student at the Inns of Court, who fails to recognize his sister in her servant's garb. Eventually the distraught fiancé Worthgood, Bellamie's guardian uncle, and the latter's game-keeper—Cicely's supposed father—locate the girls in their London retreat. After due explanations have been made, it is revealed that Cicely is not the game-keeper's daughter but Worthgood's long-lost sister and hence a gentlewoman herself. Thus she can marry Sam, Bellamie's brother. Worthgood's down-at-heel condition is redressed by an unexpected legacy, which makes him acceptable to Bellamie's uncle as her bridegroom. This framework plot, linking *Tottenham Court* not only to Shakespeare and Plautus and Terence, but also to such comedies as Jonson's *The Case is Altered, The New Inn, The Magnetic Lady, A Tale of a Tub,* Randolph's *The Jealous Lovers,* and Brome's *The New Academy,* has the merit of creating, to borrow Horace's terminology, an enveloping conventional "delight" to make more palatable the sentimental "teaching" that is Nabbes' real end. Yet he manages the teaching itself delightfully.

The teaching is in behalf of the idealistic single standard of sexual morality and the inherent wit and virtue of ordinary folk in the country and the city. This teaching is accomplished by laughing out of court the sowing of wild oats by young would-be Libertines who think they are aristocrats and humanists. The instructors are the clever milkmaid, Cicely, whose upbringing has been that of a yeoman's daughter, and the merry citizen couple, the Stitchwells. Cicely is a development of the country Luce in Heywood's *The Wise Woman of Hogsdon,* and her courtier suitor Frank may have been suggested by

132

Luce's Young Chartley. Also, Cicely may owe a little of her wit to a housemaid in Marston's *Jack Drum's Entertainment.*[7] Mrs. Stitchwell is of the same type as Dekker's merry citizens' wives in *Westward Ho* as well as Shakespeare's in *The Merry Wives of Windsor,* while Stitchwell is modeled after Mayberry in Dekker's *Northward Ho.*

There is sufficient stratification of the gallants to get something of the effect that Jonson achieves in his best social satire and that Marston matches in *The Fawn.* Frank, the courtier admirer of Cicely, occupies the top rung of the ladder. Although a philanderer, he has brought himself to admire virtue in one whom he regards as of inferior social status and masks his Libertinism in a kind of Platonism. But, as the action unfolds, both his seeming freedom from snobbery and his professed Platonism turn out to be superficial and insincere. Below him in gentility is the courtier George, who represents the worst tendencies of fashionable gallantry. Pudgy and sybaritic, he mouths the tenets of Libertinism and considers every woman his legitimate amorous prey, especially when she belongs to a lower social class. Unscrupulous, insolent, and cynical, he will not recognize virtue in either the daughters or the wives of the yeomanry and citizenry, and boasts of having had nineteen maidenheads since he set out to be a rake.[8] Subordinated to him are James, the wild young buck of the Inns of Court, and Changelove, the fantastic city amorist. Belonging to social groups that supply the court with neophytes, these young men, both convinced of their gentility, aspire to be the equals of courtiers in amorous prowess. Hence James apes George in the pursuit of Cicely, while Changelove would surpass George in the chase of Mrs. Stitchwell. James has some traits of the true humanist, such as his preference for Shakespeare and Jonson over his required law books,[9] and seems ridiculous primarily because he is too young for rakishness. But the affected Changelove is obviously a rank pretender. Sam, Bellamie's brother, both because of his genuine freedom from snobbery and his real aversion to Libertinism—the instincts of his good nature—stands in striking contrast to this group of pseudo wits as a norm character, in some respects comparable to Jonson's Manly.

Cicely, when posing as courtesan, plays Frank, George, and James

133

off against each other in a series of highly farcical situations. When James comes to her room at the Tottenham Court hostelry, she rallies him archly and hides him in a trunk, making him believe he will soon possess her. Then she tricks George into having the trunk carried away to his apartment under the belief that she is concealed in it eagerly awaiting his irresistible embraces. Finally she causes Frank, also under the illusion she is in the trunk but desiring him rather than George, to try to high-jack the trunk from George as it is in transit. While George and Frank wrangle over the trunk, James emerges from it in ordurous, odorous disarray.

The Stitchwells deal with George and Changelove in situations equally farcical. Mrs. Stitchwell, pretending she has a humour to cuckold her husband only in his very presence, persuades George to hide in a tub until she is ready. Then Stitchwell, faking illness, proposes to vomit in the tub. Instead, his wife has the tavern wench empty water into the tub, with the result that poor George, already shaken with the fear of being nastily bestrewed, emerges half-drowned. Changelove, thinking he can succeed in satisfying Mrs. Stitchwell's odd humour where George has failed, makes advances to her while her husband mimics a sleeping drunk. As Changelove tentatively fondles the apparently willing adultress, the ostensibly snoring Stitchwell cries out at regular intervals concerning his horns and his vengeance and even pulls Changelove's ears, with the result that the latter's bedroom technique is reduced to tremulous fits and starts and ultimately to total impotence. Near the end of the play Mrs. Stitchwell reveals to George and Changelove how outrageously they have been tricked, or stitched into a well-woven plot, and emphasizes for her now repentant would-be seducers the following moral:

> Henceforth account not every City Wife
> Wanton, that only loves a merry life.[10]

So much does the action of *Tottenham Court* revolve about the cleverness and merriment of Cicely and the Stitchwells that it may appear only by indirection to exalt the heart and scarcely at the expense

134

of the head. So much downright bawdry is inherent in its farcical situations designed to ridicule men's sowing of wild oats that it may seem equivocal as a lesson in behalf of the idealistic single standard of sexual morality. For these reasons some readers would perhaps deny that it may properly be termed a "sentimental comedy." I hold that sentimentalism in the early seventeenth century must be understood in a relative sense and that the ultimate drift of *Tottenham Court* is toward sentimental "teaching," however skillfully this may be disguised by an eclecticism that draws the several actions from such diverse sources toward a final impression of witty unity.

Whereas the repentance of young would-be seducers enters into the denouement of *Tottenham Court,* the reformation of a decayed rake is basic to the plot of Brome's *The Damoiselle,* probably performed in 1637 or 1638 and first published in 1653.[11] Sir Humphrey Dryground is guilty of having seduced Elinor, the sister of the citizen Brookall. She bore Dryground an illegitimate daughter, Phillis. The disgraced Elinor has disappeared. Phillis has become a waif of the London streets, begging alms from passers-by, her identity unknown. Further misfortune has descended on Brookall. Ruined by a cruel usurer, Vermine, he too tramps the streets in hunger and poverty. The Brookalls are thus pathetic symbols of the evil workings of the double standard of morality and the acquisitive spirit.

Although Dryground's reformation is belated, it is thorough and inspires him to undertake what may be called a complicated roguery of good deeds. On money borrowed from Vermine he starts, under the pseudonym of Osbright, a new kind of ordinary where entertainment is gratis. Brookall's son, Frank, a young law student, is his chief attraction in the disguise of a damoiselle named Frances, presumably Osbright's own daughter fresh from France. Frank acts as an "instructress" in French fashions, whose maidenhead, it is rumored, is shortly to be raffled off to the highest bidder. Dryground induces Vermine's cast-off son, Wat, to bring his sister, Alice, Vermine's heiress, to the ordinary and to serve as his man, a role that seems to be that of a pimp. Yet nothing vicious is intended. On the contrary, Dryground is seeking to marry Frank and Alice and to provide them with enough money not only to begin housekeeping in comparative affluence but also to retrieve Brookall from destitution. They will eventually inherit Vermine's ill-got wealth and thus bring it back to the Brookalls. Vermine will be punished into the bargain by the loss of his Alice, whom he worships alongside money.

Dryground's fantastic scheme of amends, with the aid of a wonder-working Providence, exceeds the wildest expectations of his redeemed heart. The marriage of Frank and Alice is consummated. When Dryground explains to the bidders for the maidenhead that it is all a virtuous fake, they put up their money anyway out of the impulsive goodness of their natures, which frequentation of London leaping houses and ordinaries has seemingly not seriously impaired. Brookall is rescued and cured of his bitterness. Elinor is found and married to Dryground. Phillis is restored to her parents and betrothed to Wat, Vermine's son, whose better self has come to the fore. Even the arch-villain Vermine is stirred emotionally out of what is re-interpreted to be, not inherent villainy, but a kind of moral lethargy incident to his profession. The guests of the new ordinary gather arm-in-arm around Dryground in the closing scene, as he remarks:

> So may we with a generall embrace,
> Create the Heart of Friendship, not the Face.[12]

As earlier in *The New Academy,* Brome confuses a sufficiently complicated plot with too many minor characters and actions. Valentine, Dryground's son, is newly married into the family of a country justice, Bumpsey, having followed his father's rakishness in getting Jane Bumpsey pregnant before the wedding. Valentine is now anxious to prove himself a good husband. Bumpsey decides to try him out by sharing Jane's marriage portion with him, doing with his half just what Valentine does with his. Since Valentine is a philanthropist and Jane a social-climber, the spending is rapid. Bumpsey keeps up with him, and his own wife, Magdalen, seized like her daughter with the spirit of affectation, has a chance to indulge it. Justice Bumpsey is made even more amusing by a humour of wrangling with himself. Not only do the Bumpseys gravitate to the new ordinary, but they are joined by the lusty and pet-loving old Cornish bachelor, Sir Amphilus, who got his knighthood by being dubbed in a cluster, who had been chosen by Vermine as Alice's future husband, and who goes about with a witty servant, Trebasco. There are also two typical city gallants, Oliver and Ambrose, and a supernumerary altruist named Friendly.

The most striking feature of *The Damoiselle* is its appropriation of satiric machinery from Jonson and Marston as a vehicle for sentimentalism. Dryground, the supposed Frances, and Wat owe something to the rogues of *The Alchemist,* Subtle, Doll, and Face. Frank in his disguise as the French damoiselle instructing the Bumpsey women in the latest fashions is comparable to Wittipol in *The Devil is an Ass* exploiting the Tailbush-Eitherside coterie in his disguise of the Spanish lady. Brookall rails at social injustice in emotive rhetoric like another Malevole in *The Malcontent.* Proof that Brome thought of Jonson as sanctioning such a transvaluation of values is that Valentine and Friendly are echoes of Eustace Manly.

Another feature of *The Damoiselle* has Jonsonian sanction. The crowded cast of characters contains purely capricious humours and those whose vices or follies seem to serve the ends of farcical relief more than they do the ends of satire. The Bumpseys and Sir Amphilus are cases in point.[13] Such farcical relief tends sometimes to multiply in direct ratio to the intensity of sentimentalism, as in the novels of Dickens.

The religious motivation of Caroline sentimental comedy is nowhere more clearly shown than in Nabbes' *The Bride,* performed in 1638 and published the following year.[14] Ostensibly a play about the trials and tribulations of a virtuous young citizen couple beguiled into the wicked precincts of a combined tavern and brothel, where their devotion is sharply contrasted with the falsity of those who pursue and administer to Libertinism, it is also and more fundamentally an

137

allegory of the relations of piety, chastity, evil, and benevolence in the adventure of the Christian life.

The incarnation of the virtue of benevolence is the wealthy old merchant Goodlove, who is fond of his foster son Theophilus. At the opening of the play, Goodlove is making preparations to marry a young woman known only as the Bride. Since she and Theophilus are in love with each other and yet respectfully obedient to their parents, both are plunged into deep melancholy and inner conflict between passion and duty. Actually, Goodlove's imminent marriage is a ruse to drive a better bargain with the Bride's parents in the matter of her dowry and to find out all he can concerning her father's estate. At the last moment he plans to step aside as bridegroom in favor of Theophilus and thus pleasantly surprise both the young people, who are, as their names indicate, the embodiments of piety and chastity.

Not cognizant of Goodlove's real intentions, his nephew, Raven, symbolizing evil, desiring to be Goodlove's heir, and having a humour to injure the good, persuades Theophilus and the Bride to take flight together and seek refuge in the dive or hell where he carries on his Libertine activities. The proprietor of this establishment, one Squirrel, who is used to receiving Raven's cast-off wenches in other gallants' company, is a bit puzzled by the Bride: "Yet shee lookes not like carrion of Mr. *Ravens* leaving; I have seldome known him turn over any flesh to another that hath not been sufficiently tainted."[15]

The struggle of Theophilus and the Bride against Raven is the main concern of the developing action. Theophilus, shortly after arriving at Squirrel's dive, feels remorse for the ingratitude he has shown his foster father. He thereupon asks the Bride to return to Goodlove and declares he will accept all responsibility for spiriting her away. To test his piety, which she respects, the Bride pretends she wants him to marry her at once without their parents' consent. Theophilus is firm in his conviction that their consent must be obtained first. Loving him all the more for his strength of character, she admits her dissimulation. That she has been capable even of such virtuous fooling shocks his high sense of rectitude. Touched deeply, she weeps, and he almost reciprocates.[16]

138

With their exquisite moral sensibility thus confirming that they are made for each other, Raven must inevitably be thwarted. And so he is, in a succession of somewhat melodramatic episodes. Raven hires Squirrel to have a group of roaring blades pick a quarrel with Theophilus in the hope they will kill him. The valiant Theophilus, proving the "Prologue's" thesis that a citizen can be a true gentleman, not only routs them ignominiously but also lectures them lengthily. Raven later tries to stab Theophilus from behind, but his victim is too quick for him. Thinking he has slain Raven, Theophilus philosophically weighs his predicament. Such reflection, however, is no deterrent to heroic exploit. He rescues the Bride from rape by the French cook, Kickshaw, who is employed as a kind of unifying device in the play, inasmuch as he prepared Goodlove's wedding dinner, frequents Squirrel's place in the guise of a gentleman, and steals some of the rarities collected by the antiquary, Horten, another incidental humour character.

Providence, the supreme arbiter of sentimental comedy as of dramatic romance, rewards Theophilus and the Bride lavishly and at the same time effects the reformation of the villains. Goodlove and the Bride's parents are tearfully joyful to have the young people safe and to consent to their marriage. It is discovered that Theophilus is the actual rather than the foster son of Goodlove. Raven, now fully repentant, is the agent of this disclosure. Kickshaw is pardoned for his iniquities on condition that he will no longer "play the imposter."[17]

The same tendency noted in *The Damoiselle*—the use of purely droll humours for farcical relief—is present in *The Bride*. At Goodlove's wedding dinner such guests as the Spanish merchant Maligo and the Dutch merchant Rheinish serve this function. So do the whimsical Justice Ferret and his wife, comparable to Brome's Bumpseys. Best of all is the antiquary, Horten, to whose house the Ferrets conduct the Bride for recreation and amusement while Theophilus is seeking forgiveness from Goodlove. Horten is more sympathetically portrayed than the other antiquaries who appear in Caroline comedies, such as Veterano in Marmion's *The Antiquary* and Moth in Cartwright's *The Ordinary*. Finally, characters possessing vice and folly, such as Squirrel, the tavern blades, and Kickshaw share somewhat in this drollery, and, like generally similar characters in Jonson's later comedies, are more impressive as incongruous fantastiques than as vehicles of satire.

Though the name-symbolism in relation to the pattern of the action makes the religious allegory fairly obvious, this allegory, especially toward the end of the play, is as shakily sustained and as difficult to take seriously as the quite different one in Jonson's *The Magnetic Lady*.

Brome's *A Jovial Crew; or, The Merry Beggars* was performed in 1641 and published in 1652.[18] The work of his old age and dedicated to the pioneer English historian of philosophy, Thomas Stanley, it must rank alongside *The Antipodes* as his finest and most original play.[19] One of its distinctions is that it anticipates modern musical comedy. Another is that it dramatizes on a philosophical level Brome's prophetic sense that the Caroline world, as well as his own personal life, tottered on the brink of certain destruction and that the only way to face such inevitable catastrophe was with a gayety determined, invulnerable, and unrestrained. As he puts it in his dedication to Stanley: ". . . since the times conspire to make us all beggars, let us make ourselves merry; which, if I am not mistaken, this drives at." Its peculiar interest for the understanding of Caroline sentimental comedy is that it exhibits cultural primitivism, humanitarian sensibility, and humanistic wit in curious interplay and conflict. Allowing for the passage of three centuries, it is almost Saroyanesque.

As in *The Damoiselle,* the acquisitive spirit, the double standard of morality, and repentance for wild oats sown long ago lurk in the background of the plot. The wealthy country gentleman Oldrents owes his estate to a grandfather who cheated one Wrought-on and exposed his posterity to beggary. Wrought-on's grandson, under the alias of Patrico, has become the fortune-teller of a group of beggars. Oldrents himself, in his Libertine youth, seduced Patrico's sister, beautiful despite her rags, and as a beggar the object of much dishonorable pursuit by gentlemen. Yielding only to Oldrents, she bore him an illegitimate son. Oldrents gave her a purse that contained not only a considerable sum of money but also, unknown to him, a holy relic left him by his mother. After Patrico's sister died, Patrico took care of the son and kept the relic. Later Oldrents, brooding on his guilt as a rake, became a great humanitarian, taking a young beggar named Springlove to be his steward and permitting him to throw the house open to all beggars and offer them lavish alms and entertainment. Oldrents does not know that Springlove is his son and that Patrico is Springlove's uncle, nor does Springlove. Providence, however, has shaped matters thus and has further designs, using Patrico, Springlove, and others as instruments. It is at this point that the play begins. The background story is revealed through exposition, most of it being held back until the very end.

Patrico, as fortune-teller, has initiated Providence's ultimate designs by telling Oldrents that his two legitimate daughters, Rachel and Meriel, to whom he is very much devoted, will become beggars. Oldrents is so upset by this prophecy that even his friend Hearty, who has little money but loves sack and song and is optimism personified, has to summon all his resources to dissipate the mood. Then Springlove is seized by the impulse that periodically sends him wandering with beggars as he did in his boyhood—an impulse that Oldrents indulges. Springlove turns his stewardship over to an older servant and prepares to take off. The next development is the burgeoning of a similar impulse in Oldrents' daughters and their suitors, Hilliard and Vincent. When they inform Springlove of their project, he encourages them. He is convinced that their voluntary assumption of beggars' roles for fun will fulfill the prophecy harmlessly and thus remove forever the cause of Oldrents' worry. After they have donned beggars' rags and joined him on the open road, Springlove coaches them in the art of asking alms and the science of getting along without the luxuries to which they have been accustomed. Both the girls and the two young gentlemen are too well-bred to pass inspection in their new roles and

141

are somewhat disillusioned by their first experiences, but Springlove, to whom beggary is a kind of religion and beggardom a veritable Utopia, does his best to buoy up their spirits and resolves. And the irony is that the lovers have to play up to each other, neither sex liking to be quitters.

This sequence affords Brome ample opportunity to dramatize the pros and cons of cultural primitivism. To his beggar friends Springlove remarks: "You are a jovial crew: the only people whose happiness I admire."[20] Hilliard thus supports Vincent's opinion of their felicity:

> Beggars! they are the only people can boast the benefit of a free state, in the full enjoyment of liberty, mirth, and ease; having all things in common, and nothing wanting of Nature's whole provision within the reach of their desires.

Meriel chimes in:

> Happier than we, I'm sure, that are pent up and ty'd by the nose to the continual steam of hot hospitality here, in our father's house, when they have the air at pleasure, in all variety.

Oldrents, conversing with Hearty, expresses similar sentiments:

> . . . What is an estate
> Of wealth and power, ballanc'd with their freedom
> But a mere load of outward compliment,
> When they enjoy the fruits of rich content?
> Our dross but weighs us down into despair,
> While their sublimed spirits dance i' th' air.[21]

On the other hand, Hilliard, after a taste of beggars' freedom, says to Vincent: "If I cou'd but once have dreamt, in all my former nights, that such an affliction could have been found among beggars, sure I should never have travell'd to the proof on't." And Vincent agrees: "We look'd upon them in their jollity, and cast no further." The girls, too, are having a hard time. Observes Meriel: "I am sorely sore-bated with hoofing already tho, and so crupper-cramp'd with our lodging, and so bum-fiddled with the straw, that—," whereupon Rachel interrupts: "Think not on't. I am numb'd i' th' bum and shoulders too a little; and have found the difference between a hard floor with a little straw, and a down bed with a quilt upon't." Springlove, however, seems undissuadable in his advocacy of the vagrom way. To Vincent and Hilliard he philosophizes: "The world itself had ne'er been glorious, had it not first been a confus'd chaos." And when the neophytes get into trouble, he advises them: ". . . we must therefore leap hedge and ditch now; through the briars and mires, till we escape out of this liberty to our next rendezvous, where we shall meet the crew, and then hay-toss and laugh all night."[22]

Another action involving a runaway bride-to-be now gets entangled with the adventures of Springlove and his pupils. The niece of Justice Clack, Amie, on the point of marrying Talboy, who boasts of being a gentleman, has taken to the open road with Martin, a clerk and nephew to Hearty. Gentlemen who were to attend the wedding, including Amie's forthright cousin Oliver, and the officers of the law are in hot pursuit. Springlove welcomes the runaways into his group and leads them all to the retreat of the jovial crew. Amie and Springlove are soon enamored of each other, so that poor Martin finds himself in Talboy's shoes. Meanwhile Oliver and Talboy visit Oldrents' house, where the greybearded servants are also a kind of jovial crew and Hearty has some success in reconciling the lugubriously complaining Talboy to his plight.

Not only in the drinking and singing greybeards at Oldrents', but also in a wedding at the beggars' retreat between a partly blind woman of eighty and a cripple of eighty-seven, Brome seems to be adumbrating the mood of his own confrontation of old age and death. The greybeards sing as follows:

> A round, a round, a round, boys, a round;
> Let mirth fly aloft, and forever be drown'd.
> Old sack, and old songs, a merry old crew,
> Can charm away care when the ground looks blue.

And as the old couple dance over the stage, Springlove cries, "Well hobbled bridegroom!," and Vincent exclaims, "Well grop'd bride!" Says the bridegroom: "A ha! I am lustier than I was thirty years

143

ago." The bride adds: "And I than I was threescore past. A-hem, a-hem." "What a night here's towards!" comments Vincent. Hilliard replies: "Sure they will kill one another," and the beggar Poet quips: "Each with a fear the other will live longest."[23]

The Poet proposes, in honor of the old couple, to devise an impromptu masque about "a commonwealth; Utopia with all her branches and consistencies." From the beggars and their guests he recruits his actors—a country gentleman, a merchant, a courtier, a soldier, a lawyer, and a divine. Some of the beggar actors happen to be renegades from the very professions they impersonate. The following dialog conveys the action of the masque:

> The Poet: I wou'd have the country, the city, and the court, be at great variance for superiority; then wou'd I have divinity and law stretch their wide throats to appease and reconcile them; then wou'd I have the soldier cudgel them all together, and overtop them all. Stay, yet I want another person.
> Hilliard: What must he be?
> The Poet: A beggar.
> Vincent: Here's enough of us, I think. What must the beggar do?
> The Poet: He must at last overcome the soldier, and bring them all to Beggar-Hall. . . .[24]

Here Brome seems to be symbolizing the crisis of his Caroline world facing civil war and economic and social chaos.[25]

The mood of the final act is foreshadowed earlier by a remark of Hearty to Oliver when the latter requests him to prevent Martin from marrying Amie. Hearty's response formulates in an aphorism what might be termed the credo of sentimental license: "Hang all preventions; let 'em have their destiny."[26] This is in effect the philosophy followed by Justice Clack in his dispensations, after he has had his say. Having his say at some length and at a clicking pace is his capricious humour. If any one interrupts him, he silences the offender with the remark, "Now, if we both speak together, who shall hear one another?" Brome's bringing all the characters to Clack for a final disposition of affairs recalls Jonson's similar strategy in *Every Man in His Humour* with Justice Clement and in *A Tale of a Tub* with Justice Preamble, alias Bramble. Clack, however, surpasses Clement and Preamble and also Bumpsey of *The Damoiselle* and Ferret of *The Bride* as a farcical creation. And Talboy, whose crying humour changes to a laughing one after he hears about Martin's loss of Amie to Springlove, adds convulsively to the farcical effect. The revelations of Patrico, however, in a playlet before the dozing Clack, subordinate his justice to that of "great Providence," in Oldrents' phrase,[27] and dissolve the excess foam of farce into the mellow and heart-warming body of the play's sentimentalism.

The role of sentimentalism in other comedies of the Sons of Ben than the four discussed in this chapter should not be forgotten. As in Brome's *The New Academy,* it sometimes marked the mood and meaning of a subordinate action. To such occurrences of it in the comedies still to be discussed, however, only passing attention will be necessary. What has been said of *Tottenham Court, The Damoiselle, The Bride,* and *A Jovial Crew* is sufficient to indicate some of the ways in which Thalia's prevailing temper in the eighteenth century was anticipated on the Caroline stage.[28]

CHAPTER
SIX

The Stuffed Sock

One of the most incisive of twentieth century American philosophers, Morris R. Cohen, devoted his masterpiece, *Reason and Nature* (1931), to the defense of reason against its several rivals and substitutes in contemporary thought. Much later, in his post-humously published autobiography, *A Dreamer's Journey* (1949), he mentioned his labors on a companion volume "that would deal with the role of unreason in nature." He admitted that the earlier volume "failed to deal with a large realm of human life" and "that a rationalist, if he is not to waste his energies or land in cynicism, should not underestimate the power of the many nonrational and irrational roots and sources of human behavior." Without abandoning his rationalism, he had come to view it in an altered perspective, which he defines as follows:

> The fact that reason is the most valuable of all human possessions does not imply that it is the most powerful of all human forces. The powerful forces of human life which oppose the exercise of reason, the will to illusion that stands in the way of

the will to truth, must be understood and evaluated if we are to use reason effectively.[1]

Jonson's comedy at its best attempted to hold fast to rationalism and yet to exhibit the full power of the nonrational and irrational forces in man and society. His use of the three kinds of humours shading into each other—universal human vices deeply rooted in the psyche, particular forms of vice and folly imposed by the times, and the distorting oddities of habit that everybody acquires in some degree as the special circumstances of his living stamp themselves on his individual constitution—insured fairly comprehensive coverage of unreason's power. At the same time this coverage, by its very thoroughness, involved the danger of too great concession to the varieties of incipient materialistic determinism in the transitional thought of the Counter-Renaissance.[2] If the norm characters expressing the dignity of man were replaced by cunning intriguers executing stratagems, the indignity of man might appear incorrigible, especially since much of it seemed due to those social situations or to those absurdities inherent in existence for which the individual himself could rationally be held responsible only in so limited a sense as to be morally rather meaningless. As pointed out in Chapter Three, the comedy of Middleton displayed such drift, and Jonson was not above giving in to it somewhat, under the pressure of theatrical expediency, in *The Alchemist, Bartholomew Fair,* and later comedies, just as he succumbed momentarily to sentimentalism in *The Devil is an Ass.*

As a descriptive epithet for this Middletonian-Jonsonian type of comedy, I have chosen "the stuffed sock" for several reasons. It suggests the incongruity of the padded shoe or half boot sometimes worn by professional clowns. It evokes the clodlike awkwardness of the peasant's or the citizen's over-stout sabot. It calls attention to the presence of too many capricious humours and too many sub-plots, all stuffed—so to speak—into one play. It reminds us of the derivation of the noun "farce" as the name of a form of drama from Middle English *farcen, farsen,* Old French *farcir, farsir,* and Latin *farcire,* which were verbs meaning to stuff or squeeze into, as in preparing a fowl for

147

cooking. Finally, it implies that whatever satire is included—or "sock" of vice and folly in the slang sense of a beating or a striking—is as light as the blow of a stage stocking stuffed with feathers to look like a staff or stick. Thus, as designation for a special kind of comic eclecticism, "stuffed" is more complexly expressive, I think, than Milton's "learned" or my other adjectives "sentimental" and "sophisticated" when used to modify "sock"—by which Milton was alluding, of course, to the ancient comedian's substitute for the tragic actor's buskin or cothurnus. In short, the label "the stuffed sock" is a peculiarly mixed metaphor for a peculiarly mixed kind of comedy. I might have used "absurd" or "grotesque" or "droll" instead of "stuffed," but these terms have other referents in theatrical history. To any literalist provoked to say that this is all stuff and nonsense, I would retort that it is in the best tradition of the seventeenth century conceit.

When the Sons of Ben pulled on the stuffed sock of satiric farce or farced satire entailed by combining Jonson and Middleton, or joining the general orientations represented by their respective comic worlds, they may be said to have got themselves encased beyond the knees in the kinds of ideological and aesthetic entanglements that cause talent to hobble and that only genius can cavort in gracefully. Their difficulties could be compared to those faced by a contemporary writer of fiction who might try to carry on the great normative realistic tradition of the nineteenth century novel, as Frank O'Connor has described it in his *The Mirror in the Roadway,* and yet also graft on it some of the materials and motifs of slick sensational naturalism, trimmed with Freudian fantasy and flavored with Existentialist obfuscation, that is one of the sure-fire recipes of the current best-seller. The Sons of Ben who grappled most manfully but not always successfully with what may be referred to as the problems of the stuffed sock— problems partly stated and solved in *The Muses' Looking Glass* and *The Antipodes*—were Brome, William Cartwright, and Henry Glapthorne.

Two of Brome's earlier plays, *The Northern Lass,* performed in 1629, and *The City Wit,* probably of the same year,[3] are predominantly

148

Middletonian in their concern with the inter-strata dynamics of the contemporary middle-class world. The Heywood-Dekker influence, of course, must not be left out of account, particularly inasmuch as Dekker in his commendatory verses to *The Northern Lass* speaks of Brome as his "son."[4] Both plays also possess Jonsonian features, but these must be relegated to a relatively subordinate place in the over-complicated eclecticism. Structurally, *The City Wit* is the more strikingly unified, the clearer candidate for the dubious honor of being called "well-made." Despite this distinction, *The Northern Lass* exceeded it in popularity on the Caroline stage,[5] probably because its greater infusion of sentimentalism, centering in the titular character, made it more of a novelty to all playgoers and endeared it especially to those affected by the time's sobrieties.

In *The Northern Lass* the strata of the middle-class world are represented by three groups of characters. The city-court beau monde appears in Sir Philip Luckless and his kinsman, Tridewell. The city proper meets us in the Widow Fitchow, her brother Widgine, and his tutor Captain Anvile. The country is very much in evidence in the sentimental fifteen-year-old lass herself, Constance, from the Northern town of Durham; her uncle, Sir Paul Squelch, a former grazier, whose "father whistled to a Teem of Horses"[6] but who has risen to knighthood, wealth, and the position of justice of the peace in the city; his friend, Justice Hercules Bulfinch; and the Cornishman, Master Salamon Nonsense, whom Squelch approves as his niece's suitor. Other characters—Constance's governess, Mistress Traynwell; their servant, Beavis; Sir Philip's servant, Pate; Widow Fitchow's servant, Howdie; the whore, Constance Holdup; and a Constable Vexhem and his wife—make the social picture a fairly complete one.

It is a world seething with intrigues for love, money, and social status. The Widow Fitchow seems to be one of the cleverest manipulators of others to get what she wants. Her main end in view is to better herself socially. She has almost achieved it at the beginning of the play by her engagement to Sir Philip Luckless, described as "a tender nurseling of the Court." She would also promote her brother Widgine into a marriage with the heiress, Sir Paul Squelch's niece, Constance.

149

Sir Philip, whose kinsman Tridewell has advised him not to marry the widow, is almost convinced after meeting Widgine that he is about "to mix my blood amongst a race of fools." Then an understandable error about his checkered past prompts him to hurry up the marriage. He once maintained a whore, Constance Holdup. Also, on a recent visit to Sir Paul Squelch, he happened to kiss the other Constance out of courtesy and to remark casually that he would like to make a fine lady of her. This gallant attention made too much of an impression on the teen-ager, with the result that she has come to regard herself as his betrothed and has persuaded her governess to call on Sir Philip and press the claim. Thinking that Mistress Traynwell is a bawd seeking to advance the fortunes of the other Constance, the cast-off whore, Sir Philip decides that his only safety lies in the Fitchow marriage.

Meanwhile, his kinsman Tridewell, having called on the Widow Fitchow to prevent her marrying Sir Philip, falls in love with her himself. Married to the widow, Sir Philip discovers his mistake concerning the two Constances and yearns for his immature but devoted Northern lass. Tridewell, fully cognizant of this situation, sees his chance to win the widow. But Madam Fitchow, provoked by doubt of Tridewell's sincerity and by jealousy of her new husband's nostalgic fixation, holds out both against sleeping with him and divorcing him until she gets her brother married to the lass. Tridewell then hits on the ingenious notion of palming the whore Constance off on Widgine as the heiress Constance. This stroke, he thinks, will trick the widow into divorcing Sir Philip and marrying him and will leave the lass for Luckless.

So tangled a knot only a *deus ex machina* could untie. Sir Philip's servant Pate, who earlier has demonstrated his misplaced brilliance by sending Captain Anvile disguised as Luckless to visit Mistress Traynwell and the lass under the illusion that they are bawd and whore, turns out in the end to hold unsuspected trumps. When he produces them, everybody is happily disposed of, including Mistress Traynwell, who is married to Sir Paul Squelch; Widgine, who for a handsome consideration is released from his bondage to the gold-digging Holdup; and Madam Fitchow, who can wed Tridewell.

The most definite Jonsonian features here are borrowings from *Every Man in His Humour,* although by this time they have become stock in the comedy of the period. Widgine, though he is a city rather than a country would-be, has all the simplicity of Jonson's Stephen. For example, he thus introduces himself to a new acquaintance:

> My name is *Walter Widgine* Sir, not to be denied; the only brother here of Sir *Philip Luckless* his betroth'd. She is a *Widgine* born Sir, and of the best family; our Ancestors flew out of *Holland* in *Lincolnshire* to prevent persecution.[7]

Just as Stephen is impressed by Bobadill, so Widgine looks up to Captain Anvile, thus presenting him to Luckless:

> I pray embrace my Governor, Captain *Anvile,* here. . . . He has wit, I can tell you; and breaks as many good Jests as all the wits, fits and fancies about the Town, and has train'd up many young Gentlemen, both here, and in divers parts beyond the Seas. He was dry Nurse (that's one of his own Jests upon himself) to the English youth, a dozen years together beyond Sea: And now he is my Governor, and I find profit in it; you cannot think what an Ass I was before I met with him: And I mean to travel with him, two or three years hence, my self. In the mean time, he shall spend a Hundred a year out of *Wat Widgines* purse.

Widgine's desire to be a gentleman is as pronounced as Stephen's:

> . . . then am I no sooner married, Governor, but we will set our Travels a foot, to know Countries and Nations, Sects and Factions, Men and Manners, Language and Behaviour.

When he finds that his sister intends him to pay court to the lass, he exhibits a naive connoisseurship of the chase that makes him more amusing than Stephen, a fit companion of Tim Yellowhammer in Middleton's *A Chaste Maid in Cheapside:*

> He lives not that loves a Countrey thing like me. . . . though I am a Cockney, and was never further than *Hammersmith,* I have read the Countreymans Common-wealth, and can discourse of Soccage and Tenure, Free-hold, Copy-hold, Lease, Demeans, Fee-simple and Fee-tail, Plowing, Hedging, Diking, Grubbing,

151

occupying any Countrey thing whatsoever, and take as much pleasure in't, as the best Clown born of 'hem all.

This lackwitted Libertinism reaches a crescendo when he tells his sister about the wooing of Constance the whore, whom he has of course mistaken for Constance the Northern lass, distracted by a love-melancholy for her lost Luckless:

> I promis'd her anie thing, so took her into an inner Room, to make all sure. . . . you shall hear the miracle it wrought Sister. The loss of her Maiden-head recover'd her wits. I made her right and strait in an instant. And now she loves me in my own person; knows me for a *Widgine,* and will not give her *Wat* for the best Sir *Philip* of them all. And longs for nothing but the Priest and Bed-time. . . .

Captain Anvile is another Bobadill whose pseudo gentility is fully exposed when he visits the lass' domicile as if he were in a bordello like Mrs. Holland's leaguer. The servant Beavis thus describes to Mistress Traynwell the Captain's odd behavior:

> He stayes below, and will'd me to come up first, to make his passage clear and secure. . . . he ask'd me if the house were not much haunted with Roarers or Swaggerers, poniards and pistols; whether there were not an Assurer for it, as upon the *Exchange,* as if his life were upon hazard? whether a man might come on without loss of credit, and off without need of a Chyrurgion? Much odd talk he delivers, that in my conceit, bewrayes at once, both a lascivious and cowardly disposition, and upon my understanding, cannot be so generous, or nobly spirited, as he is received.[8]

Finally, Pate is the cunning servant of classical New Comedy derived from Jonson's Brainworm, Ed Knowell's devoted master of stratagems. As for such eccentrics as Justices Squelch and Bulfinch and Master Salamon Nonsense, they resemble generally the capricious humours who are the padding of Jonsonian comedy at its most farcical.

The titular hero of *The City Wit* is appropriately named Crasy. A young merchant rooked by his debtors and ruined by the social-climb-

The Stuffed Sock

ing extravagance of his wife and her family, the Sneakups, as well as by his own honesty and generosity, he decides to mend his ways, cease being an easy mark, and teach the whole lot of them lessons they won't soon forget. With this purpose, he pretends to leave the city on a month's journey, but actually stays very much on the scene carrying out stratagems in a number of disguises with the aid of two assistants— a supposed courtesan who passes herself off as a wealthy widow and a pert young rascal named Crack. The supposed courtesan turns out to be his faithful servant, Jeremy, while Crack is Jeremy's younger brother. Their identities are surprises even to Crasy.

Crasy is obviously straight out of Middleton, suggesting Master Easy of *Michaelmas Term,* Witgood of *A Trick to Catch the Old One,* and Follywit of *A Mad World, My Masters.* The motif of the courtesan posturing as wealthy widow is used in the latter two plays. Straight out of Middleton, too, is the double-edged derision achieved by playing the social-climbing Sneakups and their hangers-on over against a group of recently fledged and very affected courtiers, Ticket, Rufflit, and Lady Ticket, who are in debt to Crasy and whom the Sneakups chase after. Dekker is very likely combined with Middleton when Crasy contrives to have both Rufflit and Ticket uproariously foiled in attempting to seduce his wife—episodes recalling what happens to Lipsalve and Gudgeon in Middleton's *The Family of Love* and Greenshield and Featherstone in Dekker's *Northward Ho.* It is important, however, to note that Brome holds strictly in abeyance Dekker's sentimental assumptions about the typical citizen's wife.

The derision aimed at the social-climbing citizens is most thoroughgoing. Josina Sneakup Crasy, as soon as she thinks her husband safely out of the city, would have amorous servants like a Court lady. She tries to entice Crasy's own servant, Jeremy. She sends her maid Bridget soliciting a chain of procuresses to provide her "an honest, handsome, secret young man; that can write and read written hand." When Crasy comes to her disguised as the quack beautician, Dr. Pulsefeel, she gives him permission to take liberties with her and requests him to find her a secretary. To Crasy posing as this secretary she is likewise

153

brazen. She is anxious to have affairs with the courtiers, explaining that "I would not be wonder'd at like an Owle among my neighbors, for living honest in my husbands absence." She comes by her spirit of affectation naturally, since her mother, Pyannet Sneakup, is an aggressive and unscrupulous promoter of her family's social position and wealth. Pyannet explains frankly to Crasy that it was not by honesty Sneakup rose from a grazier to be justice of peace. They have been in the city only three years, yet in that time have purchased their son Toby a place at Court. Crasy exploits her desire to be herself received at Court by tricking her to have Sneakup take jewels there and then to go herself with a truncheon and in a jealous rage to punish Lady Ticket for trying to seduce him. When she discovers her mistake, she seeks to make amends by a ridiculously fustian apology:

> I humbly beseech you sweet Madam, that my earnest and hearty sorrow may procure remission for my inconsiderate and causelesse Invectives. Let my confession seem satisfactory, and my contrition win indulgency to my forgetfull delinquency.

Toby Sneakup combines fawning toward courtiers with condescension toward citizens like Crasy. Farcically gulled by being wed to the supposed wealthy "widow," Jeremy, he is severely castigated by this same widow when the latter plays the strumpet Lady Luxury in an impromptu masque celebrating the occasion. The spirit of affectation has also seized a neighbor of the Sneakups, Linsy-Wolsey, who tries to learn how to be a gentleman from Toby. And it inspires even Toby's lice-ridden tutor, Sarpego, whose sights are no higher than Bridget, the maid, until Crasy makes him believe he is wanted at Court to instruct the young Prince.

It is in the elaborate stratification and detailed analysis of these social-climbing citizens that Jonson's influence is most marked in *The City Wit;* Josina has some resemblance to Fallace in *Every Man Out of His Humour,* and Pyannet is a "woman of an eternall Tongue . . . Creature of an everlasting noyse"[9] comparable to Mrs. Otter in *Epicoene.* Also Brome was apparently well aware that Jonson's use of wit-intriguers and rogue-exploiters had much in common with Middleton's technique. For this reason he has Crack remark concerning his confederacy with Crasy and the supposed courtesan: "By Indenture Tripartite, and't please you, like *Subtle, Doll,* and *Face.*"[10] This explicit reference to the intrigue machinery of *The Alchemist* is accompanied by less obvious minor borrowing from that of *Volpone* and *Epicoene* in the case of Jeremy's imposture as the presumably dying wealthy widow and the sexual surprise he springs in the denouement. In the light of such evidence, Brome's reference in the prolog to "the seal of Ben" was not a hollow gesture of conventional piety.[11]

To write comedy combining satisfactorily farce and satire means providing a fast-moving action of incongruous situations without impairing illusion through incoherence or excessive artifice and without sacrificing ethical, social, or other possibilities of meaning. What may be called the Middleton-Jonson technique of achieving the synthesis had certain drawbacks, especially when Middleton was given precedence. These drawbacks are clearly evident in both *The Northern Lass* and *The City Wit.* The intrigue of the first becomes so involved that it is at points virtually incoherent even to a most attentive audience. The intrigue of the second is easier to follow but relies too heavily on the artifice of disguise. Neither play has adequate norm characters to put into an inescapable and clear philosophic perspective the double-edged derision directed at the vices and follies of types drawn from the middle classes. The stubborn innocence of the Durham Constance and the sardonic desperation of Crasy are eccentric slants from which to contemplate and understand such odd phenomena as Widgines and Sneakups, Lucklesses and Tickets, Holdups and Sarpegos.

In *Covent Garden Weeded,* performed probably in 1632 and revived ten years later,[12] Brome retained some elements of the Middleton-Dekker comic world but gave Jonson's satire and farce primary place in his eclecticism. The aspect of contemporary life he chose for satire was the spirit of intolerance, in both its domestic and public manifestations. Impressed with Jonson's treatment of domestic intolerance in *Every Man in His Humour* and to some extent in *The Poetaster* and

Epicoene, Brome used these for models. Recognizing that Jonson's castigation of public intolerance in *Bartholomew Fair* and *The Alchemist* had established emphases and devices difficult to improve upon, he kept these plays also carefully in mind. But he still felt, as Jonson himself came to feel after his "comicall satyres," that farce should be joined and intertwined with satire to make for theatrical effectiveness. The result is that, of Brome's two chief characters, one of them, Crossewill, is as capricious in his ruling humour as Morose in *Epicoene.*[13] Whereas Morose has a fear of noise that dictates all his actions, Crossewill, as his name indicates, is hell-bent on going precisely contrary to the will of other persons, whatever it may be. The only way one can get him to do what one wishes is to demand that he do the exact opposite. The person who best understands this irrational principle in his psychology is his younger son, Mihil, a London gallant. It is Mihil, then, who becomes the other chief character, the manipulator of the action, working Crossewill for such ends as paying his debts, keeping up his gallantry, marrying the girl of his choice, and getting his sister Katherine married to the man of her choice. As an executor of successful stratagems, Mihil is more in the tradition of Middleton's cunning wit-intriguers than Jonson's normative truewits.

The most impressive feature of the play is the underlying seriousness with which, despite all its farcical machinery, Brome explores the consequences of domestic intolerance and demonstrates that it is related to public intolerance. When Crossewill, a country gentleman, comes to London with his elder son Gabriel and his daughter Katherine to take lodgings so that he can check on the activities of Mihil, it is made clear, by his own statement about his children, that his humour is actually the expression of his paternal absolutism: "They will not obey me in my way. I grant, they do things that other fathers would rejoyce at. But I will be obeyed in my own way, dee see." Later Katherine shrewdly observes: ". . . he will crosse us in all we do, as if there were no other way to shew his power over our obedience." The consequences for his niece Dorcas and for Gabriel have been disastrous. After Dorcas came to live with them in the country, Gabriel bore "the civillest and

156

the best ordered affection" toward her, "so loving to her person, so tender of her honour that nothing but too near affinity of blood could have kept them asunder." Instead of encouraging this admirable friendship, Crossewill broke it up, "fearing what youth in heat of blood might do," and sent Gabriel "from home into the service of a Reverend Bishop to follow good examples." Without Gabriel to watch over her honour, Dorcas was seduced by a London gallant who "like the slippery Trojan left her," while she "fled to what part of the world we know not." Brooding over her shame, Gabriel has become a Puritan extremist, denouncing every form of pleasure to spite his father. As for Katherine, she too has suffered from her father's tyranny. Crossewill drove away her suitor, Anthony Cockbraine, the son of a Middlesex justice of the peace, whereupon Anthony, like Dorcas, disappeared. His father, Justice Cockbraine, has been somewhat unhinged by his son's loss, and has turned into a rabid reformer of such "enormities" as exist in Covent Garden. In short, public intolerance, whether in the form of religious or legal zealotry, has psychological origins traceable to the way intolerance in one home may thwart the natural affective impulses of young people and even create unhappiness in other homes. Citizen sentimentalism enters here, to be sure, and is further woven into the action by the reunion of the still honest whore Dorcas to her reformed seducer Nick Rooksbill in quaint brothel and tavern scenes out of Dekker.[14]

The curing of the public intolerance of Justice Cockbraine is accomplished in true Jonsonian style. Covent Garden, drawn from the life, is his Bartholomew Fair.[15] Armed with a black book in which he jots down notes on "enormities," he is the reincarnation of Justice Adam Overdo. Brome leaves us in no doubt on this point. For Cockbraine thus describes his mission:

> And do not weeds creep up first in all Gardens? . . . let me alone for the weeding of them out. And so as my Reverend Ancestor *Justice Adam Overdoe* was wont to say, *In Heavens name and the Kings,* and for the good of the Common-wealth I will go about it.[16]

157

He moves from tavern to tavern in the vicinity of the Garden, snooping on roysterers and rogues, rescuing citizens from whores, leading the city watch to make raids. When he finds that his efforts in behalf of law and order have merely led him to the point of arresting his friends and his own son, he admits in despair, "Why I know not whom to commit now."[17]

The public intolerance of Gabriel's Puritan extremism is subjected to a comparable exposure and purging, recalling Jonson's treatment of Zeal-of-the-Land Busy, Ananias, and Tribulation Wholesome. At the Goat Tavern, Gabriel thus reacts to the fiddling, the swell of merriment, the cries for wine and tobacco: "O prophane tinkling of the cymbals of Satan, that tickle the eare with vanity to lift up the mind to lewdnesse. Mine eares shall be that of the Adder against the Song of the Serpent." At the Paris Tavern, however, these resolves break down under the guzzling of liquor and the proximity of blades, bawds, and broads. This convivial company he mistakes for the brethren and sisters of Amsterdam come in disguise to assist him in spying out iniquities and is ready to go to any lengths under such holy auspices. As he remarks to them all and to one in particular: "I'le drink, I'le dance, I'le kisse, or do any thing, any living thing with any of you, that is Brother or Sister. Sweet-heart let me feel thy Coney." Like Jonson contrasting his Puritans with Sir Epicure Mammon in *The Alchemist* as representing opposite deviations from the Aristotelian golden mean of temperance, so Brome brings Gabriel into similarly meaningful juxtaposition with the voluptuary Rooksbill. Crossewill underscores the point in the following observation to Rooksbill Senior concerning their sons: "I would their extream qualities could meet each other at half-way, and so mingle their superfluities of humour into a mean betwixt 'hem." Their extremes meet all right, but in a way Crossewill does not anticipate. When Gabriel is assuming the role of intoxicated whoremaster at the Paris Tavern, Nick Rooksbill exclaims, "I vow, thou art a brother after my own heart."[18] Mihil putting Gabriel through his paces in such a Covent Garden resort in the hope of restoring him to normality may even be a reminiscence of Freevill chaperoning Malhereux at the brothel in Marston's *The Dutch Courtesan*.

The Stuffed Sock

The stuffed sock will take a lot of stuffing, once a competent craftsman has caught the knack of it. Brome has come close here to making
a quite satisfactory synthesis of satire and farce. All that is lacking is
the Jonsonian norm character, but this lack is compensated for, as in
Bartholomew Fair and *The Alchemist,* by the use of contrast that
clearly implies a standard of judgment. Likewise there is a challenging
vision of existence as a disordered garden of thwarted natural affections
where one intolerance begets another.

Cartwright in *The Ordinary,* performed 1635 and published 1651,
and Glapthorne in *The Hollander,* performed 1636 and published
1640,[19] also tackled the problem of integrating satire and farce through
a synthesis of Jonson and Middleton. *The Alchemist* was for them
Jonson's most suggestive comedy. What impressed them about it was
the tripartite confederacy of Subtle, Dol Common, and Face as
machinery for the exploitation of humour characters. They also liked
Jonson's maintenance of unity of place, by having the confederacy
carry on its intrigues in one menage to which all the humours were
drawn like metal filings to a magnet or moths to a flame. Finally, they
were tantalized by the notion of endowing this menage with sufficient
topicality to afford the audience the pleasure of recognition and at the
same time presenting it as a symbolic world apart where chicanery,
license, incongruity, and whirl prevailed, with the result that it took
on philosophic overtones as an epitome of the fundamental irrationality
of existence. They were apparently cognizant, too, that Jonson's interest
in using the wit-intriguer along with the rogue-exploiter, and even
pitting these against each other, was a concession to Middleton. So
they turned to the Middletonian wit-intriguer as an extra means of
speeding up the action, holding the audience in suspense, and pointing
the moral that knavery is not the best policy since eventually it always
meets its match.

Three rogues dominate *The Ordinary*—Hearsay, an "intelligencer";
Slicer, a lieutenant; and Shape, a cheater and sharper. The ordinary
where they prey on gulls—or "ordinary gentlemen," to repeat Brathwait's pun—is owned by a grotesque hag, Joan Potluck, a vintner's

159

The Sons of Ben

widow. Although identified with no particular ordinary of the period, its atmosphere and clientele are typical enough to have been thoroughly familiar to the Caroline audience. Joan has some resemblance to Dol Common; Hearsay is like one of the rogues in *The Staple of News;* Slicer suggests Cavalier Shift of *Every Man Out of His Humour.*[20] In league with them seemingly as the action begins but actually playing a lone hand for his own ends is the wit-intriguer Littleworth, whose alias is Meanwell. He means well because he is trying to marry the daughter of Sir Thomas Bitefig against that wealthy usurer's wishes. Also he is out to punish another usurer, Sir Simon Credulous, because this villain, having brought Meanwell's father to poverty, has had him committed to jail for debt. Meanwell goes along with the rogues only so far as they are useful to his ends; after these have been served, he leads the law in a raid on the ordinary and recovers some of their spoils even though they cunningly escape arrest.

Cartwright's management of both the rogues' and Meanwell's intrigues satirizes important manifestations of the acquisitive spirit in the life of the time. The satire is amplified by the introduction of the two usurers, who appear to have something of the role here that the Puritans have in *The Alchemist,* since Sir Simon Credulous sings the following ditty:

> *My Name's not* Tribulation,
> *Nor holy* Ananias:
> *I was baptiz'd in fashion,*
> *Our Vicar did hold Bias.*[21]

The connection between the acquisitive spirit and the spirit of intolerance in domestic relations is hit off in Bitefig's tyranny over his daughter. He is reformed, of course, in the denouement. How the acquisitive spirit is bound up with the spirit of affectation is stressed by having Credulous send to the ordinary his son Andrew, a would-be whom he would have the rogues tutor in gentility to court Bitefig's daughter. This method of linking two basic trends of the period was, of course, a stock resource of comedy; one has only to recall Randolph's Worldly and Knowlittle in *The Drinking Academy* and Simo and

160

The Stuffed Sock

Asotus in *The Jealous Lovers.* Two other gulls representing obsessions of would-be gentlemen are Have-at-all, trying to learn how to pick quarrels and cow his antagonists by his military braggadocio, and Caster, a gamester who is constantly losing and therefore wants to be taught some secrets of winning. These have affinities, respectively, with Kastrill and Dapper of *The Alchemist,* but were probably drawn as much from life as from Jonson.[22] Along with them should be mentioned the members of the Ordinary Club into which the foolish Andrew Credulous is initiated. Composed of the poet Rimewell, the decayed clerk Bagshot, the curate Sir Christopher, and the cathedral singingman Vicar Cathmey, this club is somewhat like the Jeerers of *The Staple of News,* the Roarers of *The New Inn,* and the Roaring School of *A Fair Quarrel,* a play in which Middleton collaborated with Rowley. But again there may have been actual prototypes. Finally, an antiquary, Sir Robert Moth, who seems to have been drawn both from life and from Chaucer—since Cartwright was what might be termed "a scholarly realist"—has an important place among the gulls of the ordinary, obviously a substitute for Sir Epicure Mammon of *The Alchemist* and an example of old age become concupiscent.[23]

This parade of gulls represents the three kinds of humours stressed by Jonson—first, universal human vice, in the present instance avarice and lust; second, vices and follies imposed by the times—here, prodigality and the obsessions of aspiring gallants; and, third, distorting caprices or ill-got habits—especially those associated with various professions, Moth's being the most amusing. Cartwright employs so many humour characters, however, and involves them in such complications of intrigue that only a few of them receive the full and careful delineation that good satire requires, according to the recipe of the Prologue of *Cynthia's Revels:* "Words, above action; matter, above words." Hence, some of these humour characters, even those intended as realistic embodiments of vice and folly, have in certain scenes the fantasticality of purely farcical creations. The absence of genuine norm characters—for surely Meanwell lacks sufficient detachment and intellectual distinction to function in this capacity—contributes to the diminution and deterioration of the satire. But even when these defects are acknowledged, *The Ordinary,* its author's only comedy, must be pronounced a re-readable and partially effective experiment in a type of comic eclecticism admittedly difficult to bring off.

In *The Hollander* the rogues are even closer to those of *The Alchemist.* Dr. Artless is a kind of Subtle; Mrs. Mixum, wife of an apothecary, is a Dol Common; and Urinal, a pert servingman sent the doctor by the apothecary, is comparable to Face.[24] Mrs. Artless, the doctor's wife, must be counted in the confederacy because she put her husband up to their nefarious enterprise and works hard to make it a success. Their menage is a hospital for women's diseases, but is also a brothel. One of their problems is to keep their virtuous clientele, consisting at this time of two gentlewomen, Lady Yellow and her ague-afflicted sister, Mistress Knowworth, from knowing what their other clientele is about. And this problem is complicated by the presence of their daughter, Dalinea, whose innocence they would protect. Two wit-intriguers, Popingaie and Freewit, each interested for different reasons in one of the gentlewomen, participate in the action and in the course of their intricate plotting come into some conflict with the chief rogue, Dr. Artless, Popingaie out-maneuvering him in the disposition of Dalinea, and Freewit exposing the worthlessness of one of his gulling sidelines, a concoction known as the "weapon salve."[25]

Glapthorne's satire is directed chiefly at the spirit of affectation as exemplified in a naturalized young Dutchman, Sconce, and at the spirit of intolerance in domestic relations, as it blossoms wildly in Sir Martin Yellow, the jealous husband of Lady Yellow. Although this concentration on two principal humour characters, one a variation of the Jonsonian would-be, such as Stephen, and the other a refurbishing of Kitely, should have insured effective satire,[26] Glapthorne has a tendency to reduce both to purely farcical eccentrics.

Sconce introduces himself after the manner of Brome's Widgine in *The Northern Lass:*

> My name is *Sconce* sir, Master *Jeremy Sconce,* I am a gentleman of a good family, and can derive my pedigree from *Duke Alvas* time, my ancestors kept the inquisition out of *Amsterdam.*[27]

He comes to Dr. Artless' menage to discover what he can concerning the doctor's famous weapon salve, which, when rubbed on the weapon that has caused a wound, is supposed to cure this wound miraculously, without the need of surgery or medication. Sconce is quite an amorist in his way, bussing Mrs. Artless and Mrs. Mixum and making advances in French to the virtuous Lady Yellow. When the jealous Sir Martin Yellow, standing by in disguise, wounds him slightly in the arm for his effrontery to the lady, Sconce is overjoyed, for now he can test the virtues of the weapon salve. Taking Sir Martin's sword, he anoints it carefully, holding forth the while about the salve's sympathetic magic. Chosen by Artless as the husband-to-be of Dalinea, Sconce is initiated before his marriage into the order of the Twibill Knights, a club representing a kind of combination of Middleton's Family of Love, the blades of Brome's *Covent Garden Weeded,* and the quartet of tavern oddballs in Cartwright's *The Ordinary.*[28] Its leaders are two grotesque captains, Fortresse and Pirke, decadent and puppet Bobadills, one a huge tun of a man and the other a pigmy. The climax of Sconce's exploitation occurs when, instead of being married to Dalinea, he is brought in very drunk, having been wed to a young man who turns out to be a servingmaid in disguise—a homosexually suggestive reversal of a stock situation. His farcicality is accentuated by his broken English, at one moment corrupted by French and at another by Dutch; by the sustained *double-entendre* of the weapon salve; and by the slapstick of his initiation into the Twibill Knights.

One reason Lady Yellow has accompanied Mistress Knowworth to Artless' menage is to be freed from the constantly recurring jealousy of Sir Martin. More convinced than ever that his wife is a strumpet because of the quarters she has taken, he follows her there in the disguise of Popingaie's servingman and prompts Popingaie to make amorous overtures to her in order to confirm his suspicions. Lady Yellow rebuffs Popingaie, but in terms that cause Sir Martin to grow even more horn-mad. When Sconce pays court to her in French, Sir Martin can restrain himself no longer and rushes at the would-be with his sword. After Urinal has persuaded Sir Martin that his wife is virtuous, he kisses her in reconciliation. Because this kiss seems to him too passionate, his jealousy flares again.[29] Urinal, making Sir Martin believe he is being introduced to his wife's bed as her gallant and may thus prove her unchastity, causes him to lay the willing Mrs. Mixum. His dread of antlerhood thus confirmed, he brandishes his sword to slay his supposed wife, who flees insisting he should not confuse his weapons.[30] Only when he grasps his mistake is his humour cured. From situation to situation, Glapthorne has stuffed his Kitely into an uproarious clown.

The kind of synthesis found in the plays of Brome, Cartwright, and Glapthorne discussed in this chapter—a synthesis comparable in some respects to that achieved by Massinger—was not, despite the drawbacks that its authors failed to overcome, a mere decadent dead end in comic eclecticism. It established on the Caroline stage a tradition that was to be continued after the Restoration in the citizen comedies of Crowne, Wilson, and Shadwell.

Glapthorne's *The Hollander* makes a gesture, in the love story of Freewit and Mistress Knowworth, toward catering to the interest in Court Platonism, linked with the sentimental theme of the reformed rake. But their passion is not managed so as to come anywhere near true comedy of witty amorous intrigue carrying us into a more sprightly and polished world than that of citizen buffoonery, and neither character is developed into a norm to point up what satire there is.

For the development of truewits and witty women as intriguers against each other and as norms for the satire of their inferiors, it is necessary to turn to another group of comedies—by far the largest single group written by the Caroline Sons of Ben. In these comedies, I shall try to show how they sought, with varying degrees of success, to rival Shirley by drawing on the sophisticated sock.

CHAPTER
SEVEN

The Sophisticated Sock I

V. de Sola Pinto's *Sir Charles Sedley*, aside from being one of the best biographies yet written about a representative man of the Restoration, contains a short description of the Restoration "comedy of manners" or "comedy of wit" that would be difficult to improve upon:

> It was clear that the center of the new kind of comedy must be the Man of Wit and Fashion as he was conceived by the courtiers of Charles II, the ideal personage who had been to some extent embodied in the persons of such men as Rochester, Etherege, Sedley, and Buckhurst. The first and obvious method of making such a person an effective stage character was to contrast him with the false 'pretenders to wit,' the Chesterfields, Beau Hewitts, and other foolish moths who circled giddily round the lights of White-hall. He might also be appropriately contrasted with men of an older generation, who would puritanically condemn or clumsily share his pleasures. But such conflicts or contrasts between the obviously superior and obviously inferior persons (if we accept for critical purposes the standards of the Wits) are not the stuff out of which the central theme of great comedy can be evolved,

although they may provide excellent diversion in sub-plots. The perfect comedy of manners, like all good forms of drama, demands a conflict between equals—in this case equals in wit and grace and style—for these are the qualities which are the chief concern of this kind of play, as intensity of imagination and heroic magnanimity are the chief concern of poetic tragedy. To place beside the ideal Wit an equally witty and graceful woman, who could meet him on his own ground and with his own weapons, could reply to his music with an equally enchanting strain of her own, and finally, without any trace of romance or sentiment, at once conquer him and yield to him—such was the goal toward which a whole school of dramatists was half consciously groping in the reign of Charles II.[1]

One virtue of this description is that it stresses the relationship between the comic world created by Etherege, Dryden, Wycherley, and their fellows and successors and the actual world of the Court coterie, thus relegating to secondary importance the question of literary sources and influences. Another virtue of this description is that it points out clearly what gives such comedy its distinctive illusion and meaning. Basic to its effects is a gay duel of intelligence and personality between men and women adept not only in witty expression but likewise in subtle understanding of all the other demands made by their coterie's code. These characters become norms with reference to which pretenders to their excellence, contemners of its qualities, and renegades to its discipline are measured and rebuked.

Though the life of the times rather than other plays shaped this comic world, provided many of its characters and incidents, and determined its philosophy and style, nevertheless its authors, as conscientious craftsmen, sought models to help them write better what they had to write. These models were numerous and diverse, as modern scholarship has demonstrated,[2] but among them two plays stood out, if we can accept an interesting bit of evidence from Thomas Shadwell's *The Sullen Lovers*. In this play, the morose wit Stanford and the airy wit Lovel are discussing one of the interloping pretenders to wit, Sir Positive At-all. Stanford tells Lovel about Sir Positive's latest discovery:

166

This morning, just as I was coming up to look for you, Sir Positive At-all, that fool that will let no man understand anything in his company, arrests me with his impertinence. Says he, with a great deal of gravity, "Perhaps I am the man of the world that have found out two Plays, that betwixt you and I have a great deal of wit in 'em; those are, *The Silent Woman* and *The Scornful Lady;* and if I understand anything in the world, there's wit enough in both those to make one good play. . . ."[3]

What makes Sir Positive ridiculous is that he thinks his discovery is original. To Stanford and Lovel and their coterie it has long been taken for granted that Jonson and Beaumont and Fletcher are witty models for a writer of comedies to study in combination. The very plays Sir Positive has hit on are known to anybody who reads plays as the ones that show how the materials and emphases imposed on the writer by his Restoration milieu were treated in an earlier day. Had not *Epicoene; or, The Silent Woman* created a memorable trio of truewits and placed them in significant contrast with a bevy of pretenders and a pathologically anti-social old fogy? Had not *The Scornful Lady* set a wit and a witty woman head on against each other in a match of repartee and stratagem? For Sir Positive to announce solemnly as evidence of his knowledge and insight what is such old hat shows his naiveté as a man of taste. For him to expatiate on his find is insupportable to one so surfeited with folly as Stanford.

Admitting these passages as criteria, it is easy to see why the Caroline Sons of Ben, in drawing on the sophisticated sock, were making dramatic history. They were attempting the kind of eclecticism—Jonson plus Beaumont and Fletcher with possibly a look at Marston—that was to become the recognized apprentice gambit for comic writers after 1660. Shackerley Marmion, Peter Hausted, Nabbes, and William Davenant tried the gambit first after Shirley; then Brome, Glapthorne, Jasper Mayne, William Cavendish, and Thomas Killigrew followed suit. The tradition they established before 1642 explains why Shadwell's Sir Positive was so ineptly out-of-date with his Eureka.

Marmion's *Holland's Leaguer,* performed in December 1631 and published in 1632, which enjoyed a run that was "one of the longest

167

known in the Elizabethan, Jacobean, and Caroline theatre,"[4] transcends the world of citizen comedy by using verse consistently rather than prose and by bestowing foreign names, some of them borrowed from Petronius' *Satyricon,* on several of the dramatis personae.[5] Allusions throughout, however—and especially the appropriation of Mrs. Holland's well-known Bankside brothel as one of the settings—make it clear that the beau monde portrayed is that of the Court and the upper-class circles of London and that the world and underworld of the London middle classes lie in the background.[6]

Two wits of quite different temperament, as their names indicate, emerge as norm characters. The first of these, Snarl, is a fleering censor, comparable to Shadwell's Stanford. His righteous indignation at the vices of the Court, his scorn for the ubiquitous spirit of affectation, his distrust of women's virtue, his "itching humour to see fashions," and his skill at barbed and polished "charactery" suggest that Jonson's Asper, Crites, and Truewit have all contributed to his conception. His friend, Fidelio, also has wit, but it has been overlaid and sobered by his slightly insecure Platonism. He has long been devoted to the lady Faustina, like Kenelm Digby to his Venetia Stanley. After they fell in love, her father forbade her to marry any one for seven years, six of which have now passed. Although her father is dead, she lives in seclusion still, out of deference to his wishes, and will admit no one to her presence but Fidelio, and only on the most decorous footing. When Snarl slurs all women's virtue, Fidelio is quick to parry, "You are deceived,/There are a thousand chaste." He is really trying to bolster up his faith in Faustina, because he soon jumps at the chance to test her constancy.[7]

One way for the writer of comedy to come to terms with the anti-comic trend of Court Platonism was to take it seriously, endow fictitious exponents of it with some worldly cleverness, and employ them as critics and purgers of pretenders to wit and gentility. This compromise Marmion has attempted in his portrayal of Fidelio and Faustina. Fidelio persuades her, partly as a trial of her virtue and philosophy, to cure the mannered Libertinism of one of the most overblown poseurs of the play, her own brother Philautus, a courtier married to the affected

168

Triphoena. Fidelio and Faustina, however, fall far short of the wits and witty women of Beaumont and Fletcher, Shirley, and Restoration comedy in that they are overromanticized, relegated to a sub-plot that seems cribbed from tragi-comedy, and not pitted against each other in sprightly conflict.

Philautus' major vice, from which his other vices and follies spring like mushrooms from dank soil, is the self-love signalized by his name and reminiscent of that possessed by the courtiers in Jonson's *Cynthia's Revels*. He refers to his person as a tree loaded with "tempting fruit" and a "building nature has solemnised/With . . . magnificence," boasts of his "strange attractive power/Over your females," maintains that, if he had taken the place of Paris on Mt. Ida, all three goddesses would have fallen together "by the ears" for his love and chased him as if they had drunk aphrodisiacs, and asserts that his present ambition is to bathe his limbs in the same well with Diana, "get the foremost of her troupe with child,/And turn the rape on Jupiter."[8] Brought to Faustina, who has been transformed into a goddess by "delusive art,"[9] he endeavors to undermine her scruples by the conventional Libertine arguments, entirely unaware that she is his sister. She counters with the usual Platonic distinction between love and lust, "pure affection" and "beastly appetites." Her most effective stroke subtly flatters his self-love:

> I wonder, one
> So complete in the structure of his body,
> Should have his mind so disproportioned,
> The lineaments of virtue quite defaced.

Her insistence that he "seek . . . fame/In brave exploits," rather than "stay at home,/And dress [himself] up, like a pageant/With thousand antic and exotic shapes," puts the finishing touches on his reformation. He leaves for the wars with this speech to his friends:

> . . . hug your ignominies,
> And whilst we spoil the enemy, may you
> Be pil'd [pli'd?] by pimps, cheaters intrench upon you.
> Let bawds and their issues join with you. Marry
> With whores, and let projectors rifle for you.[10]

169

When he returns in the last act as the complete gentleman, he thus thanks Faustina for the metamorphosis:

> Lady, you are a good physician,
> It was your counsel wrought this miracle,
> Beyond the power of Esculapius.
> For when my mind was stupified, and lost
> In the pursuit of pleasures, all my body
> Torn and dissected with close vanities,
> You have collected me anew to life;
> And now I come to you, with as chaste thoughts
> As they were first adulterous, and yield
> A due submission for the wrong I did
> Both to yourself and sex.[11]

The main plot uses Snarl along with a group of rogue-exploiters—the projector Agurtes and his disciple Autolicus, who resemble Meercraft and Everill in *The Devil is an Ass;* the bawd Margery; Agurtes' daughter Milliscent; and the pander and whores of the notorious brothel—as somewhat too cumbersome machinery to satirize most of the other pretenders of the play. Ardelio, a parasite who lives on Philautus and puts his patron's Libertinism into practice on a less fashionable level, and Philautus' wife, Triphoena, a pseudo lady, are not so fully delineated as are Triphoena's hanger-on, Trimalchio, the prodigal son of a rich usurer; her older brother from the country, Capritio, whom she would like to make a courtier; and Miscellanio, the tutor she has engaged for him. The latter three are put through their paces in true Jonsonian style, suggesting *Every Man Out of His Humour.* Trimalchio's pretensions are summed up in his name, as he explains:

> Indeed, my father's name
> Was Malchio; for my three additions
> Of valour, wit, and honour, 'tis enlarg'd
> To Mr. Trimalchio. . . .

He also describes himself quadruply, with reference to "four nations," "the four elements," and "the four humours":

170

The Sophisticated Sock I

I am in my compliment, an Italian,
In my heart a Spaniard,
In my disease a Frenchman,
And in mine appetite an Hungarian.

. . . . .

I am hot in my ambition,
I am dry in my jests,
I am cold in my charity,
And moist in my luxury.[12]

Capritio, who tends to display farcical whims, as his name suggests, looks up to Trimalchio and follows his example in a succession of amusing scenes. He courts Margery while Trimalchio is courting Milliscent; is rooked of a diamond ring just as Trimalchio is of a watch; and with Trimalchio is uproariously victimized in the course of their pseudo-valorous assault on the leaguer. Miscellanio, who pretends expertness in Court etiquette, is taken in by Trimalchio's false gentility, but, after challenging him to a duel later, exhibits more genuine valor. The scheme of Agurtes to advance his daughter Milliscent by marriage to Trimalchio permits Marmion to comment satirically through Autolicus, himself a climber, on the extent to which the spirit of affectation has spread to all levels of Caroline society. Autolicus thus addresses Milliscent:

Thou hast a noble wit, and spirit, wench,
That never was ordained for any skinkard
T' engender with, or mechanic citizen,
Unless it were to cuckold him; thou shalt
Be still i' th' front of any fashion,
And have thy several gowns and tires, take place,
It is thy own, from all the city wives
And summer birds in town, that once a year
Come up to moulter, and then go down to th' country
To jeer their neighbors, as they have been served.[13]

Marmion's second comedy, *A Fine Companion,* performed and published in 1633, surpasses *Holland's Leaguer* in sophisticated eclecticism.[14] His chief models were probably Jonson's *Epicoene,* Beaumont

171

and Fletcher's *The Scornful Lady,* and Shirley's *The Witty Fair One.* Most of the characters represent the upper stratum of the London *bourgeoisie.* Prose supplements verse. Gone are the rogue-exploiters as satirical machinery. Two contrasted pairs of lovers, one more soberly dedicated and the other wildly witty, serve as norm characters. So busy are both couples in overcoming obstacles to the consummation of their love and in furthering the exposure of folly that the counterpointing of the sexes achieved in Restoration comedy and in some of Marmion's models is not a major concern. Collaboration rather than conflict marks the relations of each pair of lovers, even the wittier ones.

Marmion's advance over his first comedy can be seen in the way the graver pair of lovers, Aurelio, the disinherited elder brother, and Valeria, the elder daughter of the citizen Littlegood, function in the elaborate satirical portrayal of the pseudo wit Spruse, preferred by Valeria's father as her suitor. Tender-hearted and soberly constant as Aurelio and Valeria are, their Platonism is not stressed. Although Valeria takes cues from her witty younger sister, Aemilia, and Aurelio can too easily be moved to distrust, both show intelligence and enterprise in getting the better of Spruse and Littlegood. Spruse, who is comparable to Sir Amorous La-Foole of *Epicoene* and fit company for the amorists of Marston's *The Fawn,* is more keenly drawn than Philautus of *Holland's Leaguer.* A fop to his fingertips, he is distressed at the most trifling impairment of his elegance. Entering Careless' apartment with one garter untied, he explains:

> I met with a disaster coming up. Something has ravisht the tassel of my garter, and discompos'd the whole fabric, 'twill cost me an hour's patience to reform it; I had rather have seen the Commonwealth out of order.

He carries a black box containing form love-letters, "ready penned with as much vehemency of affection, as I could get for money," that he can dispatch speedily to any lady just after meeting her. One of his boasts is that he has culled his wit and repertoire of mannerisms from "the dust of antiquity"; as he caps one of his long speeches about it, "I

172

still affect a learned luxury." His exit from the apartment is as
ridiculous as his entry, for he says to Careless: "I took your lodging
by the way. I am going to dazzle the eyes of the ladies with my ap-
parition." When Valeria tells him that his protestations of love "savour/
Of art, more than of passion," he concludes she wishes him to play
the Libertine, which he most airily attempts to do. Her ironical reproof—"I am very sorry,/The time's disease has so prevailed upon
you"—causes him to return to her a Platonist. His approach this time
smacks of Cavalier heroic drama:

> Now, by that sacred shrine, brighter than Venus,
> To whom I pay my orizons, that form,
> That fair Idea, that rules all my thoughts,
> Thyself I mean, that spotless seat of pleasure—
> The continent of all perfection,—
> This spring of love, that issues from my soul
> Runs in a stream as pure as are your virtues,
> Full fraught with zeal, immaculate and free
> From all adulterate mixtures.

Valeria, coached by the shrewd Aemilia, refuses to be impressed. "I can
not frame me to believe one word" and "But 'tis all shew; and nothing
serious" are her quietly devastating remarks.[15]

Careless, Aurelio's younger brother, having entered spiritedly into
the special gallantry of the time, is addicted, as he puts it, to "new
plays, new mistresses, new servants, new toys, new fangles, new friends,
and new fashions. . . ." He is thus reminiscent of Beaumont and
Fletcher's younger Loveless of *The Scornful Lady* and Shirley's
Fowler of *The Witty Fair One*. His sweetheart Aemilia recalls Marston's Crispinella of *The Dutch Courtesan* as she sets forth her credo of
pleasure and independence to the more conventional Valeria:

> . . . For my part,
> When I have stretcht my brains, made all the shifts
> The wit of woman can be pregnant of,
> And shew'd my love by such experience
> As shall outstrip belief, all for his sake
> That shall enjoy me, which is Master Careless;

And when he has me, if he shall presume
On former passages of my affection
To oversway me in the least desire,
To contradict, and tempt my patience,
I'll shake off all obedience, and forget it.

This wild pair have quick, realistic minds grasping all the nuances
of the code they live by, knowing how to get what they want, seeing
through the absurdities and weaknesses of others. Their social intelligence is admirably suited to put in proper perspective the various
pretenders to gentility as well as an eccentric oldster who, though he is
out of step with the times, would marry to cut his nephew off from a
goodly inheritance. The pretenders, with Spruse at the top, are stratified
in the Jonsonian manner. Of the two town pseudo wits, Captain
Whibble and Lieutenant Sterne, it is Whibble who is more reminiscent
of Jonson's Bobadill and Shift. One of his talents is the minting of new
oaths—"by the soul of Hercules!" "Fire of my blood!" "Sulphur of
Styx!" "body of Jupiter!" "By the womb of Bacchus!" and the like.
In his charge is the citizen would-be Lackwit, descendant of Jonson's
Stephen, Sogliardo, Fungoso, Plutarchus, and a host of others. Careless
neatly hits off Lackwit's character: "Well, 'tis the truest spaniel that!
I put a hundred jeers upon him, and yet he loves me the better. I can
pawn him as familiarly as my cloak." Like most would-bes, Lackwit is
much concerned with his ancestry, thus describing to his mother a
volume he has been studying:

> This is a book of Heraldry, forsooth, and I do find by this book
> that the Lackwits are a very ancient name, and of large extent,
> and come of as good a pedigree as any is in the city; besides they
> have often matcht themselves into very great families, and can
> quarter their arms, I will not say with Lords, but with squires,
> knights, alderman, and the like, and can boast their descent to be
> as generous as any of the Lafools, or the John Daws whatsoever.

Lackwit's father and mother, Littleworth and Fondling, are social-
climbing citizens more in the tradition of Middleton than of Jonson.[16]
Lackwit's explicit reference to the prize pseudo wits of *Epicoene*

suggests that Dotario, the oldster turned gallant, may owe something to Morose. Littlegood, Aemilia's father, who has chosen Dotario to be her husband, thus describes him:

> Look you, here comes the old lecher! he looks as fresh as an old play new vampt. Pray see how trim he is, and how the authors have corrected him; how his tailor and his barber have set him forth; sure he has received an other impression.

To frighten him Aemilia's strategy is to unloose her tongue in abuse and to draw up a proviso itemizing what some of his problems will be in a marriage to a young woman. He concocts a counter proviso, a "syngraphus," upholding a lamentably archaic conception of a wife's subservience to her husband. After being as royally gulled by Careless as was Amphitryon by Jupiter, Dotario is willing to make any bargain to keep from becoming a laughingstock in the ordinaries, including the restoration to Aurelio of the estate rightfully his. Although hints from other sources, especially Beaumont and Fletcher, have probably figured in Dotario's portrait, the pattern of his exploitation, allowing for changes in the basic action, roughly parallels that of Morose. More importantly, the contrast he offers to the witty and the pretentious among the younger generation serves a function similar to Morose's.[17]

Marmion's last comedy, *The Antiquary*, performed probably in 1635 and published in 1641, while less well-made than *A Fine Companion*, shows he was endeavoring to perfect the eclecticism he had already experimented with.[18] Here his world is most remote from that of London citizen comedy, with Pisa as setting and with the Duke of Pisa and his chief courtier Leonardo disguised as gallants to study the manners of the age. These two become associates of Lionell and Aurelio, the young wits of the play, and the quartet is one of norm characters in some respects comparable to the trio in *Epicoene*. The conflict of wit and witty woman, which lends sprightliness to the comedies of Beaumont and Fletcher, Shirley, and the Restoration, emerges here in the relations of Aurelio and Lucretia. In carefully placed scenes of the second, third, and fourth acts,[19] they put each other out of countenance and finally make it up, Aurelio striving to

175

assert his superiority, Lucretia to exact his respect. Brought into contrast with the wits and the witty woman are an arch pseudo wit, Petrutio, priding himself on his physique, his manners, his poetaster's talents, his appeal to the fair sex, and his capacity for honour, but lacking any understanding of true friendship, piety, or love; and two oldsters, the antiquary Veterano, fantastically out of touch with his own day, and Aurelio's rival Moccinigo, clumsily seeking to keep pace with contemporary gallantry. In Petrutio Marmion has repeated the type drawn in Philautus of *Holland's Leaguer* and Spruse of *A Fine Companion,* as speeches like the following show:

> It draws near noon, and I appointed certain gallants to meet me at the five-crown ordinary: after, we are to wait upon the like beauties you talk'd of, to the public theatre. I feel of late a strong and witty genius growing upon me, and I begin, I know not how, to be in love wtih this foolish sin of poetry.[20]

In the oldsters Marmion has doubled the character of Dotario in *A Fine Companion* to achieve a more complex contrast.

It is the effort toward complexity, toward the many-actioned whole, that causes *The Antiquary* to fall short of what it might have been. The Duke's disguise, taking us back to Shakespeare's *Measure for Measure;* the involvement of Petrutio in a tragi-comic imbroglio with Lionell's sister, Angelia; the use of the disguised Angelia in a domestic triangle featuring Lucretia's father and mother; and Moccinigo's melodramatic tactic of hiring a bravo to kill Aurelio—these diversions, although perhaps appropriate to the Italianate setting, distract our attention from the concerns of genuine comedy of wit or manners and create an atmosphere hostile to it. Furthermore, the emphasis on Veterano's caprices is carried so far that it amounts to pulling the stuffed sock over the sophisticated one.

Hausted's *The Rival Friends,* performed for the King and Queen on the occasion of their visit to Cambridge in March 1632 and published later that year,[21] has the invidious distinction of being one of the most chaotic hybrids among Caroline comedies. Tragi-comedy, pastoral romance, and Jonsonian comedy of humours confusingly compete for dominance of the action, with the consequence that each corrupts the other's effects. The country setting makes for freshness. The satire aimed at simony as one of the contemporary manifestations of the acquisitive spirit, in the character of Sacrilege Hook, the mean-spirited justice and holder of mortgages who owns most of the community, shows considerable originality. Sophisticated eclecticism, although certainly not a major feature of this medley, is present to some extent in the norm characters, in the pretenders to wit whom they subject to satirical and farcical gulling, and in the mocking treatment of one of the favorite themes of Platonic serious drama—the self-sacrificing rivalry of ideal friends. Although there are more women than usual, none is genuinely witty. Pandora, the object of the Platonists' strange rejective devotion, jilts them both for another swain, but fickle passion and facile sentiment rather than wit dictate her behavior.

There are three norm characters so diversified as to muddle the satire. Bully Lively, "just fourscore," is a Falstaffian humanist, whose philosophy is summed up in the following remark: "This laughing/ Surely's restorative above your gold/Or all your dearer drugs." He is used to expose the acquisitive spirit in Hook and in the suitors of Hook's supposed daughter, Mistress Ursely, deformed and foolish but baited by her father with the dowry of "an impropriate parsonage." Also, Lively participates in intrigue designed to reduce the sublimity of the Platonic rivals to what may best be described as homosexual ridiculousness. In prying into others' affairs, he discovers, as he puts it, "more than e'er Columbus/Or our own waterfowl, Drake." Another norm character is Anteros, whose point of view—that of the confirmed woman-hater and satirist—is embodied in his name. A lover of sack, he compares his nose to "the ivy bush unto a tavern/Which tells us there is wine within." The third norm character is Jack Loveall, whose humour, as his name also indicates, is the exact opposite of his friend's—that of the rakish woman-chaser. Thus Anteros greets him: "What, my little ubiquitary Loveall? My page of the smock? My commodity above stairs? My court Shuttlecock, tossed from one lady

177

to another?" This raillery is affectionate rather than abusive, for Anteros adds: ". . . though it be an humor contrary to mine, who care for none, yet I like it far above your whining constancy as savoring more of the man." Loveall's response to this remark defends Libertinism with a salacious "metaphysical conceit" in prose:

> True. For why should I confine my love to one circle? We see that laborious creature the bee, which is often set before us for a copy of industry, not always droning upon one flower, but as soon as she has sucked the sweetness from one throws her little airy body upon a second, and so to a third, till at last she comes home with her thighs laden with that pretty spoil.

Anteros and Loveall spend most of the third act entertaining each other, after the fashion of Wellbred and Knowell in *Every Man in His Humour* and Truewit and his friends in *Epicoene,* with would-be wits of their special finding. They also offer contrast to the Platonists. Toward the end of the play Anteros is himself satirized as the two ugliest and stupidest women of the cast pursue him by love possessed.[22]

The suitors of deformed Mistress Ursely "for the parsonage's sake" include two Puritans—Zealous Knowlittle, "a box-maker," and Hugo Obligation, "a precise scrivener"; two "robustious football players," Arthur Armstrong and Stutchell Leg; "a decayed cloth-worker" Tempest Allmouth; and "a pretender to a scholar," Ganymede Fillpot. The would-bes egged on to quarrel over their gentlemanly superiorities and tricked through their fears into imprisonment in dog kennels, a chest, and a hogsty are William Wiseacres, "a quondam attorney's clerk"; Noddle Empty, an Inns of Court Man; Hammershin, "a bachelor of arts";[23] and Mongrel, who thus describes himself:

> My name, sir? Why, sir, I am not ashamed of my name, sir. My name is, sir, M. Mongrel, sir. A poor elder brother, sir. And yet not very poor neither, sir. Heir to six or seven hundred a year, sir. My father is a gentleman, sir. I have an uncle that is a justice of peace, sir. I can borrow his white mare when I please, sir. She stood him in thirty pieces, sir.[24]

When Anteros asks, "But how shall we dispose of them?", Loveall replies: "We'd best/Barrel them up and send them for New England." Anteros quips back: "A pox, there's fools enow already there./Let's pickle them for winter salads."[25]

Hausted on purpose exaggerates beyond belief the lengths to which Lucius and Neander, the Platonic rivals for Pandora, are each willing to go so that the other may ultimately enjoy her charming person. Although she likes both at the beginning of the play, neither will marry her on the ground that he will wrong his friend. Lucius whines to disgust her so she will turn to Neander, who scorns her to send her back to Lucius. When she folds Lucius' arms around her, he calls her "thou prostitute immodest" to the relief of Neander. As Pandora leaves in tears, Lucius and Neander embrace.[26] Neander is willing to wed a supposed man to insure Lucius' marriage to Pandora, whereupon Lucius insists he is a eunuch. This is not only farced satire of Court Platonism but also parody of its literature. Little wonder that King Charles and especially Queen Henrietta, despite the reverent tributes to them in the prolog in the eighth scene of Act I, and in the epilog, preferred Randolph's *The Jealous Lovers!*

Nabbes in *Covent Garden,* performed probably in 1633 and published in 1638,[27] rose to the defense of Court Platonism by shaping his comic action to put two ideally virtuous women of sober intelligence and gracious manners in conflicts of varying significance with their contrasted aspiring lovers, one a Platonist and the other a Libertine. At the same time he advanced toward a truly sophisticated eclecticism in comedy by using all four of these characters as norms to satirize the spirit of affectation in a carefully chosen and stratified group of pretenders to wit and gentility.

Dorothy Worthy, the daughter of a knight, has a philosophic cast of mind and has learned caution about marriage from her step-mother, who is near Dorothy's age and who, having failed to exercise choice in her marriage, is not too happy with the much older Worthy. Dorothy thus formulates her credo:

179

There is a power
Call'd Fate, which doth necessitate the will,
And makes desire obedient to it's rule.
All the resisting faculties of reason,
Prevention, feare and jealousie are weake
To disanull what in it's firme decrees
Is once determin'd. Yet my heart is free;
Unbounded by the stricter limits of
Particular affection: so I'le keepe it.
No proud ingratefull man shall ever triumph
O're the captiv'd sweets of my Virgin love;
Nor a vain-glorious gull that offers service
To every noted beauty, boast my favour.
I'le cloath my thoughts in humorous observation;
And if on any that sollicits love
I fixe a liking, I'le refer my selfe
To what is destin'd for me.[28]

Her suitor, Theodore Artlove, described in the dramatis personae as "a compleat gentleman," tends toward Court Platonism, as this speech to his Libertine friend, Hugh Jerker, makes clear:

    . . . where there is an union
Of loving hearts, the joy exceed's expression.
That love is vertuous whose desires doe never
End in their satisfaction, but increase
Towards the object; when a beautious frame
Garnish't with all the lustre of perfection
Invite's the eye and tells the searching thoughts
It holds a richer minde, with which my soule
Would rather mixe her faculties.

Despite Artlove's fine sincerity, Dorothy mocks him gently in order to test him. But the duel thus auspiciously begun is not sustained. Dorothy succumbs too soon to "what is destin'd" for her, and his conflict with her meddling brother is substituted for dramatic interest.

Hugh Jerker, the Libertine wit, is trying to persuade Lady Worthy to commit adultery. He states his credo in the following speeches to Artlove:

Nothing comes from thee but documents. I sweare I should love
thee much better if thou hadst lesse virtue. I prethee leave thy
Stoicisme, and become an Epicure with me. . . . drinking and
wenching are the onely virtues in a gentleman of the last edition;
to be excellent at them is a master-piece of education. Besides, they
are the only *acumens* of wit.

> 'Tis a blisse above the faign'd *Elysium*
> To clasp a dainty waste; to kisse a lip
> Melts into *Nectar;* to behold an eye
> Shoot amorous fires, that would warme cold Statues
> Into a life and motion; play with hayre
> Brighter then that was stellifyed;
> And when the wanton appetite is cloy'd
> With thousand satisfactions of this kind,
> Then follow's th' absolutenesse
> Of all delight. But were desire restrain'd
> From variation, soone 'twould satiate,
> And glut it selfe to loathing.[29]

Since Lady Worthy loved Hugh before her unfortunate marriage, she
cannot be harsh with him but is much too sensible and virtuous to take
seriously his solicitations. Consequently she employs her wit to reform
his Libertinism and to cure her husband of jealousy. This action is one
of the stock resources of citizen sentimental comedy, but Nabbes so
portrays Lady Worthy that she is unusually mature, dignified, and witty
as an exponent of the idealistic single standard of sexual morality. Court
Platonism and citizen sentimentalism are thus merged, on a sophisticated social plane.

The pretenders, some of them resembling amorists in Marston's
The Fawn,[30] include Hugh Jerker's cousin, Jeffrey, who has come to
London "to learne wit and the fashion."[31] His unsubtle putting into
practice of Hugh's credo brings out fully its inherent absurdity. Every
woman Jeffrey meets he invites forthrightly, without preliminaries,
to go "vaulting" with him; he has no discrimination, making similar
propositions to Mrs. Tongall, the Covent Garden gossip, match-maker,
and genteel pandress; to Susan, Lady Worthy's sack-loving and not
unamorous waiting-woman; and even to Lady Worthy herself! An-

181

other would-be gallant, Littleword, is Jeffrey's antithesis. Speaking only one word in the course of the play—and that the monosyllable "no"—,[32] Littleword pursues Dorothy Worthy, but has to depend on Mrs. Tongall to describe his qualifications. Although she asserts that he comes of ancient descent, that his ancestors were great philosophers, that he is a wit and a poet and possesses a great estate, he can only stand mute, racking his brain futilely for appropriate compliments. Dorothy observes, "Sure, Mrs. *Tongall,* your friend would make an excellent midwife; he can keepe secrets."[33] Later, at Dasher's Ordinary, he industriously copies down in a notebook all the remarks he over-hears, hoping no doubt that some of them will lend sparkle to his wit should it ever grow articulate. Mrs. Tongall remarks that he must be "taking a humour for a Play. . . ."[34] Warrant, Worthy's clerk, and Spruce, Lady Worthy's gentleman usher, are lesser would-bes addicted to quarreling and tricked by Susan—after the manner of Maria in Shakespeare's *Twelfth Night*—into farcical exhibition of their false courage[35] Finally Nabbes gives us one of the best country would-bes of Caroline comedy in Dungworth, just arrived in London with his two servants, Dobson and Ralph. He thus explains his mission to them:

> I am resolv'd to forsake the Countrey profession of mine Aunces-tors; and meane to turne Gallant. Ile sell some few dirty Acres, and buy a Knighthood; Ile translate my Farme of *Dirt-all* into the Mannor of *No-place*.[36]

Ralph, the wittier of the servants, comes up in the last scene with the following "character" of his master, when, in a typical Jonsonian denouement, they all appear before Justice Worthy, who whimsically appoints Ralph to do the judging:

> You are a Countrey Gentleman: a Gallant out of fashion all the yeare; but especially at Sessions, and upon High Holi-dayes, when your sattin doublet drawes away the eyes of the simple, and distracts their devotion almost into Idolatry: giving it more worship then the Heraulds ever gave your Auncestors. You intend as I understand to come forth in a new Edition: and when the Mercers and Tailors have new printed you and that some gentile wit may be read in your Character, to marry a Wife in the

182

City. You shall then have a passe sealed upon her by a Courtier; and be ship't at Cuckolds haven, and so transported into *Cornwall*.

A noteworthy feature of *Covent Garden* is its "place-realism" and its use of documentary, reportorial scenes, such as that in Dasher's Ordinary, where the wits appear in an upper room while the pretenders to wit congregate in a lower one, thus symbolizing the Jonsonian stratification so important in their portrayal.[37]

By the middle of the 1630's Davenant did his part toward a sophisticated eclecticism in comedy. *The Wits,* performed in 1634 and published in 1636, ran the longest of all his plays and was the most frequently revived. *News from Plymouth,* performed 1635 and not published until 1673, was apparently little noticed. To these must be added one of his tragi-comedies, *The Platonic Lovers,* also performed in 1635, published the following year, and moderately successful.[38]

The only one of these to employ a London setting is *The Wits.* Its greatest distinction lies in juxtaposing a wild wit, Younger Pallatine, with one of the wittiest young women of Caroline comedy, Lady Ample, as accomplices in the execution of stratagems and as norms to satirize humours. They seem generally to be modeled on characters in Beaumont and Fletcher and Shirley.[39] Instead of making them lovers, Davenant attaches Younger Pallatine to Lucy, who flees from her aunt to stay with Lady Ample and assumes a distinctly subordinate role to her benefactress. Younger Pallatine, who welcomes to town two friends from the war in Holland—Meager and Pert, is interested in gulling his brother, Elder Pallatine, heir to all their father's estate and just arrived in London with another older country knight, Sir Morglay Thwack, to recapture the disorderly gallantry of their long fled youth. Lady Ample, in possession of both wealth and social position, is to be freed within the next twenty-four hours from the wardship of her usurer uncle and guardian, Sir Tyrant Thrift, and is resolved to defeat his scheme to provide her at the last moment with a husband of his choice. The scheme strikes her as absurd:

183

He choose a husband, fit to guide and sway
My beauty's wealthy dowry, and my heart!
I'll make election to delight myself. . . .

She advises Lucy to be less subservient to the will of her lover, contrasting her own management of men:

I led my fine
Trim-bearded males in a small subtle string
Of my soft hair; made 'em to offer up
And bow, and laugh'd at the idolatry.[40]

When she hears of Younger Pallatine's gulling of his brother, she is quick to praise:

. . . why, there was wit enough
In this design to bring a ship o' fools
To shore again, and make them all good pilots.

But she is a bit piqued that the design was not hers and threatens to so far outdo him and his friends that they will "degrade" themselves "from all prerogatives/Above our sex" and "singe off with tapers" their "trim beards" "As a just sacrifice to our supremacy."[41] She keeps her word and is so successful that she enables Younger Pallatine and Lucy to marry and at the same time ropes in Elder Pallatine for herself. This latter outcome somewhat lowers her status as a witty woman, however, since the best embodiments of the type never marry any but their equals in intelligence. Neither Elder Pallatine nor Sir Morglay Thwack is quite so naive as Jonson's Stephen or Sogliardo, but both are capricious old lechers with few brains to speak of. Elder Pallatine, for example, thus faces London after all these years:

What beauties, girls of feature, govern now
I' th' town? 'tis long since we did traffic here
In midnight whispers, when the dialect
Of love's loose wit is frighted into signs,
And secret laughter stifled into smiles;
When nothing's loud, but the old nurse's cough.
Who keeps the game up, ha! who mislead now?[42]

And Thwack makes the following wry commentary on his gulling:

> Cozen'd in my youth! cozen'd in my age!
> Sir, do you judge, if I have cause to curse
> This false inhuman town. When I was young,
> I was arrested for a stale commodity
> Of nut-crackers, long-gigs, and casting-tops:
> Now I am old, imprison'd for a bawd.[43]

Here the stuffed sock is on!

The setting of *News from Plymouth* takes us into an atmosphere quite different from that of most Caroline comedies, a seaport town where two fashionable and wealthy London ladies, Loveright and her cousin Joynture, are living at the house of the rich Mrs. Carrack, widow of a sea captain. They represent prize cargoes to three witty and rakish sea-captains, Seawit, Cable, and Topsail, who all aspire at first to win Lady Loveright. But the ladies are skillful maneuverers. Widow Carrack sets her cap for Cable. When he rebuffs her, she disguises as a courtesan and lures him to an assignation, where his resistance shows signs of weakening. Pressed by his creditors, he would rush her into marriage, but she discovers the extent of his debts and rejects him. In the end she agrees to take him, on condition that he will bring her a good prize back from sea. Mistress Joynture, making a play for Seawit, meets with initial failure but eventually cajoles him into being her servant. Lady Loveright keeps Topsail dangling only to jilt him for the scholarly soldier, Sir Studious Warwell, whose presence permits Davenant to have side-splitting fun with maritime and martial valor. The intrigues are generally reminiscent of *The Wild-Goose Chase* with curious overtones from *The Magnetic Lady*.[44]

Caught up in the intrigue-paced action are humour characters definitely Jonsonian and serving the ends of both satire and farce. Sir Solemn Trifle, Lady Loveright's uncle, has an eccentric argumentative prolixity and gravity derived from his occupation as justice. At the same time he pretends to a knowledge of affairs of state comparable to that of Sir Politick Would-Be in *Volpone* and operates a news-mongering agency like that in *The Staple of News*, with three bed-

185

lamite "intelligencers," Scarecrow, Zeal the Wrong Way, and Prattle. Sir Furious Island, a country knight, has the quarreling humour of Kastril in *The Alchemist* and takes it out on the Dutch sea-captain, Hans van Bumble, whose broken English adds much to the uproarious-ness of certain situations.[45] Again, the sophisticated sock is swallowed up by the stuffed one.

Going to the opposite extreme in *The Platonic Lovers,* Davenant escapes to Sicily and deals more critically with Court Platonism, under the pretext of a pastoral romance, than do Jonson, Marmion, Hausted, and Shirley.[46] The norm characters include a pair of lovers represent-ing the average healthy man and discreet woman under the double standard of sexual morality. Phylomont is frank about desiring Ariola physically, even before marriage. When she meets his ardor with "virtuous scorn," making it clear that she will yield only in marriage, he is thoroughly willing and requests her brother Theander's permis-sion. She has no excessive idealism about the state of virginity, as she indicates to Theander:

> Sir, it is excellent, and free, but, I
> Am told, the next degree of happiness,
> The married challenge and enjoy.[47]

A third norm character is the physician Buonateste, who regards Platonic love as an unnatural folly:

> My Lord, I still beseech you not to wrong
> My good old friend Plato, with this Court calumny;
> They father on him a fantastic love
> He never knew, poor gentleman. Upon
> My knowledge, sir, about two thousand years
> Ago, in the high street yonder
> At Athens, just by the corner as you pass
> To Diana's conduit,—a haberdasher's house,
> It was, I think,—he kept a wench![48]

Contrasted with these norm characters are different exponents of the Platonic folly. Theander and Eurithea are sincere, highly self-con-scious Platonists, but wholly absurd in the denial of their animal natures. Fredeline, who turns into the tragi-comic villain, is the hypocritical Platonist, using the cult as a stalking horse for Libertinism at its worst. Lastly, in Gridonell appears the unconscious Platonist, who is such an innocent about sex as the result of a youth spent in rigorous military training that he acts like a ninny in the presence of a woman. To cure Theander and Gridonell, Buonateste administers them aphrodisiacs, with the consequence that the first agonizes over his irrepressible new impulses to carnality and the latter roars for a wench like a young bull in heat. The sensible Ariola, incongruously to reverse these incongruities, catches her brother's Platonism at its most toploftical—more a matter of catching cold than catching fire—and leads the flabbergasted Phylomont a merry dance until Buonateste comes to the rescue. If Davenant had injected his satire into a comedy of London life and held in check his rampageous penchant for farce, he might have worn the sophisticated sock more impressively than any of his colleagues.

Even though none of the plays considered in this chapter effects a synthesis of Beaumont and Fletcher and Jonson so neat as Shirley's in meeting most of the criteria of the later Restoration comedy of wit or manners, all satisfy at least some of them. The new look in humour comedy had come to stay. Such successes as *Holland's Leaguer, A Fine Companion, Covent Garden,* and *The Wits* could not but spur Brome and other Sons of Ben to emulation.

CHAPTER
EIGHT

The Sophisticated Sock II

So complete was Brome's commitment to the sentimental sock and the stuffed sock, to the blending of one or the other mode of citizen comedy with Jonson, that his wearing of the sophisticated sock was never more than partial, a motley makeshift to stay in fashion, instead of a real change in theatric footgear. His comic world was already complicated enough in every play. Insistent on retaining it and adapting to its crowded mechanism of plots and sub-plots parts of the world being created by Marmion, Nabbes, Davenant, and Shirley, he ran the risk of reducing his eclecticism to a wholly inartistic chaos. Could his talent manage to achieve anything resembling unity out of such diversity?

The Sparagus Garden, performed in 1635 and published in 1640,[1] the first of several plays in which Brome sought to incorporate elements of his colleagues' synthesis, provoked Swinburne, one of his most charitable critics, to this curiously qualified generalization:

> It is surely a very bad fault for either a dramatist or a novelist to cram into the scheme of a story, or to crowd into the structure of a play, too much bewildering ingenuity of incident or too

much confusing presentation of character; but such a fault is possible only to a writer of real if not high ability.[2]

Swinburne's generalization is equally relevant to the three other plays of Brome that more or less follow the lead of *The Sparagus Garden*— *A Mad Couple Well Match'd,* performed sometime during 1636–39 and published in 1653; *The English Moor,* performed in 1637 and published in 1658; and *The Court Beggar,* performed either in 1639 or 1640 and published in 1653.[3] That Brome knew what he was doing, however, is shown by the fact that *The Sparagus Garden,* as Caroline box-office receipts go, and assuming, of course, that our data are not grossly exaggerated, was "a spectacularly popular play."[4]

What most interested Brome here, as the title indicates, was to outdo Marmion's *Holland's Leaguer,* Nabbes' *Covent Garden,* and Shirley's *Hyde Park* in putting on the stage a fashionable resort of contemporary gallantry with reportorial or documentary realism. The Sparagus or Asparagus Garden was a plantation of two acres with a house where guests could rent private rooms for whatever diversion they desired, an arbor where they could dine and drink at pleasantly dispersed tables, and a spacious promenade where they could meander amongst the neatly tended asparagus beds. Since the speciality of the establishment—asparagus—was reputed in the folklore of the age to have aphrodisiac properties comparable to oysters, lovers and married couples from the upper classes, especially the city-court beau monde, made up the bulk of the clientele.

In Act III the intricate intrigue-sped action is interrupted, almost forgotten. The citizen "gardner" and his wife chat with their guests. A couple of gentlefolk too penurious in their pursuit of pleasure complain to them of the high prices. At one of the tables in the arbor three witty young gallants foregather. Two waiters cover the table and set down wine, sugar, and asparagus. Soon the gallants are exchanging badinage with a perverted old knight who has come to the garden to stalk and ogle and drool over the ladies. Some of these, with their courtier escorts, promenade in close converse and dance gracefully to music. Presently a pair of rogues with their country gull in tow and

189

a restless upper class couple, the wife with the stance and swing of the insatiate wanton and the husband looking strained and hounded like a jealous impotent, surge into the foreground. Having tasted some of the supposedly potent asparagus, the couple wrangle about renting one of the rooms. A gentleman squiring a citizen's wife argues with a waiter over their reckoning, the wife finally paying what is asked, while her paramour passes a blasé quip at the cozenry of all such hostels to gourmandizing, thirst, and lust. This act-long panorama is unsurpassed in Caroline comedy for the local color of its place-realism.[5]

Another of Brome's interests in *The Sparagus Garden* was to recast the Middletonian wit-intriguer into the likeness of the Jonsonian true-wit. A gallant, Sam Touchwood, son of a crabbed justice of the peace, is faced with a problem comparable to that of Witgood in Middleton's *A Trick to Catch the Old One:* to marry the girl of his choice and at the same time gain the inheritance that is rightfully his. Two young gallants, Gilbert and Wat, assist him to realize these hopes. In the Asparagus Garden panorama of Act III, the trio might easily pass for Truewit, Dauphine, and Clerimont of Jonson's *Epicoene.* Gilbert favors us with a memorable satiric portrait of the perverted old knight, Sir Arnold Cautious, and Sam launches into an inspired defense of poetry and poets.[6] The genuineness of their wit provides a good contrast to the grotesque efforts at wit made by the country would-be, Tim Hoyden, in the company of his rogue-exploiters, who bilk him of several hundred pounds, bleed and diet him to give him blue blood, and cause him to look down the nose at his rustic-garbed and dialect-mumbling brother, Tom, by coaching him in such principles of gentility as the following:

> To commend none but himselfe: to like no mans wit but his owne: to slight that which he understands not: to lend mony, & never look for't agen: to take up upon obligation, & lend out upon affection: to owe much, but pay little: to sell land, but buy none: to pawn, but never to redeem agen: to fight for a whore: to cherish a Bawd, and defie a tradesman.[7]

The one all-important feature of the new comic synthesis that Brome fails to do much with in *The Sparagus Garden* is the witty woman.

Sam's sweetheart Annabel finally forces her guardian grandfather into approval of her marriage to Sam by stuffing her clothes with pillows to simulate pregnancy. Although this is so clever a ruse that it seems to have had quite a vogue in seventeenth century comedy, passing from Marston's *The Fawn* to Thomas May's *The Heir* to Brome's *The Sparagus Garden* to Dryden's *The Wild Gallant*,[8] it is suggested to Annabel by Sam and is thus no evidence of her resourcefulness. She remains, in fact, relatively undeveloped as a heroine.

The two chief intriguers of *A Mad Couple Well Match'd* are Careless and Lady Thrivewell. Careless, a down-at-heel city wit, is trying to climb back into the good graces of his uncle, Sir Oliver Thrivewell. Lady Thrivewell, the uncle's clever wife, seeks to reform Libertines, get debauched virgins married, and cure her husband's jealousy. Both the nephew and the Lady are types drawn from the citizen comedy of Middleton, Dekker, Heywood, and Massinger. But there are important differences. Probably inspired by Marmion's *A Fine Companion* and Shirley's *The Lady of Pleasure,* Brome has created relationships for Careless and Lady Thrivewell that lift them into the world of the Restoration comedy of manners and endow them with some of the dimensions of its norm characters.

Careless is an unpolished preliminary version of such a Libertine wit as Etherege's Dorimant in *The Man of Mode.* When he is introduced to us at the outset of the play, his servant Wat proposes that he recoup his shattered fortunes by setting up a "male bawdy house." Thereafter Careless is shown trying to get rid of his former mistress Phoebe, whom he is guilty of seducing from virginity; overcome the scruples of his aunt, Lady Thrivewell; and win in marriage the wealthy and witty widow Anne Crostill, the only woman he respects. When he writes in insolent mockery to Phoebe and in fawning compliment to Anne, the letters get mixed, much to his embarrassment. The wholly unconventional letter that Anne receives, however, pleases her own perverse taste, with the result that she pursues him. When he puts her off, partly out of masculine stubbornness and partly because Lady Thrivewell has stirred in him a dim sense of his duty to Phoebe, Anne is all the more eager to have him. Toward Lady Thrivewell he is

191

astonishingly uninhibited. When she tricks him into cohabiting with Phoebe under the illusion that he has possessed herself, she almost loses the gambit and her virtue. As he leaves Phoebe in Lady Thrivewell's darkened bedroom, he encounters the Lady outside, thinks she has come to him again, and would have her a second time by force. In the end he palms Phoebe off on his servant Wat so that he can marry the widow Anne. Swinburne passes the following interesting judgment on Careless: "A more brutal blackguard, more shameless ruffian, than the leading young gentleman of this comedy will hardly be found on the stage of the next theatrical generation."[9]

Lady Thrivewell is brought into striking contrast with the promiscuous, unscrupulous, social-climbing citizen's wife, Alicia Saleware, whose husband is as willing to be cuckolded for the enjoyment of prestige and luxury as Middleton's Allwit of *A Chaste Maid in Cheapside*. Alicia has already committed adultery with Sir Oliver and is anxious to become the kept mistress of Lord Lovely. Lady Thrivewell is clever enough to gull her out of the 100 pounds Thrivewell has paid her for her favors and to win Lord Lovely away from her so that he can marry the nice girl who loves him. Lady Thrivewell, in her thorough understanding of the double standard of sexual morality, her seemingly unethical manipulation of others in the interests of ethics, and her ability to see through pretense and falseness, is a kind of Celestina, a virtuous lady of pleasure. Alicia corresponds to Shirley's Lady Arentina Bornwell, on a slightly lower social plane—the unvirtuous woman of pleasure. Lady Thrivewell's maturity as a witty woman links her definitely with the more impressive Restoration versions of the type.[10]

The English Moor has a tragi-comic action that marks it as a hybrid; its truly comic action adapts Jonson's treatment of Morose in *Epicoene* with some reference to Marmion's handling of Dotario in *A Fine Companion*.[11] Like Dotario, Brome's elderly eccentric is a usurer, Quicksands. Instead, however, of courting a witty young woman like Aemilia, he is shown married to one, in this instance Millicent, who has been forced to become his wife by her tyrannical father Testy. Like

Morose, Quicksands is driven by three young wits, Banelass, Vincent, and Edmund, in conspiracy with Millicent, to abhor his marriage and assent to any proposal that will release him from its hazards, chiefly cuckoldry. Millicent, through the help of the wits and her maid Phillis, escapes, still virgin, to her lover Theophilus, a character very much involved in the tragi-comic action. Both Millicent and Phillis, at different times, disguise themselves as a blackamoor lady.

Brome counterpoints effectively the Libertine gayety of the wits with the social aversion of Quicksands. A crusty representative of the older generation, he has made his money chiefly by cheating the younger and believes it is composed of hellions. Banelass and his companions play up to this belief, and Banelass goes far to justify it merely by being himself. His concupiscence, if his own braggadocio about it can be credited, has included women of all ages, statures, conditions, opinions, features, and shapes.[12] Leading the persecution of Quicksands, he winds a horn outside the usurer's menage, enters with a group of masquers whose impersonations of a stag, a ram, a goat, and an ox are calculated to fill their victim with terror as to the future condition of his forehead, sends him a paper signed by many town gallants faithfully averring they intend to lay his wife, brings to his menage two disguised servants pretending to be Quicksands' idiot bastard from the country and his yokel keeper, and finally manages to be caught *flagrante delicto* with the blackamoor, whom Quicksands believes to be Millicent. Convinced now that his horns have sprouted, Quicksands rushes about the stage crying, "Oh . . . oh . . . oh . . . oh!", after the manner of Morose, with Banelass remarking, "It is the Cuckolds howlde. A common cry about the City."[13] Here is the sort of bawdy satirical farce that Restoration comedy, even at its most sophisticated, found uses for.

Brome's effort to move in two separate comic worlds at the same time is nowhere more evident than in *The Court Beggar*. One complicated action centers about the family of Sir Andrew Mendicant, the titular character. A combination of the social-climbing Fitzdottrel and the rogue Meercraft of Jonson's *The Devil is an Ass,* Mendicant has sacrificed his country estate and come to London to act as go-

193

between for a group of projectors who seek Court monopolies and patents for a whole series of fantastic ways to make money. He has to depend for Court influence upon one Sir Ferdinando, to whom he would like to marry his daughter Charissa. Ferdinando, however, is hot after a Court widow, Lady Strangelove, and is interested in Charissa only as a possible incidental seduction. Charissa, for her part, is content with a middle-class status and loves a young citizen with noble connections, Frederick, who emerges as an accomplished wit-intriguer of the Middleton type. Not only does he expose some of the deceptions practiced by Sir Ferdinando but also enlists Lady Strange-love's wit in forcing the courtier to aid him in winning Charissa. Brome is here wearing ably the stuffed sock of Middleton and Jonson to satirize both the acquisitive spirit and the spirit of affectation.

There is, however, a second, equally complicated action, that conceives Sir Ferdinando in quite different terms and foreshadows the more sophisticated comic world of the Restoration dramatists. As this action unfolds, Sir Ferdinando is not a mere pseudo wit of the Court but a resourceful Libertine truewit endeavoring like the Elder Loveless in Beaumont and Fletcher's *The Scornful Lady* or Fowler of Shirley's *The Witty Fair One* to provoke the pleasure-loving but mockingly aloof Lady Strangelove to drop the shield of her humour and show real emotion and passion. He would like to seduce her, or take her by force, in order to assert his masculine superiority. With such a consummation in view, he pretends to be out of his wits and hires a quack doctor to prescribe a tête-à-tête with her as his only feasible cure. Lady Strangelove, however, who amuses herself with masques and the baiting of her various suitors' foibles, is more than a match for Sir Ferdinando. Having reformed him, she has enough respect for his intelligence and devotion to accept him as her husband.

Brought into the duel between them to be measured by their distinctions of personality are a bevy of social pretenders. Three of these are nicely stratified to flay the spirit of affectation on every level. Court-wit is so snobbish that he thinks courtiers ought to have a monopoly on the writing of plays; Citwit spouts derogatory "characters" of all his acquaintance and pretends to a courage that he utterly lacks; and Swainwit is full of military bluster and the conceit of his powers as a stallion. A fourth pretender, Sir Raphel Winterplum, is a caricature of the Court Platonist, a castrated bachelor horrified at every allusion to sex. Finally, there is Dainty, a fashionable painter of bawdy pictures, who turns out to be a cutpurse in masquerade. If Brome had devoted the entire play to the development of this second action, he would have produced one of the sprightliest comedies of manners in the period. As it stands, *The Court Beggar* as a whole is sharply bifurcated rather than even loosely unified, and is seriously flawed by the resultant inconsistency in the characterization of its leading wit.[14]

The displacement of one mode of Caroline comic eclecticism by the other is well illustrated in Glapthorne's *Wit in a Constable,* performed sometime during 1636–38, revised in 1639, and published in 1640, and Jasper Mayne's *The City Match,* performed in 1637 or 1638 and published in 1639.[15] As their titles imply, both plays are Bromesque in their preoccupation with citizens. But more than Brome, Glapthorne and Mayne saw the necessity of leaving Middleton, Dekker, Heywood, and Massinger almost entirely behind, save perhaps for an occasional minor borrowing, and giving the combination of Jonson, Beaumont and Fletcher, and Shirley full opportunity to assert its possibilities, without the handicap of hybrid form or proliferating sub-plots from tradition.

Wit in a Constable has three truewits—Thorowgood-Freewit, Valentine, and Knowell—and places them in contrast with two would-bes, Jeremy Holdfast and Sir Timothy Shallowit. Since Knowell is not introduced until later and the name of Freewit is not used until after Act III, it suffices to speak of Thorowgood and Valentine as initiating the satire on social pretension.[16]

Jeremy Holdfast is Thorowgood's cousin, just arrived in London from Cambridge with the intention of courting Clare, the ward and niece of Alderman Covet. Jeremy's way of passing for a gentleman is to make an ostentatious display of his academic learning. Thorowgood, visiting him at his lodging, is frank to tell him his limitations as a suitor and how to correct them. Thorowgood's motive, however, is not genuinely altruistic. He himself wants to marry Clare but knows that the only way he can win her guardian's approval is to pass himself off as Jeremy. So the disparity between himself and Jeremy must to some extent be lessened. Hence he advises his cousin:

> . . . you're not now
> Amongst your cues at Cambridge, but in London,
> Come up to see your mistris beautious Clare,
> The glory of the city; goe and court her,
> As does become a gentleman of carriage,
> Without your Tropes and figures Inkehorne terms,
> Fit only for a Mountebanke or Pedant. . . .

Instead of his customary assigned reading, Jeremy must look into the Bibles of gallantry—"*Aretins* Politicks, and *Ovids* Art." Thorowgood and his friends "will refine/Thy Academicke wit with bowles of wine." Lastly Jeremy must be provided with both dress and language "fit to accost your mistris."[17]

As coincidence would have it, Sir Timothy Shallowit has come up from the country to court Grace, Alderman Covet's daughter. Valentine, who is interested in Grace, takes him in tow and introduces him to Thorowgood, who immediately perceives his assininity and ribs him unmercifully, without Sir Timothy suspecting irony in such remarks as the following: "I know you for the most Egregious knight/In all the country," and "right witty, and right honor'd sir . . ./Are you come up to learne new fashions?" Sir Timothy's stock replies are "Very right" and "Right agen."[18]

It is in courting Clare and Grace that Jeremy and Sir Timothy appear most ridiculous. Transmogrified from scholar into gallant, Jeremy so astounds Alderman Covet that he has to go to some trouble to prove his identity. Grace pokes such fun at Sir Timothy that he and Jeremy agree to switch girls. After this switch, Clare and Grace have a field day terrifying their foolish suitors with fantastically witty descriptions of what will happen to them after marriage. Clare, for example, lays down this proviso:

And if a Lord or courtly gentleman,
Whom we stile servant, out of love sometimes
Gives us a visit, you shall not repine:
If we foresake your bed to goe to his.

And Grace tops it off thus:

And if you chance, as fooles will oft be peeping
To spye us coupling, with respective silence
You shall depart, not daring to bedew
Your eyes with tears for grief that you are cuckolds. . . .[19]

The cooperation Clare and Grace seem to be giving Thorowgood and Valentine is, however, deceptive. They of course prefer these truewits, but would not be won too easily. So they provoke a lively duel of the sexes. The mettlesome counter-pranking of the truewits proves so outrageously effective that the girls seek help from Constable Busie to avenge themselves. So strong is their resentment that they are at one point even willing to accept the would-bes as husbands if Busie will trick Thorowgood and Valentine into marrying his own bouncing daughters, Nell and Luce. But Busie has a wiser head than that and so conducts his intrigue that the would-bes become his own sons-in-law and the wits and witty women are appropriately and happily paired. He thus justifies to Clare and Grace his betrayal of their expressed wishes:

. . . faith I thought
There was no wit in't, that you two should cast
Your selves away on two such gulls, your portions
Deserv'd more noble husbands. . . .[20]

By elevating a constable to the role of *deus ex machina* and arch wit and wag, Glapthorne lowered somewhat the tone of his comedy and lost the note of sophistication he had struck at the outset. The presence of this note perhaps explains why *Wit in a Constable* was revived for a brief run after the Restoration. The failure to sustain this note may account for the brevity of the run and Pepys' censure. On May 23, 1662, he wrote: "To the Opera, where we saw 'Wit in a Constable,' the first time that it is acted; but so silly a play I never saw I think in my life."[21]

197

The city wit Plotwell, who dominates Mayne's *The City Match,* is more than the wit-intriguer that his name suggests. Although his stratagems to prevent his uncle from disinheriting him as well as to accomplish other ends keep the action moving, his main function is that of a Jonsonian truewit exploiting both pretension to wit and the opposite humour of social aversion.

The citizen would-be Timothy Seathrift is the chief example of the former. Shown in company with two town pseudo gentlemen, Captain Quartfield and Salewit, obvious imitations of Jonson's Bobadill and Matthew, Timothy is presently exhibited drunk at an ordinary in the guise of a strange fish, a scene that is an expanded adaptation of Peregrine's gulling of Sir Politick Would-Be in Jonson's *Volpone.* Salewit thus comments on the spectacle that Timothy affords: "You must think a fish like this/May be taught Machiavel, and made a state-fish."[22] Plotwell's sister, disguised as the fashionable witty woman Aurelia, also participates in the castigation of Timothy. He begins courting her with such speeches as the following:

> Lady, let me taste the Elysium of your lips.
> Nay, they say
> You have a good wit, lady, and I can find it
> As soon as another. I in my time have been
> O' th' university, and should have been a scholar.

Aurelia's reply reduces Timothy, by his own admission, to "a dumb parrot":

> By the size of your wit, sir, had you kept
> To that profession, I can foresee
> You would have been a great persecutor of nature
> And great consumer of rush candles, with
> As small success as if a tortoise should
> Day and night practice to run races. Having
> Contemplated yourself into ill-looks,
> In pity to so much affliction,
> You might ha' pass'd for learned; and 't may be
> If you had fallen out with the Muses, and
> 'Scap'd poetry, you might have risen to scarlet.[23]

198

The Sophisticated Sock II

Aurelia, however, needs a husband with an estate, so she compromises her status as a witty woman by finally marrying him, as Lady Ample marries the Elder Pallatine in Davenant's *The Wits*. After the wedding, her brother locks up the bridegroom, rampant on aphrodisiacs, to await the bride.

The merchant Warehouse, Plotwell's uncle, is as averse to the ways of contemporary society as Jonson's Morose. For this reason, when he marries to disinherit his nephew, he chooses Dorcas, Timothy's sister, a girl who has had a strict Puritan education and seems decorum personified. The truth is that she is now a witty rebel against Puritanism, has secretly been already married to Plotwell, and is conspiring with him to gull Warehouse. Following the fake ceremony with the old merchant, they go to his menage, where she begins to rail at him, refuses to lie with him, threatens to make his forehead look like a trophy room, and has two fashionable paramours carried in by footmen. After these and other outrages to his sense of propriety and decency, Warehouse, like Morose, is willing to sign any document that will free him from his connubial scourge.

Penetrating satire of both Puritan extremism and Court Platonism heightens the sophistication of *The City Match*. When Dorcas takes the job of being Aurelia's waiting-woman and companion, she still bears the marks of her education. Aurelia thus describes her:

Never
Poor lady had so much unbred holiness
About her person; I am never dress'd
Without a sermon; but am forc'd to prove
The lawfulness of curling-irons, before
She'll crisp me in a morning. I must show
Texts for the fashions of my gowns. She'll ask
Where jewels are commanded? or what lady
I' th' primitive times wore ropes of pearl or rubies?
She will urge councils for her little ruff,
Call'd in Northamptonshire; and her whole service
Is a mere confutation of my clothes.

199

The Sons of Ben

She can't preserve
The gift, for which I took her; but, as though
She were inspir'd from Ipswich, she will make
The *Acts and Monuments* in sweetmeats, quinces
Arraign'd and burnt at a stake: all my banquets
Are persecutions; Dioclesian's days
Are brought for entertainment, and we eat martyrs.

She works religious petticoats; for flowers
She'll make church-histories. Her needle doth
So sanctify my cushionets; besides,
My smock-sleeves have such holy embroideries,
And are so learned, that I fear in time
All my apparel will be quoted by
Some pure instructor. Yesterday I went
To see a lady that has a parrot: my woman,
While I was in discourse, converted the fowl;
And now it can speak nought but Knox's works;
So there's a parrot lost.[24]

Later, when Dorcas is putting the finishing touches on the exploitation of Warehouse, the paramours brought to her by the footmen are said to be pictures she has ordered. Warehouse, already horn-mad, imagines they must be bawdy pictures:

. . . methinks,
It should be Mars and Venus in a net;
Aretine's postures, or a naked nymph
Lying asleep, and some lascivious satyr
Taking her lineaments. These are pictures which
Delight my wife.

A curtain covers the supposed pictures. When it is drawn back, Bright and Newcut—two young Inns of Court men who are friends of Plotwell—are found dressed and posed to simulate the high sobriety of rapt Court Platonists. Warehouse cries out:

Why this is far beyond example rare.
Now I conceive what is Platonic love.
'Tis to have men, like pictures, brought disguised,
To cuckold us with virtue.[25]

200

It remained for the courtiers, William Cavendish and Thomas Killigrew, at the very end of the Caroline period, to climax the efforts of the Sons of Ben to wear the sophisticated sock. Cavendish's *The Varietie,* performed probably sometime during 1641–42 and published in 1649, is filled with Jonsonian echoes as well as reminiscences of Shirley and Brome, particularly of *Love Tricks, The New Academy,* and *The Damoiselle.*[26] Killigrew's *The Parson's Wedding,* probably composed in 1639–40, published in 1663, and in all likelihood not performed until after the Restoration, in 1664,[27] strikingly combines Jonson with Beaumont and Fletcher as well as showing the influence of other Sons of Ben, especially Brome and probably Marmion.

Milieu rather than intrigue is all-important in *The Varietie.* The entire action centers about the fashionable townhouse of the Lady Beaufield and her daughter Lucy. The Lady, reputed to be a wit, has some resemblance to Jonson's Lady Loadstone of *The Magnetic Lady* and is in fact referred to as "the only magnetick widdow i'th Town."[28] To dominate the social scene, she is playing patroness to a matrimonial expert and fortune-teller, Mistress Voluble, and to a French dancing-master, M. Galliard. She permits these two to conduct a kind of academy at her townhouse, where truewits, pseudo ladies, pseudo wits, and even a country would-be and his mother are equally welcome.

The truewits consist of Sir William, who is courting Lady Beaufield; his friend, Jack Manley; and Newman, Lucy's suitor. Through Manley and Newman, Cavendish raises the question as to what wit really is. Manley distinguishes between true wit as a rare personal gift and false wit as a facile fashionable acquisition. Newman challenges the two pseudo wits, Jeerer Major and Jeerer Minor, and the would-be, Simpleton, to come forward with a satisfactory definition of wit or, in lieu of that, to "speake something that is witty." To the Jeerers, wit is railing and vituperation; to M. Galliard, it consists largely in dressing like a coxcomb and making "de reverence Alamode"; to Formall, Lady Beaufield's gentleman-usher, it is knowledge of all the latest rumors and supposed secrets of state; to the pseudo ladies, it is the lore of ensnaring men that Mistress Voluble expounds in her lectures; and to Simpleton, it means dubbing every remark of others "a clinch" and producing spontaneous repartee by turning oneself around until the head is dizzy and then speaking whatever pops into it. Of the pseudo ladies, Sir William remarks: ". . . you may live to see another University built and only women commence Doctors." Of the Jeerers and Simpleton, Newman quips: "They have a gunpowder-plot to blow up sence. . . ."[29]

Through Manley, Cavendish raises another issue—the difference between the Elizabethan conception of the gentleman and one that evolved in the Caroline period. Manley dramatizes this difference by impersonating the historical Lord Leicester in every detail of dress and manner and condemning those of M. Galliard, in the following rhetorical passage:

> . . . which of our two habits . . . is the more grave and manly, his leane upper chinne, or this goodly promontory? my Trunkes with a round walke pav'd with gold and silver, or your trouses, cut close to your dock, and drawne on with a screw? in which if you venture but halfe a crowne, lookes like a poltisse, or a swelling in the groine; your habit is phantasticall as the time, you squirt into your dublet, which you weare so carelesse as you had not button'd it since you came from a bawdy house, where men of this garbe, coming from the stewes, march with that gravity as they came from a conventicle, so soberly they would carry it.

In other words, the Elizabethan conception of the gentleman was thoroughly English and masculine; the new Caroline conception is Frenchified and effeminate. Both Lady Beaufield and Lucy, at first somewhat taken aback by Manley's archaic dignity, become his converts. Says the Lady: ". . . there wants but such a noble leader to . . . make this habit fashionable." And Lucy observes to Simpleton: "I do not like your new phantasticall shapes, that transforme a man from his masculine aspect; you appear to me like a Jackanaps. . . ."[30] The opposition of Manley to M. Galliard looks ahead to Etherege's contrast between Dorimant and Sir Fopling Flutter in *The Man of Mode*.

Toward the end *The Varietie* distintegrates into pure farce. Nothing

attests this collapse more than the way the truewits lose their normative function. Sir William, for example, is married to Simpleton's
cross-eyed mother, who has been tutored in gentility by the courtesan,
Mrs. Nice. Newman, although he ultimately wins his Lucy, does so by
rescuing her from abduction at the hands of Simpleton. Furthermore
Newman succumbs to a ludicrous melancholy induced by one of
Mistress Voluble's ominous prophecies and goes on a tavern binge
to escape it.[31] Manley is replaced by a whimsical Jonsonian justice
who acts as *deus ex machina* in the denouement, handing down
eccentric sentences, dallying amorously with the rescued Lucy, and
finally deciding to marry Mistress Voluble because of her wit. Too
servile imitation of Jonson's technique in his "dotages" may account
for Cavendish's inability to sustain sophistication.

Killigrew's *The Parson's Wedding* is more of a piece. There is little
question that he sustains strongly the eclecticism with which he begins.
If this cannot truly be called a sophisticated comedy, comparable to
Etherege's or Dryden's or Wycherley's or Congreve's at their best,
the fault lies in having made the wits too outrightly ruffian in their
Libertinism, the witty women too obviously restive in their sexuality,
and the outsider and the pretenders too blatantly illustrative of follies
that require subtler ridicule.

As in *The Varietie*, milieu takes precedence over intrigue. The
fashionable townhouse of the widow, Lady Wild, and her niece,
Mistress Pleasant, is the principal setting. It is before this house in
Act I that the four wits—Tom Careless and Ned Wild (the widow's
nephew), just returned from foreign travel; the courtier Jolly, back
from an expedition to the country; and the Captain, veteran haunter
of the town's purlieus—meet to exchange gossip and philosophy. It is
at an oyster collation in the house, preceding the dinner to which they
have been invited, that the wits are brought into most striking juxtaposition with the two witty women and two pretenders to wit, Constant
and Sadd.[32] Other vivid settings for important scenes are the Devil
Tavern, site of the famous Apollo Room, and Ned Wild's lodgings,
where the wits are holding high carnival when the witty women come

to them for refuge after having been turned away from their own house presumably because it is under quarantine for the plague.

Careless, who is interested in Lady Wild, is a Libertine to the hilt, with a technique of seduction he explains at some length, a conviction that having venereal disease is trivial in comparison to being a fool, and a lively interest in other women than his bride as soon as he is married. He is clearly descended from Shirley's Fowler in *The Witty Fair One,* Marmion's Careless in *A Fine Companion,* Hausted's Jack Loveall in *The Rival Friends,* Nabbes' Hugh Jerker in *Covent Garden,* Davenant's Younger Pallatine in *The Wits,* and Brome's Careless in *A Mad Couple Well Match'd.* Wild, who is very much drawn to his cousin, Mistress Pleasant, shares Careless' credo. His attitude toward women before he is married is summed up in the following remark: "I believe none fair, none handsome, none honest, but the kind."[33] After he is married, he sees nothing wrong in keeping an eye on pastures beyond his own. He thus reproves Lady Wild for being shocked at Careless' promiscuous fancy:

> Why, you're a fool, aunt; a widow, & dislike a longing Bride-groom! I thought you had known better; do you love a spurr'd horse, rather than a Duker, that neighs and scrapes?[34]

Jolly thus describes his sexual code: "Madam, we do not glory in Fornication; and yet I thank God, I cannot live without a woman." Bigamy plus is his notion of felicity: "I'd have the state prescribe two Wives and a Mistress."[35] The Captain, who keeps a young whore named Wanton, describes his ideal of pleasure in a lengthy passage unmatched for bawdry in all Caroline comedy. It begins:

> A Girl of Fifteen, smooth as Satten, White as her Sunday Apron, Plump, and of the first down: I'le take her with her guts in her Belly, and warm her with a Countrey-dance or two, then pluck her, and lay her dry betwixt a couple of sheets; There pour into her so much oyl of Wit as will make her turn to a man. . . .[36]

Mistress Pleasant has a high ideal for a husband, but the imagery she uses in describing him bespeaks a subconscious that is anything but pure:

. . . if I marry, it shall be a gentleman that has wit and honour, though he has nothing but a sword by his side; such a one naked is better than a fool with all his Trappings, Bells and Baubles.

Widow Wild pretends at first to have little interest in Careless, or any of his friends, but her comment gives her away with a vengeance:

Him! marry, God bless all good women from him; why, he talks as if the Dairy-maid and all her Cows could not serve his turn; then they wear such baudy-breeches, 'twould startle an honest woman to come in their company, for fear they should break, and put her to count from the fall of them; for I'le warrant, the year of the Lord would sooner out of her head than such a sight.[37]

Although Killigrew does not develop a duel of the sexes involving a series of stratagems and counter-stratagems, he gives us enough insight into the minds of his wits and witty women for us to see that their relations will always be spirited even when they are in close accord. And he makes the most of the one major stratagem by which the wits finally think they have won a stunning victory. When the ladies seek refuge at Wild's lodgings, Wild and Careless make them comfortable in a private room, send out Captain and Jolly to round up wedding serenaders, then let themselves into the private room, embrace the surprised and rudely awakened ladies in virtual nudity, and hale the serenaders outside as if they were bridegrooms in the zenith of the first night's ascension. Thus compromised, the ladies have no choice but to marry them. It is to be noted, however, that when the latter were turned away from their own house through a ruse engineered by their other suitors, they did not accept these suitors' offer of a haven, but came instead straight to Wild's, where they must have known Careless would also be. Perhaps, then, they really chose a predicament wherein they hoped they would have no choice!

The satire of *The Parson's Wedding* is directed primarily at Puritan extremism and Court Platonism, the two chief enemies of the Caroline comic spirit, and thus adds a fillip to Mayne's *The City Match*. The Parson of the title is of the Puritan persuasion. He is treated as a kind of Morose, violently averse to the gallantry of the wits. They take him

205

in tow, however, as Mihil takes Gabriel in Brome's *Covent Garden Weeded*. Married to the Captain's whore, Wanton, he is put to bed with Wanton's bawd, is haled to Wild's lodgings as to a constable's on a charge of adultery, and is finally made a hanger-on of the wits after he has agreed to let Wanton do pretty much as she pleases, which is, in her own words, to "bring wenching to that perfection, no age could ever have hoped."[38] Careless would like to "forbid the spiritual Nonsence the age calls *Platonick* Love."[39] This nonsense has three advocates in the play—the pseudo wits Constant and Sadd and an old nymphomaniac widow, Lady Love-all. Constant and Sadd originally came from the country and occasionally return for glimpses of the dunghill. They affect the Platonic views and airs in order to stay in the fashion. How deep their idealism lies is apparent when they engineer the ruse that backfires on them by sending the ladies to Wild's lodgings. As for Lady Love-all, Platonism is a genteel mask for her stallion-hunting propensities. She is hiding behind it when she makes such observations as the following: "I'll swear 'tis strange, the state doth not provide to have all Whores hang'd or drown'd," and ". . . there's none that sacrifices more to friendship-love than I."[40]

CHAPTER
NINE

A Concluding Note

James Branch Cabell, who had a passion for
Thalia and for the Restoration, apparently held a low opinion of the
Caroline Sons of Ben in comedy. In *Beyond Life* his spokesman, John
Charteris, makes the mistake of measuring them against Shakespeare
and Congreve. Inevitably, then, he must dismiss them with a depreca-
tory witticism: "It should always be remembered in favor of the
Puritans that when they closed the theatres 'realism' was sprawling
upon the stage."[1] This is equivalent to saying that here was a tribe of
traffickers in carpentry rather than aesthetics who lacked the creative
imagination to transcend the stock topicality of the Jonsonian tradition
and the artistry to endow their works with "the auctorial virtues of distinction and clarity, of beauty and symmetry, of tenderness and truth
and urbanity."[2]

My effort in this study has been to re-create, through interpretative
synopsis, the illusory world and life of the Sons' thirty-two so-called
"realistic" comedies and to relate these to the challenge of their authors'
time, the premises of their comic theory, and the forces in their heritage

shaping their comic practice. Such a review justifies a somewhat different estimate of the Caroline Sons of Ben as a group—an estimate both historical and critical—than is implied in the oblivion to which they have been consigned by Cabell, most of the professional students of English drama, and that mysterious posterity of "general readers" who are the ultimate arbiters of all literary reputations.

Historically, the Sons deserve praise for keeping Thalia alive and racy during a period none too hospitable to her in either the role of beadle or the role of hoyden. Their eclecticism explored the rich resources of satire and farce in the classical and the English Renaissance theater and experimented with a variety of choices and combinations. Randolph's *The Muses' Looking Glass* and Brome's *The Antipodes* have the unique distinction of being thought-provoking comedies about the art of comedy. Randolph's *Aristippus* and *The Jealous Lovers* are among the more sprightly imitations in English, respectively, of Aristophanes and Plautus. Brome's *A Jovial Crew* is a minor masterpiece of the drama of sensibility written long before this genre was invented. Brome's *Covent Garden Weeded* and Cartwright's *The Ordinary* are re-readable satiric farces perpetuating some of the philosophic overtones in Jonson's *Bartholomew Fair* and *The Alchemist* and helping to transmit to the Restoration a lesser but lusty tradition of citizen buffoonery. Marmion's *A Fine Companion,* Nabbes' *Covent Garden,* Brome's *The Sparagus Garden* and *A Mad Couple Well Match'd,* Mayne's *The City Match,* and Killigrew's *The Parson's Wedding* are perhaps the spiciest of a sizeable ragout of plays that develop patterns and meanings later revived and perfected in the Restoration comedy of manners.

A just critical estimate of these Sons of Ben must acknowledge that their greatest weakness is one of style or language. The verse of Randolph or Marmion or Nabbes or Davenant or Cartwright or Glapthorne is competent but uninspired read alongside that of Jonson at his best. The prose of Brome or Cavendish or Killigrew is awkward or flat or coarse when one comes to it after the ease of Etherege, the grace of Dryden, the vigor of Wycherley, or the brilliance of Congreve. A second of their weaknesses is construction. In the majority of their comedies, the effort to achieve unity of inclusion results only in too great inclusiveness, so that variety or medley or olla-podrida and the manic-depressive anarchy of the sub-plot prove besetting sins. A third weakness is the monotony of too many stock characters and situations. And a fourth is the excessive topicality that all drama seeking to put the life of its time on the stage must necessarily fall into now and then, as surely as a forager in a quagmire will sink occasionally to his midriff.

Yet it cannot be denied that, if significant drama must give us "the concrete universal,"[3] many of these comedies have some survival value. The follies and vices they mirrored from the Caroline Court- and city- and country-worlds were universal human failings. The spirit of intolerance, the acquisitive spirit, the spirit of affectation, and the ludicrosities of concupiscence are all very much with us in contemporary society. Stock characters and situations are to be found in every considerable body of comedy, even in the canons of such original geniuses as Shaw or James Bridie or Cabell himself in prose fiction. Indeed, there is ground for believing that one of the secrets of laughter is "the peep-bo situation," the periodic popping up of more of the same with only incidental changes.[4] Granting this substratum of the mechanical and repetitive in all comic experience, it is arguable that the thirty-two comedies of the Caroline Sons of Ben—if it is possible to keep them in mind for a while as entities—are unusually rich in ingenious twists to well-worn plots and in clever variations of familiar dramatis personae. For their priceless name-symbolism alone, their endlessly merry parade of Freewits and Newcuts and Sneakups and Dungworths, they deserve some lease on immortality. After more than three centuries, they can still make us ask ourselves the question that all real comedy should make us ask, according to Benjamin DeCasseres: "Hey there, little mannikin that once I thought a giant Thor, what deviltry will you be up to tomorrow?"[5]

NOTES AND
REFERENCES

Chapter One

1. Alfred Harbage, *Cavalier Drama* (New York and London, 1936), pp. 72–172.

2. *Ben Jonson,* ed. C. H. Herford, Percy and Evelyn Simpson (11 vols., Oxford, 1925–52), VIII, 638. Hereafter cited as *BJ.*

3. *The Poems of Robert Herrick,* ed. F. W. Moorman (Oxford, 1915), p. 289; cited *BJ,* XI, 416. For an account of the Sons of Ben, see *BJ,* I, 108–114.

4. This room is the scene of the fourth act of Jonson's *The Staple of News* (*BJ,* VI, 345–362). Over the entrance door were painted in gold letters on a black ground English verses of welcome by Jonson and over the mantelpiece within the room were engraved his *Leges Convivales,* twenty-four rules in Latin verse for convivial procedure (*BJ,* VIII, 656–657). For comment on these rules and the Apollo Room, see *BJ,* XI, 294–300.

5. Act II, sc. iv. The passage from Marmion is cited in *BJ,* XI, 361. G. G. Smith, *Ben Jonson,* "English Men of Letters series" (London, 1926), pp. 276–277, cites the Marmion with the Herrick passage.

6. William Haller, *The Rise of Puritanism* (New York, 1938), p. 72.

7. L. J. Potts, *Comedy,* Hutchinson University Library (London, n.d.), pp. 25, 44.

8. Hausted, *Ten Sermons* (London, 1636), p. 199.

9. Brome, Prolog to *The Antipodes,* ed. G. P. Baker, in *Representative English Comedies,* ed. C. M. Gayley (3 vols., New York, 1914), III, 435. Hereafter cited as Gayley III. Harbage, pp. 68 and 154, cites this and other comments by Brome on Court drama. R. J. Kaufmann, *Richard Brome: Caroline Playwright* (New York, 1961), pp. 109–130, makes a strong case for the view that Brome's *The Love-sick Court* (probably 1633–34), usually regarded as an attempt at Platonic drama, is actually a burlesque of it.

10. *The Autobiography and Correspondence of Sir Simonds D'Ewes, Bart.,*

During the Reigns of James I and Charles I, ed. J. O. Halliwell (2 vols., London, 1845), I, 279; hereafter cited as D'Ewes. See Godfrey Davies, *The Early Stuarts 1603–1660* (Oxford, 1938), p. 44. My account of the political crisis follows Davies (pp. 33–44) closely.

11. D'Ewes, I, 301; cited by Davies, p. 44.

12. Davies, p. 41.

13. D'Ewes, I, 402; cited by Davies, p. 44.

14. G. M. Trevelyan, *History of England,* Anchor Books (3 vols., New York, 1953), II, 167, stresses this conflict between systems of law.

15. Harold J. Laski, *The Rise of Liberalism* (New York, 1936), pp. 1–179, and George Soule, *The Coming American Revolution* (New York, 1935), pp. 23–30, present popularized summaries of this economic-social interpretation of English history.

16. My phrasing here is indebted to R. A. Knox, *Enthusiasm* (Oxford, 1950), p. 1.

17. David Mathew, *The Age of Charles I* (London, 1951), pp. 122–123.

18. Kathleen M. Lynch, *The Social Mode of Restoration Comedy,* "University of Michigan Publications, Language and Literature," Vol. III (New York, 1926), pp. 43–52, discusses the origins of Caroline Court Platonism.

19. On the tranquillity of England during this period, see William McElwee, *England's Precedence* (London, 1956), p. 111.

20. *The Familiar Letters of James Howell, Historiographer Royal to Charles II,* ed. Joseph Jacobs (2 vols., London, 1892), I, 317–318.

21. Act III, sc. i.

22. Cited by Ethyn Williams Kirby, *William Prynne: A Study in Puritanism* (Cambridge, Mass., 1931), p. 20. My summary of Prynne's career is based on this study.

23. William Prynne, *Histrio-Mastix: The Players Scourge, Or, Actors Tragaedie* . . . (London, 1633), "To the Christian Reader," and p. 6. Cyrus L. Day, "Randolph and Prynne," in *Modern Philology,* XXIX (1932), 349–350, discusses the origin of Prynne's classification.

24. Prynne, pp. 70, 71, 499–500, 290.

25. The sheets of the first edition, London, 1662, were apparently used to make up the second edition, London, 1670, which has a new title-page and title, *Theatrum Triumphans.* The date of composition can be established with reasonable accuracy from a statement in the text itself. In refuting Prynne's contention that plays demoralize a society, Sir Richard resorts to the evidence of history. He first cites Rome in the age of Augustus as a place and time of great dramatic activity and admirable public and private morality. Then, apparently desirous of driving his point home without emulating Prynne's prolixity, he turns abruptly

to contemporary England: "Come to our own Country, which is better known to us; take the Time from the beginning of our late famous Queen Elizabeth, to the present, almost fourscore years, a large time likewise for probation; and were ever any times known in this State more Civil, or more virtuous?" (*Theatrum Redivivum*, pp. 68, 69). This statement definitely places the date of Baker's writing between 1633, the year in which *Histrio-Mastix* appeared, and 1638, fourscore years after Elizabeth's accession.

26. R. Baker, pp. 83, 24f; see also pp. 26, 37, 38f.

27. R. Baker, pp. 36, 31, 33, and 130. For these important passages, see my "The Case for Comedy in Caroline Theatrical Apologetics," in *PMLA,* LVIII (1943), 366.

28. R. Baker, p. 62.

29. See Prynne, pp. 545 and 688, for these phrases; R. Baker, p. 120, presents his authorities, including also Cicero, Marcus Aurelius, and Sidney.

30. R. Baker, pp. 98, 100f, and 133–135, attempts to reconcile drama and theology and on pp. 137–138 presents his "delight" argument; Davis, pp. 368f.

31. R. Baker, pp. 125–126.

32. R. Baker, "To the Reader."

33. See S. L. Lee, *DNB,* III, 14–16.

34. My sketch of Digby's career leans heavily on R. T. Petersson, *Sir Kenelm Digby: The Ornament of England 1603–1665* (Cambridge, Mass., 1956).

35. See Petersson, pp. 38–40, for the poems from which these couplets are taken.

36. Petersson, p. 73, and John Aubrey, *Brief Lives 1669–1696,* ed. Andrew Clark (2 vols., Oxford, 1898), I, 230–232.

37. E. W. Bligh, *Sir Kenelm Digby and His Venetia* (London, 1932), pp. 285–300.

38. Petersson, p. 261, compares Digby's Powder of Sympathy to Bacon's Grains of Youth, Browne's Gallow Chips, and Berkeley's Tar Water.

39. The quotes are from *Private Memoirs of Sir Kenelm Digby,* [ed. A. N. Nicholas] (London, 1827), pp. 6–278; hereafter cited as Digby. The entire speech to Aristobolus is on pp. 261–293.

40. Digby, pp. 2 and 228. The terms "Libertine" and "Libertinism" are capitalized throughout this study to indicate that they are being used in a special seventeenth century sense as synonyms for "Don Juan" and "Don Juanism" as well as "hedonist" and "hedonism." See Dale Underwood, *Etherege and the Seventeenth-Century Comedy of Manners* (New Haven, 1957), pp. 10–40, for a full discussion of this problem of definition.

41. Digby, p. 242.

42. Petersson, p. 44.

43. Bligh, p. 285.

44. Digby, pp. 52–53, 95. Mardontius' identity is fully discussed by Bligh, pp. 29 and 102–104.

45. Digby, pp. 84, 88.

46. Digby, pp. 205, 206.

47. In "The Castrations"; Bligh, pp. 294–297.

48. Digby, pp. 206–209, 306, 319.

49. Lynch, p. 52, remarks that "Digby seems to have anticipated by several years the court enthusiasm regarding Platonic fashions," while Harbage, p. 117, speaks of the courtship in the romance as "strangely compounded of platonic and unplatonic impulses"; his n. 54 on p. 126 indicates that he has the Libertine touches of "The Castrations" in mind. His discussion of Cavalier plays, pp. 28–47, defines their atmosphere well; see particularly his recapitulation, p. 41.

50. S. N. Behrman, *No Time for Comedy* (New York, 1939), pp. 33, 188–189. Copyright 1938, 1939, 1966 by S. N. Behrman. Reprinted by permission of Brandt & Brandt.

51. Brathwait, *Whimzies* (London, 1631), "The Epistle Dedicatorie."

52. Brathwait, *The English Gentleman* (London, 1630), pp. 305f. Hobart Sidney Jarrett, "The Character-Writers and Seventeenth-Century Society: 1608–1658" (Syracuse University Ph.D. dissertation, 1954), pp. 155–159, points out that the character-writers generally upheld moderation.

53. Brathwait, *Whimzies,* pp. 200, 201, 174, 190.

54. John Stephens, *New Essayes and Characters* (London, 1631), p. 102.

55. William Gouge, *Of Domesticall Duties* (London, 1622), p. 229.

56. Eli F. Heckscher, *Mercantilism,* trans. M. Shapiro, rev. ed. E. F. Soderlund (2 vols., London, 1955), II, 301.

57. Henry Peacham, *The Worth of a Penny, or a Caution to Keep Money* (London, 1647 [1641]), p. 15; quoted from L. C. Knights, *Drama & Society in the Age of Jonson* (London, 1937), p. 123.

58. Samuel R. Gardiner, *History of England from the Accession of James I to the Outbreak of the Civil War 1603–1642* (10 vols., London, 1883–84), IV, 1–107.

59. W. R. Scott, *The Constitution and Finance of English, Scottish and Irish Joint-Stock Companies to 1720* (3 vols., London, 1912), I, 167; quoted from Knights, pp. 135–136.

60. Roger Williams, *The Bloudy Tenent of Persecution for Cause of Conscience* . . . (London, 1644), Ch. 6; quoted from A.S.P. Woodhouse, ed., *Puritanism and Liberty* (London, 1938), p. 267.

61. Wye Salstonstall, *Picturae Loquentes* (London, 1631), the thirteenth Character, quoted from Knights, pp. 165–166.

62. Brathwait, *Whimzies,* pp. 48–49.

63. Gerald Eades Bentley, *The Jacobean and Caroline Stage* (5 vols., Oxford, 1941–56), IV, 747.

64. Nicholas Goodman, *Hollands Leaguer, or, An Historical Discourse of the Life and Actions of Dona Britanica Hollandia the Arch-Mistris of the wicked women of Eutopia* (London, 1632), pp. C4f.

65. Knights, pp. 123–126, stresses the reliability of early seventeenth century satirists as witnesses to some of these manifestations of the acquisitive spirit in the life of the time; for his comment on projectors, see pp. 78–81 and 211–218. For comment on alchemy and astrology, monopolies, and news-mongering, see Davies, *The Early Stuarts,* pp. 366–367, 328–333, and 409–410. Jarrett, pp. 66–154, shows the comprehensive critical realism of the character-writers.

66. Philip Lee Ralph, *Sir Humphrey Mildmay, Royalist Gentleman: Glimpses of the English Scene 1633–1652* (New Brunswick, 1947), pp. 41, 53, 59–60.

67. David Mathew, *The Social Structure in Caroline England* (Oxford, 1948), pp. 35–58.

68. Davies, pp. 264, 265.

69. Brathwait, *The English Gentleman,* four unnumbered pages after p. 456 [pp. 457–460].

70. Brathwait, *The English Gentlewoman* (London, 1631), eight unnumbered pages after p. 221 verso [pp. 223–230].

71. Brathwait, *The English Gentleman,* pp. 195, 221.

72. Brathwait, *Whimzies,* pp. 130–131, 149–150.

73. Brathwait, *The English Gentleman,* pp. 249, 293–294.

74. Brathwait, *The English Gentlewoman,* pp. 10–11, 20.

75. Stephens, pp. 169, 359–360, 234, 210–211, 214–215.

76. Edmund Cobbes, *Mundanum Speculum, or, The Worldlings Looking Glasse* (London, 1630), pp. 193–196, 240, 242; the dedicatory epistle to this volume is "written from my study at Low Layton in Essex, January 1, 1630."

77. See Carroll Camden, *The Elizabethan Woman* (Houston, New York, and London, 1952), especially pp. 241–271; Chilton Latham Powell, *English Domestic Relations 1487–1653* (New York, 1917), especially pp. 147–178; Louis B. Wright, *Middle-Class Culture in Elizabethan England* (Chapel Hill, 1935), pp. 465–507; and Jean Elisabeth Gagen, *The New Woman: Her Emergence in English Drama 1600–1730* (New York, 1954), especially pp. 9–39.

78. Mathew Griffith, *Bethel: or, A forme for families* (London, 1634), p. 166.

79. Gouge, pp. 209–210. For a short comparison of Gouge and Griffith, see Powell, pp. 137–138.

Chapter Two

1. G. C. M. Smith, *Thomas Randolph* (London, [1927]), p. 18; Bentley, *The Jacobean and Caroline Stage,* I, 241, and V, 986–988.
2. C. E. Andrews, *Richard Brome,* "Yale Studies in English," XLVI (New York, 1913), p. 15; Bentley, III, 55–57; Kaufmann, *Richard Brome: Caroline Playwright,* pp. 61–66, 181–182.
3. Andrews, pp. 122–123.
4. Richard Hurd, *Works* (8 vols., London, 1811), II, 53, regards *Every Man Out of His Humour* as a main source of Randolph's play; Andrews, pp. 122–125, stresses *The Roman Actor* and *The Lover's Melancholy* as possible sources for Brome's play.
5. *Poetical and Dramatic Works of Thomas Randolph,* ed. W. C. Hazlitt (2 vols., London, 1875), I, 179, n. 1. Hereafter cited as *Randolph's Works.*
6. The quotations are from *The Muses' Looking Glass,* Act I, sc. i.
7. Act I, sc. ii.
8. Act V, sc. iv.
9. Cf. Andrews, pp. 124–125.
10. Petersson, *Sir Kenelm Digby,* p. 28.
11. That Dr. Hughball has had carnal relations with Barbara and is probably carrying on such relations at the time of the play is implied in Act I, sc. i, vv. 99–101 and 109–110, and in Act V, sc. iv, vv. 5–21.
12. Act I, sc. v.
13. See "The Persons in the Play" for the epithet "Phantasticke"; Act I, sc. v and Act II, sc. ii for Letoy's views of acting.
14. Act V, sc. vii.
15. See Act I, sc. vi for his reactions to Hughball's remarks; Act II, sc. ix for his agreement with Byplay.
16. Act III, sc. vi and Act IV, sc. vi.
17. Act IV, scs. ix, xi, xiii.
18. Jonson used this term on the title pages of *Every Man Out of His Humour, Cynthia's Revels,* and *Poetaster.* See Oscar James Campbell, *Comicall Satyre and Shakespeare's Troilus and Cressida* (San Marino, Cal., 1938), pp. vii, 1–8, 54–134.
19. Act I, sc. iii.
20. Act I, sc. iv; Cyrus L. Day, "Randolph and Prynne," in *Modern Philology,* XXIX (1932), 349–350, and Bentley, V, 987–988, differ on Randolph's possible revision of this scene to answer Prynne.
21. Act I, sc. iv.

22. "Dramatis Personae"; Banausus and Microprepes are omitted by error.

23. Act II, sc. i. Randolph prefers the Latin *Comitas* to the Greek φιλία (friendliness) as the name for the mean state from which flattery and quarrelsomeness are deviations; he ignores the other excess that Aristotle associates with this virtue, namely ἀρέσκεια or obsequiousness. See Aristotle, *Nicomachean Ethics,* trans. J. E. C. Welldon (London, 1892), pp. xx–xxi, for a convenient table of the excesses, deficiencies, and mean states.

24. See Aristotle, *Ethics;* flattery and quarrelsomeness as opposed to friendliness appear tenth on the list.

25. Emil Koeppel, *Ben Jonson's Wirkung auf zeitgenössiche Dramatiker und andere Studien,* "Anglistische Forschungen," Vol. XX (Heidelberg, 1906), p. 139, notes a striking verbal parallel between one of Colax's speeches and one of Macilente's, tending to confirm my contention. It is important to remember that where Colax praises, Macilente damns: this is my reason for saying that Colax more effectively conveys satire in terms of irony and is thus a more ingenious creation.

26. Act II, sc. ii.

27. Act II, sc. iii.

28. Koeppel, p. 165, and Karl Kottas, *Thomas Randolph: sein Leben und seine Werke,* "Wiener Beiträge zur Englischen Philologie," Vol. XXIX (Wien und Leipzig, 1909), pp. 58–59, identify Acolastus with Sir Epicure Mammon.

29. Act II, sc. iv.

30. Kottas, p. 59, points out that this Asotus resembles the Asotus of Randolph's *The Jealous Lovers.* The relation of the Asotus of *The Jealous Lovers* to Knowlittle of Randolph's *The Drinking Academy,* who is based on three of Jonson's characters—Pennyboy Junior of *The Staple of News,* Asotus of *Cynthia's Revels,* and Sogliardo of *Every Man Out of His Humour,* should be borne in mind.

31. Act III, scs. i–iv; Act IV, scs. i and ii.

32. Act IV, sc. iii.

33. In the *Ethics,* Book V, Chs. 1–13, Aristotle discusses justice as a mean and, as Welldon notes, p. xxi, shows in his *Rhetoric,* trans. J. E. C. Welldon (London, 1886), Book II, Ch. 9, that envy and malice are not opposites.

34. Agroicus is exploited individually in Act IV, sc. iv; Bomolochus in Act IV, sc. v.

35. Act V, scs. i and ii.

36. Act V, scs. i and iv.

37. Andrews, pp. 114–121.

38. See *BJ,* VI, 13, line 8, for Jonson's reference to "his man, Master Broome, [*sic*] behind the Arras" in "The Induction." Cf. Alwin Thaler, "Was Richard

Brome an Actor?" in *Modern Language Notes,* XXXVI (1921), 88–91, with Bentley, II, 389, who is skeptical that Brome acted in *Bartholomew Fair.* The most thorough discussion of Brome's personal and literary relations with Jonson is in Kaufmann, pp. 35–46. Also consult E. K. R. Faust, *Richard Brome* (Halle, 1887), pp. 3–5, Andrews, pp. 1–5, and Charles E. Guardia, "Richard Brome as a Follower of Ben Jonson" (Louisiana State University M.A. thesis, 1938), pp. 2–16.

39. Ray L. Heffner, Jr., "Unifying Symbols in the Comedy of Ben Jonson," in *English Stage Comedy,* ed. W. K. Wimsatt, Jr., "English Institute Essays" (New York, 1955), pp. 89–96, offers one of the best analyses of Trouble-all's importance in *Bartholomew Fair.*

40. Philip Aronstein, *Ben Jonson,* "Literarhistorische Forschungen," Vol. XXXIV (Berlin, 1906), pp. 157–159, strikingly elucidates this underlying philosophic idea or *Weltanschauung* in *Bartholomew Fair.*

41. *The Antipodes,* Act II, scs. vi–viii.

42. Act III, scs. ii–iv.

43. Act IV, scs. i–iii.

44. Act IV, scs. vi–viii. This theme is continued in sc. ix, where a sedanman is introduced to converse with the carman and the waterman.

45. Act IV, sc. x.

46. See Baker in Gayley III, 426–427, for comment on *The Antipodes* as an anticipation of Gilbertian farce.

47. A. C. Swinburne, "Richard Brome," in *The Complete Works of Algernon Charles Swinburne,* Bonchurch edition, ed. Sir Edmund Gosse and Thomas James Wise (20 vols., London and New York, 1925–27), XII, 334f; hereafter cited as *Works,* Bonchurch.

48. Act IV, sc. xiii.

49. *The Muses' Looking Glass,* Act I, sc. iv.

50. *The Antipodes,* Act V, scs. xi and xii.

51. *The Muses' Looking Glass,* Act I, sc. iv.

52. Act I, sc. ii.

53. Act I, sc. iii.

54. Marie-Henri Beyle (De Stendhal), *The Red and the Black,* trans. C. K. Scott-Moncrieff, Modern Library (2 vols. in 1, New York, 1929), [Vol. II], pp. 166–167; for the original passage, see Stendhal, *Le Rouge et le Noir,* ed. P. Jourda (Paris, 1929), [Vol. II], p. 159.

55. These passages are all from *The Muses' Looking Glass,* Act I, sc. iii.

56. Robert Burton, *The Anatomy of Melancholy,* ed. F. Dell and P. Jordan-Smith (New York, 1928), p. 477.

57. *The Antipodes,* Act II, sc. ii.

218

Chapter Three

1. Honoré de Balzac, *Cousin Bette,* trans. Katharine Prescott Wormeley (Boston, 1928), p. 326. For the original see Balzac, *La Cousine Bette,* ed. Maurice Allem (Paris, n.d.), p. 239.

2. Allen Tate, *The Man of Letters in the Modern World: Selected Essays, 1928–1955,* Meridian Books (New York, 1955), p. 11.

3. William Cartwright, "In the Memory of the most Worthy BENJAMIN JOHNSON," in *Jonsonus Virbius, BJ,* XI, 455, lines 19–26.

4. Falkland (Lucius Cary), "An Eglogue on the Death of Ben. Johnson, betweene Melybaeus and Hylas," in *BJ,* XI, 432–433, lines 116–120.

5. Edmund Waller, "Upon Ben: Johnson, the most excellent of Comick Poets," in *BJ,* XI, 447–448, lines 5–12.

6. James Clayton, "To the Same," in *BJ,* XI, p. 450; note on p. 451 corrects attribution of this poem to John Cleveland in *The Works of Ben Jonson,* ed. W. Gifford and F. Cunningham (9 vols., London, 1875), IX, 450.

7. The date of the Globe performance is 1598; whether it was performed earlier at the Rose is uncertain. The quarto edition of 1601 is the Italianate version; the English version appears in the folio edition of Jonson's plays in 1616.

8. Act IV, sc. x and sc. ii.

9. Act III, sc. ii.

10. For Quarlous' "character" of him, see Act I, sc. iii, lines 135–158; for the Rabbi's confutation, see Act V, sc. v.

11. Act IV, sc. i shows Overdo put in the stocks; Act II, sc. iii shows Overdo taken in by Edgworth; Act IV, sc. iv shows Mistress Overdo in bad company.

12. Act V, sc. vi: "I invite you home, with mee to my house, to supper: I will have none feare to go along, for my intents are *Ad correctionem, non ad destructionem; Ad oedificandum, non ad dirvendum:* so lead on."

13. Act V, scs. i–v.

14. Tate, p. 11.

15. Cf. Knights, *Drama & Society in the Age of Jonson,* pp. 200–227.

16. Act I, sc. iii; Act III, scs. vii–viii.

17. This formulation occurs later in Jonson, *The Devil is an Ass,* Act I, sc. v, line 26; Wittipol is speaking of Fitzdottrel.

18. Act II, sc. i.

19. Cf. Knights, pp. 210–218, for an interesting analysis of *The Devil is an Ass* from this point of view.

20. Act V, sc. vi, especially Pecunia's closing speech, lines 60–66.

21. This metaphor is involved in the names of the characters in relation to their

219

actions: Sir Moth Interest, usurer and guardian, seeks the treasure in a well; Lady Loadstone, match-making widow, is the magnetic lady, drawing to her supposed niece, Placentia Steele, various suitors, and marrying Captain Ironside herself; Needle, her steward and tailor, points the way to the treasure and is the father of Placentia's bastard; Compass, the wit-intriguer, gets the real Placentia and out-points them all.

22. See the exchange of verse about *The Magnetic Lady* in *BJ*, XI, 346–349, and VIII, 410–411. Alexander Gill's destructive critique was answered by Zouch Townly and by Jonson himself. Knights, pp. 218–227, has interesting analyses of both *The Staple of News* and *The Magnetic Lady* as comedies attacking the acquisitive spirit.

23. See Campbell, *Comicall Satyre*, pp. 56–71, for the best discussion of these characters as substitutes for the censor-author of formal verse satire.

24. *The Devil is an Ass*, Act IV, sc. vi, especially Manly's speech beginning, "O friend! forsake not/ The brave occasion, vertue offers you,/ To keepe you innocent . . ." (lines 28–30), and Wittipol's reply beginning, "Vertue shall never aske my succours twice;/ Most friend, most man; your *Counsells* are commands . . ." (lines 35–36). Sir Friendly Moral, of Colley Cibber's *The Lady's Last Stake* (1707), helped establish this type on the eighteenth century stage.

25. *The Staple of News*, Act I, sc. iii, especially Pennyboy Cantor's aside, lines 40–41: "The Covetous man never has money! and/ The Prodigall will have none shortly!"

26. Quarto of 1601, Italianate version, Act III, sc. i, lines 157–158.

27. Folio of 1616, Act III, sc. iv, lines 20–22.

28. John J. Enck, *Jonson and the Comic Truth* (Madison, 1957), p. 42, has a slightly different view of this textual change. For an excellent critique of Riesman's three forms of direction, see Dennis H. Wrong, "Riesman and the Age of Sociology," in *Commentary*, XXI (1956), 331–338.

29. *Every Man Out of His Humour*, Act II, sc. i; the phrase is used to characterize the would-be wit Sogliardo.

30. Act II, sc. iii. In the introductory character sketches (*BJ*, III, 423 and 426), Puntarvolo is described as a fantastically "Vaine-glorious Knight, over Englishing his travels," and Clove and Orange are called "an inseparable case of Coxcombs, City-borne" and "Twins of foppery."

31. Act I, sc. v.

32. Act II, sc. iii, lines 123–145, for a "character" of Crites.

33. Peregrine's satiric function with reference to Sir Politick Would-Be is best seen in Act II, sc. i and V, sc. iv.

34. Heffner, "Unifying Symbols in the Comedy of Ben Jonson," pp. 79–89, presents a striking analysis of Morose's importance in *Epicoene*.

35. Act III, sc. ii.

36. Campbell, pp. 145, 156, and 176 uses the term "wit-intriguer."

37. John Galsworthy, "Some Platitudes Concerning Drama," in *The Inn of Tranquillity* (New York, 1928), p. 189.

38. See Heffner, pp. 87–88, and Enck, p. 147, for interesting comment on the roles of Truewit, Clerimont, and Dauphine.

39. Cf. Freda L. Townsend, *Apologie for Bartholomew Fayre: the Art of Jonson's Comedies* (New York, 1947), pp. 91–97, and T. S. Eliot, "Ben Jonson," in *Elizabethan Essays* (London, 1934), p. 77.

40. For this three-fold classification of Jonson's humours and the types of comedy that emphasis on each gives rise to, I am indebted to Paul Mueschke and Jeannette Fleisher, "Jonsonian Elements in the Comic Underplot of *Twelfth Night*," in *PMLA*, XLVIII (1933), 722–740. For an unsatisfactory critique of their classification (pp. 723–724), see Cary Bates Graham, "The Influence of Ben Jonson on Restoration Comedy" (Ohio State University Ph.D. dissertation, 1936), pp. 13–14 and n. 21. Enck, pp. 45–48, has a different and challenging view of the humours.

41. *BJ*, VIII, 547. Thomas B. Stroup, *Microcosmos: The Shape of the Elizabethan Play* (Lexington, Ky., 1965), pp. 67–70, comments on Jonson's "encompassing actions."

42. *The Plays and Poems of George Chapman: The Comedies*, ed. T. M. Parrott (London, [1914]), pp. 689–690; hereafter cited as *Chapman's Comedies*. Aaron Michael Myers, *Representation and Misrepresentation of the Puritan in Elizabethan Drama* (Philadelphia, 1931), pp. 118–119, regards Florilla as a mild satiric portrait of a Puritan.

43. Sc. viii.

44. *Chapman's Comedies*, p. 808, for the resemblance of Lemot, Rinaldo, Lodovico, and Tharsalio; pp. 702–708 and 798–801 for the sources.

45. *Chapman's Comedies*, pp. 894–896; 775–778; 780–781; also see Esther Cloudman Dunn, *Ben Jonson's Art*, "Smith College Fiftieth Anniversary Publications," Vol. III (Northampton [Mass.], 1925), pp. 122–125.

46. *Chapman's Comedies*, pp. 708–709 and 707–708, for analyses of Cornelio and Valerio; p. 736, for comments on Jonson's influence on Quintiliano.

47. *Chapman's Comedies*, p. 893, and Dunn, pp. 122–123, disagree as to the Jonsonian nature of these characters.

48. Dunn, pp. 123–124.

49. *Chapman's Comedies*, pp. 779–780, after pointing out that Monsieur D'Olive is possibly derived from Brisk, calls him "one of the most original figures in our comic drama."

50. *Chapman's Comedies*, p. 804, designates Tharsalio as "a plain anticipation of the roués and fortune-hunters of Restoration comedy."

51. For discussions of Marston's early satiric plays, see Campbell, pp. 135–184. For high praise of *The Dutch Courtesan,* see M. C. Bradbrook, *The Growth and Structure of Elizabethan Comedy* (Berkeley, 1956), pp. 152–154.

52. Act II, sc. i; *The Works of John Marston,* ed. A. H. Bullen (3 vols., London, 1887), II.

53. Act V, sc. i.

54. See Morse S. Allen, *The Satire of John Marston* (Columbus, 1920), pp. 152–153.

55. Act II, sc. i; see Campbell, pp. 176–181, particularly p. 180.

56. Act I, sc i; Act III, sc. i; and Act V, sc. iii. Cf. J. Sainmont, *Influence de Montaigne sur Marston et Webster* (Louvain, 1914), cited by Allen, p. 141. Both Freevill and Crispinella voice Libertine concepts borrowed from Montaigne. For interesting comment on Malheureux as a character expressive of Marston's temperament, see Samuel Schoenbaum, "The Precarious Balance of John Marston," in *PMLA,* LXVII (1952), 1077–1078.

57. Act I, sc. i and Act II, sc. ii.

58. This folio, issued in London by William Sheares, omits *The Malcontent.*

59. Wilbur Wright Dunkel, *The Dramatic Technique of Thomas Middleton in His Comedies of London Life* (Chicago, 1925), pp. 5–7, presents cogent reasons for limiting a discussion of Middleton's realistic comedy to the six plays I discuss; his plot charts are on pp. 28–47.

60. Cf. Knights, pp. 256–269, "Middleton and the New Social Classes."

61. Act III, sc. iv; *The Works of Thomas Middleton,* ed. A. H. Bullen (8 vols., London, 1885–86), I.

62. Cf. Dunkel, p. 57.

63. Act V, sc. iv. When Tim discovers that his Welsh bride is a whore, he consoles himself for the loss of the Welsh mountains supposed to be his inheritance with the reflection that, at any rate, he has a "mount."

64. Louis I. Bredvold, "A Note in Defense of Satire," in *ELH,* IV (1940), 253–264, regards derision as inferior to the righteous indignation of the best satire.

65. This title is probably borrowed from Nicholas Breton's didactic dialog, *A Mad World my Masters, Mistake me not* (London, 1603).

66. Cf. Knights, pp. 228–255, "Dekker, Heywood and Citizen Morality"; Bradbrook, pp. 119–137, "Pastime and Good Company: Dekker and Heywood."

67. Act V, sc. iv; *Thomas Heywood,* ed. A. Wilson Verity, Mermaid Series (London, 1888).

68. See Knights, pp. 270–300, "The Significance of Massinger's Social Comedies with a Note on 'Decadence.' "

69. Emil Koeppel, *Quellen-Studien zu den Dramen George Chapman's,*

Philip Massinger's, und John Ford's, "Quellen und Forschungen zur Sprach- und Culturgeschichte der Germanischen Völker," Vol. LXXXII (Strassburg, 1897), pp. 137–140; A. H. Cruickshank, *Philip Massinger* (Oxford, 1920), pp. 205–208.

70. Robert Hamilton Ball, *The Amazing Career of Sir Giles Overreach* (Princeton, 1939), pp. 3–25; Knights, pp. 274–275 and n. 2 on p. 275; *The Plays of Philip Massinger,* ed. William Gifford (4 vols., London, 1813), III, 516–518; hereafter cited as *Massinger's Plays.*

71. Maurice Chelli, *Le Drame de Massinger* (Lyon, 1923), p. 281, is impressed by the relationship between *Volpone* and Massinger's conception of "le caractère fort."

72. Knights, pp. 282ff, points out parallels with *Eastward Ho.*

73. *The City Madam,* Act III, sc. iii for Luke Frugal's soliloquy, which identifies him with Sir Epicure Mammon.

74. Puzzled by the Macilente-like nature of Luke, Gifford (*Massinger's Plays,* IV, 119, note) comments as follows: "The moral purpose of the Play is accomplished, even upon moral principles, by its most flagitious character. Luke is a declared villain, and a reformer too! He allows revenge to be the motive of his cruelty, yet he rises up a 'new satirist' against the vices of the city!—it is obvious that Massinger has forgot himself." Cf. Knights, pp. 288–290.

75. Although there is some parallelism between the dramatic functions of Stargaze and Subtle, it must not be forgotten that Massinger may have had actual astrologers like John Lambe and William Lilly in mind; for comment on their popularity, see Davies, *The Early Stuarts,* p. 367.

76. See Jonson, "Prologue" to *Every Man in His Humour,* for his attack on romantic drama. Cf. Madeleine Doran, *Endeavors of Art: A Study of Form in Elizabethan Drama* (Madison, 1954), pp. 148–151, and Bradbrook, pp. 61–116.

77. *Wit Without Money,* Act III, sc. i; *The Works of Beaumont and Fletcher,* Variorum Edition (4 vols., London, 1905), II.

78. C. R. Baskervill, "The Source of the Main Plot of Shirley's *Love Tricks,*" in *Modern Language Notes,* XXIV (1909), 100–101, shows its indebtedness to a short story in Barnabe Riche's *Farewell to the Military Profession.*

79. *Love Tricks,* Act III, sc. v; *The Dramatic Works and Poems of James Shirley,* ed. William Gifford and Alexander Dyce (6 vols., London, 1833), I.

80. W. H. Hickerson, "The Significance of James Shirley's Realistic Plays in the History of English Comedy" (University of Michigan Ph.D. dissertation, 1932), pp. 84–87.

81. See Hickerson, pp. 102–103, for the influence of Beaumont and Fletcher. The best discussion of Shirley's sentimentalism is that by Robert A. Reed, Jr., "James Shirley, and the Sentimental Comedy," in *Anglia,* LXXIII (1955), 149–

170; see p. 155 for a summary of the six formulas of eighteenth century sentimental comedy.

82. See Hickerson, pp. 137–140; 146–150.

83. *Hyde Park*, Act I, sc. i.

84. Cf. Harbage, *Cavalier Drama*, p. 83. For this type of scene, see Sir George Etherege, *She Wou'd if She Cou'd*, Act III, sc. i; *The Works of Sir George Etherege*, ed. H. F. B. Brett-Smith, the Percy Reprints No. 6 (2 vols., Oxford, 1927), II.

85. Shirley, *The Lady of Pleasure*, Act II, sc. ii.

Chapter Four

1. *BJ*, III, 436–437, lines 228–270.

2. Eliot, *The Sacred Wood* (London, 1920) and *Selected Essays, 1917–1932* (London, 1932).

3. Brathwait, *The English Gentleman*, pp. 183 and 194.

4. Bentley, *The Jacobean and Caroline Stage*, V, 973.

5. Cyrus L. Day, "Thomas Randolph and *The Drinking Academy*," in *PMLA*, XLIII (1928), 800–809, and Samuel A. Tannenbaum and Hyder E. Rollins, in the introduction to their edition of Thomas Randolph's *The Drinking Academy* (Cambridge, Mass., 1930), pp. ix–xxv, accept the skit as indisputably Randolph's; likewise Fredson T. Bowers, "Problems in Thomas Randolph's *Drinking Academy* and Its Manuscript," in *Huntington Library Quarterly*, I (1938), 189–198. G. C. Moore Smith, "The Authorship of *The Drinking Academy*," in *Review of English Studies*, VIII (1932), 212–214, makes out a case for Robert Baron as author. The most distinguished authority is Bentley, V, 976–980.

6. Tannenbaum and Rollins, p. xxiii: ". . . a date of 1626 perhaps better fits all the known facts."

7. Bentley, V, 980–982.

8. Katherine Lever, *The Art of Greek Comedy* (London, 1956), pp. 110–124, presents one of the best descriptions of Aristophanic Old Comedy.

9. *Randolph's Works*, I, 6–23. Cf. Shakespeare's *Henry IV, Part One*, Act V, sc. iii and Act I, sc. ii. Kottas, *Thomas Randolph*, pp. 26–27, suggests other sources for Aristippus.

10. *Randolph's Works*, I, 10, 12, 32, 33, and 4.

11. Cited by Bentley, V, 972.

12. *Randolph's Works*, I, 9, 11, and 10.

13. I am indebted to Perry Miller, *The New England Mind: The Seventeenth Century* (New York, 1939), pp. 449–500, for these data.

14. Norman E. Nelson, *Peter Ramus and the Confusion of Logic, Rhetoric, and Poetry*, "University of Michigan Contributions to Modern Philology," No. 2 (Ann Arbor, 1947), p. 22.

15. "An Eclogue to Master Jonson"; *Randolph's Works*, II, 609–610.

16. "An Eclogue on the noble Assemblies revived on Cotswold Hills by Master Robert Dover"; *Randolph's Works*, II, 622.

17. In the poem "Lord Alcohol"; *The Complete Works of Thomas Lovell Beddoes*, ed. Sir Edmund Gosse (2 vols., London, 1928), II, 396.

18. Act I, scs. i and iii; Act II, sc. i; and Act V, sc. v.

19. Tannenbaum and Rollins, p. xv, suggest some of these relations. A striking verbal parallel between *The Drinking Academy*, Act IV, sc. iii, lines 626–630, and Beaumont and Fletcher's *The Scornful Lady*, Act I, sc. i, lines 169–177, establishes Randolph's use of *The Scornful Lady*.

20. For a good discussion of Middle Comedy, see Lever, pp. 160–185.

21. Act I, sc. i.

22. Act I, sc. ii. The Middleton referred to is Sir Hugh Middleton, ancestor of the Middletons of Chirk Castle, according to *Randolph's Works*, II, 391, n. 1.

23. Act I, sc. ii.

24. See n. 59 for Ch. One.

25. The quotes are from Act IV, sc. i and sc. ii (misnumbered iii) and Act V, sc. i.

26. Act II, sc. v.

27. *Randolph's Works*, II, [vi].

28. Concerning the use of Menander by Plautus and Terence, William Beare, *The Roman Stage* (2nd ed., London, 1955), p. 54, remarks: "Liveliness of plot and abundance of farcical situations seem to have been what Plautus sought, not that interest in theme and in personality which attracted Terence to Menander." Daniel C. Boughner, *The Braggart in Renaissance Comedy* (Minneapolis, 1954), pp. 8–9, sharply contrasts Plautus and Terence.

29. Cf. Lever, pp. 186–205, and Beare, pp. 40–59 and 81–102, for the characteristics of Greek and Roman New Comedy.

30. For data concerning the performances of Hausted's and Randolph's plays, see Bentley, IV, 534–536, and V, 982–986, respectively. The official who committed suicide was Dr. Butts, Vice-Chancellor of Cambridge; see Bentley, V, 984.

31. *The New Academy* is entered in Stationers' Register for Aug. 4, 1640. Cf. Bentley, III, 81 and Kaufmann, *Richard Brome: Caroline Playwright*, pp. 53–57, who thinks the play was written shortly after July 1635, when Brome signed a contract with the Salisbury Court theater (see p. 181).

32. Kottas, pp. 43–44. Cf. Mina Kerr, *Influence of Ben Jonson on English Comedy, 1598–1642* (New York, 1912), p. 84.

33. Randolph's scholarship is at fault, for Athens, not Thebes, paid tribute to the Minotaur.

34. Kottas, pp. 44–46.

35. *The Jealous Lovers,* Act III, sc. vii.

36. Kottas, pp. 48–49.

37. Insertion by W. C. Hazlitt, editor of *Randolph's Works.*

38. The quotes are from Act IV, sc. iii.

39. Karl von Reinhardstoettner, *Plautus: Spätere Bearbeitungen plautinischer Lustspiele* . . . (Leipsig, 1886), pp. 346–357, discusses *The Case is Altered* as a "Kontamination zweier plautinischer Stücke, der *Aulularia* und der *Captivi.* . . ." See W. E. Selin, ed., *The Case is Altered,* "Yale Studies in English," Vol. LVI (New Haven, 1917), pp. xliii–xlvi. C. R. Baskervill, *English Elements in Jonson's Early Comedy,* "Bulletin of the University of Texas," No. 178 (Austin, 1911), p. 81, points out that *A Tale of a Tub* belongs to a group of English comedies which owe their general conception of comic action to the influence of the *Menaechmi.* The date of *A Tale of a Tub* is that of the revised version; the original version was probably composed before 1598. Enck, *Jonson and the Comic Truth,* p. 24, does not think the foreign setting of *The Case is Altered,* which he regards as the first important Jonsonian comedy of humours rather than *Every Man in His Humour,* is of any real significance. Frank L. Huntley, "Ben Jonson and Anthony Munday, or, *The Case is Altered* Altered Again," in *Philological Quarterly,* XLI (1962), 205–214, argues against Jonson's authorship.

40. Koeppel, *Ben Jonson's Wirkung* . . . , p. 154, notes this indebtedness.

41. Kerr, *Influence of Ben Jonson* . . . , pp. 70–71, remarks: "The School of Compliment in *The New Academy* takes us back to *The Devil is an Ass* and *Epicoene* with their expositions of fashion and compliment." Faust, *Richard Brome,* pp. 35–36, points out that Brome's Cash has much in common with the apprentices of Massinger's *The City Madam.*

42. Andrews, *Richard Brome,* pp. 105–106, calls attention to the importance of *Westward Ho* and *Northward Ho* as influences on Brome's comedy and notes their influence in the sub-plot of *The New Academy.*

43. The quotations are from Act II, sc. i and Act V, sc. ii.

44. T. S. Eliot, "Ben Jonson," in *Selected Essays 1917–1932,* p. 157.

45. Swinburne, "Richard Brome," in *Works,* Bonchurch, XII, 336, passes the following judgment on *The New Academy:* ". . . a tangled and huddled comedy of unattractive and improbable intrigue, not unrelieved by glimpses of interest and touches of humour; worth reading once as a study of manners and language, but hardly worth tracing out and unravelling through all the incoherent complications and tedious convolutions of its misshapen and misconstructed plot."

Chapter Five

1. Hiram Haydn, *The Counter-Renaissance* (New York, 1950), pp. xi–xvii, distinguishes "the counter-renaissance" from what he calls "the classical renaissance" or "the humanistic revival" and "the scientific reformation."

2. For the changing status of the concept of grace in the seventeenth and eighteenth centuries, see my "Mystical Versus Enthusiastic Sensibility," in *Journal of the History of Ideas,* IV (1943), 311–314; for the Christian background of eighteenth century sentimentalism, see R. S. Crane, "Suggestions Toward a Genealogy of the 'Man of Feeling,' " in *ELH,* I (1934), 205–234.

3. For the difference between the terms "cultural primitivism" and "chronological primitivism" and the changing status of the term "nature," see A. O. Lovejoy and George Boas, *Primitivism and Related Ideas in Antiquity,* Vol. I of *A Documentary History of Primitivism and Related Ideas* (Baltimore, 1935), *passim.* Also consult Haydn, pp. 461–554.

4. *Cynthia's Revels,* Act II, sc. iii.

5. Jonson, *Epicoene,* Act II, sc. ii and Act IV, sc. i.

6. See Charlotte Moore, *The Dramatic Works of Thomas Nabbes* (Menasha, [Wisconsin], 1918), p. 11, n. 36, for the dating of Nabbes' first comedy, *Covent Garden,* as well as *Tottenham Court;* also Bentley, *The Jacobean and Caroline Stage,* IV, 940–942.

7. Marston's housemaid Winifride tricks John fo' de King into carrying John Drum away in a sack under the illusion that she will be in it; *Jack Drum's Entertainment,* Act IV; reprint of 1601 edition in Tudor Facsimile Texts Series, ed. John S. Farmer (London, 1912), no scene division and no pagination.

8. Nabbes, *Tottenham Court,* Act IV, sc. iv.

9. Act III, sc. i.

10. Act V, sc. iii.

11. Bentley, III, 65–67, and Kaufmann, *Richard Brome,* p. 182.

12. Act V, sc. i. Kaufmann, pp. 138–150, treats *The Damoiselle* as an antiusury play.

13. Andrews, *Richard Brome,* p. 89, relates Bumpsey to Jonson's Justices Clement (*Every Man in His Humour*), Overdo (*Bartholomew Fair*), Eitherside (*The Devil is an Ass*), and Preamble (*A Tale of a Tub*). Although Faust, *Richard Brome,* p. 69, identifies Sir Amphilus with Don Adriano de Armado in Shakespeare's *Love's Labour's Lost,* Puntarvolo of Jonson's *Every Man Out of His Humour* is the more likely source. Guardia, "Richard Brome as a Follower of Ben Jonson," pp. 32–34, finds some indebtedness to Jonson's *The Staple of News* in *The Damoiselle.*

14. Cf. Moore, p. 11, n. 36, and Bentley, IV, 929–932.
15. Act II, sc. v.
16. Act II, sc. iii.
17. Act V, sc. vii.
18. Bentley, III, 70–73.
19. Thomas Stanley (1625–1678) published in 1655 the first *History of Philosophy* written in the English language. Swinburne, "Richard Brome," in *Works*, Bonchurch, XII, 337, and Ronald Bayne, "Lesser Jacobean and Caroline Dramatists," in *The Cambridge History of English Literature*, ed. A. W. Ward and A. R. Waller (14 vols., New York and Cambridge, 1907–1917), VI, 258, regard *A Jovial Crew* as Brome's best play. Giles Roberts Floyd, "A Critical Edition of Brome's *A Jovial Crew*" (State University of Iowa Ph.D. dissertation, 1942), pp. xl–lxxxviii, after thoroughly discussing its sources, especially Middleton and Rowley's *The Spanish Gipsy* and Fletcher's *Beggars' Bush*, ends by stressing its originality. Robert Dodsley edited and published the play in *A Select Collection of Old Plays* (2nd ed., 12 vols., London, 1780), X; citations from the play are to this edition.
20. Act I.
21. Act II.
22. Act III.
23. Act IV, [sc. i] and sc. ii.
24. Act IV, sc. ii.
25. There is some possibility that the passages describing the masque were added after the Civil Wars had become a reality, the theaters were closed, and actors, playwrights, and many anti-Puritan families were in distress. Incidentally, Kaufmann, pp. 169–173, is the only critic of *A Jovial Crew* who has adequately related it to the impending collapse of Brome's world.
26. Act IV, [sc. i].
27. Act V for Clack's remark and Oldrents' phrase.
28. Ernest Bernbaum, *The Drama of Sensibility*, "Harvard Studies in English," Vol. III (Boston and London, 1915), pp. 37–48, comments on sentimentalism in some Elizabethan, Jacobean, and Caroline comedies.

Chapter Six

1. Morris R. Cohen, *A Dreamer's Journey* (Boston, 1949), pp. 189–190.
2. Hadyn, *The Counter-Renaissance*, pp. 20–26, 139–160, 434–453.
3. Bentley, *The Jacobean and Caroline Stage*, III, 81–84 and 59–61; cf. Kaufmann, *Richard Brome*, pp. 47–52, 179, who inclines toward a slightly later date for *The City Wit*.

4. *The Dramatic Works of Richard Brome* (R. H. Pearson reprint, 3 vols., London, 1873), III, xi.

5. Cf. Bentley, p. 82.

6. Act II, sc. i.

7. Act I, scs. i and ii for this and preceding short quotations. Kerr, *Influence of Ben Jonson* . . . , p. 73, links Widgine with both Stephen and Matthew, and Anvile with Bobadill.

8. The quotations are from Act I, sc. ii; Act II, sc. i; Act V, sc. vi; and Act II, sc. ii.

9. The quotations are from Act I, sc. i; Act IV, scs. i and ii; and Act V.

10. Act III, sc. i. Noted by Koeppel, *Ben Jonson's Wirkung* . . . , p. 166, and Kerr, p. 70.

11. In the first published version:
> For it was written when
> It bore just Judgement, and the seal of Ben.

12. Cf. Bentley, III, 89–92 with Kaufmann, pp. 68–74. The alternate title, preferred by Bentley, is *The Weeding of the Covent Garden; or, The Middlesex Justice of Peace*.

13. The elder Knowell, Ovid Senior, and Morose are the characters that seem telescoped in Crossewill. Koeppel, pp. 144–145, points out an interesting verbal parallel between *Covent Garden Weeded* and *The Poetaster;* on p. 174 he identifies Crossewill with Waspe of *Bartholomew Fair.* Andrews, *Richard Brome,* pp. 90–91, compares Crossewill with Morose.

14. Act I, sc. i and Act III, sc. ii. Dorcas has some affinities with Bellafront in Dekker's *The Honest Whore.* Kaufmann, pp. 74–87, presents a challenging analysis of *Covent Garden Weeded* and suggests that Brome included political allegory in his treatment of Crossewill's paternalism.

15. Theodore Miles, "Place-Realism in a Group of Caroline Plays," in *Review of English Studies,* XVIII (1942), 432–433, comments on the topicality of the setting in *Covent Garden Weeded.*

16. Act I, sc. i.

17. Act V, sc. iii.

18. The quotations are from Act II, sc. ii and Act IV, sc. ii. E. N. S. Thompson, *The Controversy Between the Puritans and the Stage,* "Yale Studies in English," Vol. XX (New York, 1903), pp. 236–237, and Myers, *Representation and Misrepresentation of the Puritan in Elizabethan Drama,* pp. 80–81, regard Gabriel as too abusive and overdrawn to be an effective satiric portrait of a Puritan.

19. Cf. Bentley, III, 132–134 and IV, 482–483 with Harbage, *Cavalier Drama,* pp. 265–266.

229

20. Friedrich Gerber, *The Sources of William Cartwright's Comedy The Ordinary* . . . (Berne, 1909), pp. 62–73; Koeppel, pp. 162–164; Kerr, pp. 94–100; and G. Blakemore Evans, ed., *The Plays and Poems of William Cartwright* (Madison, 1951), pp. 263–264, discuss the Jonsonian elements in *The Ordinary*. Middleton's influence is noticed by Margery Fisher, "Notes on the Sources of Some Incidents in Middleton's London Plays," in *Review of English Studies*, XV (1939), 293, n. 1, and by Gerber, pp. 60–61.

21. Act IV, sc. i.

22. Bentley, III, 134, comments on the tendency of scholars to neglect material from life in such Jonsonian imitations as *The Ordinary*.

23. Gerber, p. 61, proposes *The Fair Quarrel* as probable source and, pp. 53–58, stresses Cartwright's use of Chaucer in creating Moth.

24. Max Zwickert, *Henry Glapthorne* (Halle, 1881), pp. 28–29, and Chester Linn Shaver, "The Life and Works of Henry Glapthorne" (Harvard University Ph.D. dissertation, 1937), pp. 243–247, discuss the indebtedness of *The Hollander* to *The Alchemist*. Koeppel, p. 121, and Zwickert, p. 33, identify Urinal with Brainworm in *Every Man in His Humour*.

25. Act I, sc. i.

26. Zwickert, p. 33, identifies Sir Martin Yellow with Kitely.

27. Act I, sc. i.

28. Koeppel, p. 170, n. 34, comments on the parallelism with the Order of the Blade and Batton in *Covent Garden Weeded*.

29. Act IV, sc. i.

30. Act V, sc. i.

Chapter Seven

1. V. de Sola Pinto, *Sir Charles Sedley* (London, 1927), p. 259; quoted by permission of the publisher, Constable and Company. Cf. John Palmer, *The Comedy of Manners* (London, 1913), *passim*, with Thomas H. Fujimura, *The Restoration Comedy of Wit* (Princeton, 1952), *passim*, and especially pp. 3–38.

2. Among the more impressive special studies of the sources or origins of Restoration comedy are Lynch, *The Social Mode of Restoration Comedy;* John Harold Wilson, *The Influence of Beaumont and Fletcher on Restoration Drama,* "Ohio State University . . . Contributions in Languages and Literatures," No. 4 (Columbus, 1928); Paul Mueschke, "Prototypes of Restoration Wits and Would-Bes in Ben Jonson's Realistic Comedy" (University of Michigan Ph.D. dissertation, 1929); and John Wilcox, *The Relation of Molière to Restoration Comedy* (New York, 1938).

3. Act I, sc. i.

4. Bentley, *The Jacobean and Caroline Stage,* IV, 745–748; the quotation is from p. 746. Bentley does not ascribe this long run to any intrinsic merits in the play but to accidental extrinsic factors.

5. Sue Maxwell, "Shakerley Marmion, Poet and Dramatist" (Yale University Ph.D. dissertation, 1941), p. 180, points out that the names of Trimalchio, Triphoena, and Quartilla are taken from *The Satyricon* and discusses other borrowings from this source, pp. 180–185.

6. Miles, "Place-Realism in a Group of Caroline Plays," p. 431, comments on the play's use of Mrs. Holland's brothel. Maxwell, pp. 153–179, treats fully the relationship of Marmion's play to the actual brothel and the extant literature about it.

7. Act I, sc. i.

8. Act I, sc. iv.

9. Act II, sc. ii.

10. Act III, sc. iv.

11. Act V, sc. i.

12. Act II, sc. i and Act III, sc. ii.

13. Act II, sc. iii.

14. Cf. Bentley, IV, 742–745 and Harbage, *Cavalier Drama,* p. 264. Marion Jones, "The Life and Works of Shakerley Marmion 1603–1639" (University of Oxford B. Litt. thesis, 1956), pp. 104–107, shows that the structure and handling of place and time in *A Fine Companion* are more competent than in *Holland's Leaguer.*

15. These several passages are from Act I, sc. v; Act II, sc. i; and Act III, sc. ii.

16. The quotations in this paragraph are from Act I, sc. iv; Act III, sc. i; Act I, sc. vi; Act III, sc. iv; Act IV, sc. i; Act I, sc. v; and Act II, sc. v.

17. For Dotario's role, see Act II, sc. iv; Act III, sc. v; and Act V, sc. ii. Lackwit, confusing the disguised Careless with Dotario, remarks concerning the former: ". . . there was another changling as like to him in shape as Jupiter to Amphitruo. . . ." Maxwell, pp. 217–219, presents evidence to show the influence of Apuleius and Juvenal on Marmion's portrayal of Dotario and, pp. 224–226, traces him and Aemilia to Sir Humphry and Luce in Beaumont's *The Knight of the Burning Pestle.* Dotario may also be linked with Morecraft of *The Scornful Lady.*

18. Bentley, IV, 739–741. Jones, pp. 112–123, treats *The Antiquary* "as the most highly polished of all his productions."

19. The first of these scenes suggests Beaumont and Fletcher, *The Scornful Lady,* Act I, sc. i; the second, Shirley, *The Witty Fair One,* Act III, sc. iv; the third, Beaumont and Fletcher, *Wit Without Money,* Act V, sc. v.

20. *The Antiquary,* Act I.
21. Cf. Bentley, IV, 534–536 and Harbage, p. 263.
22. The quotations in this paragraph are from Act I, sc. vii; Act IV, sc. i; Act III, sc. iv; and Act I, sc. viii.
23. These phrases are from the play's "Dramatis Personae."
24. Act III, sc. i.
25. Act V, sc. xi.
26. Act I, sc. vi.
27. Cf. Bentley, IV, 932–934 and Harbage, p. 263.
28. Act II, sc. iv. Moore, *The Dramatic Works of Thomas Nabbes,* p. 13, points out that this passage illustrates regulation of affection "according to the best seventeenth century tenets."
29. Act I, sc. iv includes both Artlove's and Jerker's credos.
30. Cf. J. Koch, "Thomas Nabbes, ein zu wenig beachteter Dichter," in *Anglia,* XLVII, Neue Folge XXXV (1923), 352.
31. Act I, sc. iv.
32. Act IV, sc. vi. F. G. Fleay, *A Biographical Chronicle of the English Drama 1559–1642* (2 vols., London, 1891), II, 119, comments on Nabbes' Little-word as a stock character.
33. Act II, sc. v.
34. Act IV, sc. v.
35. Kerr, *Influence of Ben Jonson . . .* , pp. 108–109, stresses the point that Warrant and Spruce are Jonsonian characters; cf. Mueschke and Fleisher, "Jonsonian Elements in the Comic Underplot of *Twelfth Night,*" in *PMLA,* XLVIII (1933), 722–740.
36. Act I, sc. i.
37. Cf. Miles, p. 433, for comment on its "place-realism."
38. Cf. Bentley, III, 222–225, 209–211, and 211–212 and Harbage, pp. 264–265.
39. Younger Pallatine recalls Younger Loveless of *The Scornful Lady,* Mirabel of *The Wild-Goose Chase,* Valentine of *Wit Without Money,* and Fowler of *The Witty Fair One.* Lady Ample recalls Niece of *Wit at Several Weapons,* the Lady of *The Scornful Lady,* and Penelope of *The Witty Fair One.*
40. These two passages are from Act II, sc. i.
41. Act III, sc. ii.
42. Act I, sc. ii.
43. Act IV, sc. ii.
44. In Act II the Widow Carrack soliloquizes:

O, my brave Cable! if thou wouldst but hold
Thy Carrack to an anchor, she would seek
No other port. This quarrel must be tane up
Or I am shipwrack'd.

232

Such allegorical "conceitism" figures in the love-intrigue of *The Magnetic Lady*. Also, the duel between Warwell and Seawit has its parallel in that between Sir Diaphanous Silkworm and Captain Ironside, although Warwell is not satirized after the fashion of Silkworm. Cf. Jonson, *The Magnetic Lady*, Act III, sc. iii [i] in *BJ*, VI, 549–553.

45. Bumble resembles Hans van Belch, the Dutch merchant in the sub-plot of Dekker's *Northward Ho*. Arthur H. Nethercot, *Sir William D'Avenant* (Chicago, 1938), pp. 126–128, stresses the Jonsonian influences mentioned here.

46. Jonson's *The New Inn* and Shirley's *The Lady of Pleasure* are anti-Platonic. Lynch, p. 88, calls Davenant's satire against Platonic love in this play "daring." Cf. Nethercot, pp. 128–131, and Alfred Harbage, *Sir William Davenant* (Philadelphia, 1935), pp. 235–237.

47. Act II, sc. i and Act III, sc. i.

48. Act II, sc. i.

Chapter Eight

1. Bentley, *The Jacobean and Caroline Stage*, III, 87–89; Kaufmann, *Richard Brome: Caroline Playwright*, pp. 57–61, 181.

2. Swinburne, "Richard Brome," in *Works*, Bonchurch, XII, 329.

3. Bentley, III, 80–81, 67–69, and 61–65; Kaufmann, pp. 33, 182, 181, 168, n. 34. Bentley dates the first performance of *A Mad Couple Well Match'd* between 1637 and 1639; Kaufmann dates it shortly after April 1639. Fleay, *A Biographical Chronicle of the English Drama 1559–1642*, I, 39; Andrews, *Richard Brome*, p. 36; and Henry W. Wells, *A Chronological List of Extant Plays Produced in or about London 1581–1642* (New York, 1940), p. 15, give 1636 as the date.

4. Bentley, III, 88, suggests that data on receipts are exaggerated.

5. Miles, "Place-Realism in a Group of Caroline Plays," p. 434, says *The Sparagus Garden* offers "the most striking example of detached local colour." Richard H. Perkinson, "Topographical Comedy in the Seventeenth Century," in *ELH*, III (1936), pp. 280–282, comments on the realism of *The Sparagus Garden*.

6. Act III, scs. iv and v.

7. Act IV, sc. ix.

8. *The Fawn*, Act IV, sc. i. John Genest, *Some Account of the English Stage* (10 vols., Bath, 1832), X, 40; Felix E. Schelling, *Elizabethan Drama 1558–1642* (2 vols., Boston, 1908), II, 272; and Andrews, p. 111, suggest that Brome borrowed this incident from *The Heir*, which Allan Griffith Chester, *Thomas May: Man of Letters, 1595–1650* (Philadelphia, 1933), p. 78, dates as having been composed shortly before or during 1620; also see Ned Bliss Allen, *The Sources of John Dryden's Comedies* (Ann Arbor, 1935), p. 9, n. 29, and p. 37, n. 95.

9. Swinburne, *Works,* Bonchurch, XII, 329–330.

10. The best treatment of *A Mad Couple Well Match'd* as an anticipation of The Restoration comedy of manners is by Richard Jefferson, "Some Aspects of Richard Brome's Comedies of Manners: A Re-interpretation" (University of Wisconsin Ph.D. dissertation, 1955), pp. 156–183; his interpretations of Lady Thrivewell and Careless, however, differ somewhat from mine.

11. Guardia, "Richard Brome as a Follower of Ben Jonson," pp. 30–31, points out the indebtedness of *The English Moor* to *Epicoene;* Andrews, p. iii, suggests Brome's use of *A Fine Companion.*

12. Act III, sc. iii.

13. Act IV, sc. v. Kaufmann, pp. 136–138, treats *The English Moor* as an anti-usury play.

14. Kaufmann, pp. 151–168, makes an interesting case for *The Court Beggar* as a comedy of personal satire, identifying Sir Ferdinando as Sir John Suckling and Courtwit as Sir William Davenant.

15. Bentley, IV, 494–497 and 847–850; *The City Match* was intended for presentation before the King and Queen when they visited Oxford in August 1636 but was crowded out by other selections. Wells, p. 16, and Harbage, *Cavalier Drama,* p. 267, accept 1637 as certain.

16. Joseph Quincy Adams, Jr., "Some Notes on Henry Glapthorne's *Wit in a Constable*," in *JEGP,* XIII (1914), 299–304, and D. L. Thomas, "Concerning Glapthorne's *Wit in a Constable*," in *JEGP,* XIV (1915), 89–92, discuss textual peculiarities.

17. Act I, sc. i.

18. Act I, sc. i.

19. Act IV, sc. i.

20. Act V, sc. i.

21. Helen McAfee, *Pepys on the Restoration Stage* (New Haven, 1916), p. 106.

22. Act III, sc. ii.

23. Act II, sc. iii.

24. Act II, sc. ii.

25. Act V, sc. vii.

26. Bentley, III, 149–151, discusses the date. Harbage, p. 269, assigns it tentatively to 1639. Cavendish collaborated with Shirley in *The Country Captain* (or *Captain Underwit*) of 1639–41. Henry Ten Eyck Perry, *The First Duchess of Newcastle and Her Husband as Figures in Literary History,* "Harvard Studies in English," Vol. IV (Boston and London, 1918), p. 113, stresses the influence of Shirley's *Love Tricks.*

27. Bentley, IV, 701–705. Although *The Parson's Wedding* was apparently

intended for production late in 1639 or in 1640, there is no evidence of its performance until 1664; also see Alfred Harbage, *Thomas Killigrew: Cavalier Dramatist 1612-83* (Philadelphia, 1930), pp. 178-179, who thinks the play was composed in the summer of 1641; he discusses its stage history, pp. 189-190.

28. Act I, sc. i.
29. Act II, sc. i.
30. Act III, sc. i.
31. Act II, sc. i and Act IV, sc. i. The tavern, resembling the Old Devil with its Apollo Room, is described in Act III, sc. i in Formall's speech to Lucy.
32. Act II, sc. vii.
33. Act II, sc. v.
34. Act V, sc. iv.
35. Act II, sc. vii.
36. Act III, sc. ii.
37. Act I, sc. ii for these two speeches.
38. Act IV, sc. i.
39. Act I, sc. iii.
40. Act II, sc. iv and Act II, sc. ii.

Chapter Nine

1. James Branch Cabell, *Beyond Life,* in *The Works of James Branch Cabell* (18 vols., New York, 1927-30), I, 26. This sentence does not appear in earlier editions of *Beyond Life.* Cabell mentions no plays of the Sons of Ben but cites Shirley's *Hyde Park,* Dekker and Middleton's *The Roaring Girl,* and Jonson's *The New Inn* as depressing examples of the growth of realism.

2. Cabell, pp. 13 and 19; the phrases recur as motifs in *Beyond Life* expressing Charteris' standards for fine literature.

3. On this term, see W. K. Wimsatt, Jr., *The Verbal Icon* (Lexington, Ky., 1954), pp. 69-83.

4. J. Y. T. Greig, *The Psychology of Laughter and Comedy* (London, 1923), pp. 54-56, 136-138, discusses "the peep-bo situation."

5. Benjamin DeCasseres, *Chameleon: Being the Book of My Selves* (New York, 1922), p. 88.

SELECTED

BIBLIOGRAPHY

Primary Sources

(Limited to editions of the Sons of Ben used in this study.)

BROME, RICHARD. *The Antipodes,* ed. G. P. Baker, in Vol. III, *Representative English Comedies,* ed. C. M. Gayley (3 vols., New York, 1914).

———. *The Dramatic Works of Richard Brome* . . . (R. H. Pearson reprint, 3 vols., London, 1873).

———. *A Jovial Crew* in Vol. X, *A Select Collection of Old Plays,* ed. Robert Dodsley (2nd ed., 12 vols., London, 1780), and in Giles Robert Floyd, "A Critical Edition of Brome's A Jovial Crew" (State University of Iowa Ph.D. dissertation, 1942).

CARTWRIGHT, WILLIAM. *The Plays and Poems of William Cartwright,* ed. G. Blakemore Evans (Madison, 1951).

CAVENDISH, WILLIAM. *The Country Captaine, And The Varietie, Two Comedies, Written by a Person of Honor* . . . (London, 1649).

DAVENANT, WILLIAM. *The Dramatic Works of Sir William D'Avenant,* ed. James Maidment and W. H. Logan (5 vols., Edinburgh and London, 1872–74).

GLAPTHORNE, HENRY. *The Plays and Poems of Henry Glapthorne* . . . [ed. R. H. Pearson] (2 vols., London, 1874).

HAUSTED, PETER. *Peter Hausted's The Rival Friends,* ed. Laurens J. Mills, "Indiana University Publications, Humanities Series" No. 23 (Bloomington, Indiana, 1951).

KILLIGREW, THOMAS. *The Parson's Wedding* in *Restoration Comedies,* ed. Montague Summers (Boston, 1922).

MARMION, SHACKERLEY. *The Dramatic Works of Shakerley Marmion,* ed. James Maidment and W. H. Logan (Edinburgh and London, 1875).

MAYNE, JASPER. *The City Match* in Vol. XIII, *Dodsley's Old English Plays,* ed. W. Carew Hazlitt (14 vols., London, 1875).

237

Selected Bibliography

NABBES, THOMAS. *The Works of Thomas Nabbes,* ed. A. H. Bullen, in Vols. I and II, *Old English Plays: New Series* (3 vols., London, 1887).
RANDOLPH, THOMAS. *The Drinking Academy,* ed. Samuel A. Tannenbaum and Hyder E. Rollins (Cambridge, Mass., 1930).
————. *Poetical and Dramatic Works of Thomas Randolph,* ed. W. C. Hazlitt (2 vols., London, 1875).

Secondary Works

(This annotated list is limited to a few basic and recent items and does not include most of the specialized books and articles cited in my "Notes and References.")

ACKERMAN, CATHERINE A. "Fashionable Platonism and Sir Kenelm Digby's *Private Memoirs,*" in *College Language Association Journal,* V (1961), 136–41. An interesting analysis by an authority on Caroline Court Platonism.
BARISH, JONAS A., ed. *Ben Jonson: A Collection of Critical Essays* (Englewood Cliffs, New Jersey, 1963). A paperback in Prentice-Hall's Twentieth Century Views series providing a fine collection of recent Jonson criticism.
————. *Ben Jonson and the Language of Prose Comedy* (Cambridge, Mass., 1960). An approach to Jonson that suggests new possibilities of research into the comedies of the Sons of Ben.
BARNARD, DEAN STANTON, JR. *"Hollands Leaguer* by Nicholas Goodman: A Critical Edition" (University of Michigan Ph.D. dissertation, 1962: See *Dissertation Abstracts,* XXIV, 737). Shows that Goodman's description of Mrs. Holland's brothel is a satire on the Church of England.
BENTLEY, GERALD EADES. *The Jacobean and Caroline Stage* (5 vols., Oxford, 1941–56). This still unfinished monumental work of reference so far gives dramatic companies and players in Vols. I and II (1941) and plays and playwrights in Vols. III–V (1956).
CECIL, C. D. "Libertine and *Précieux* Elements in Restoration Comedy," in *Essays in Criticism,* IX (July, 1959), 239–53. Although not concerned with Caroline comedy, clarifies in Restoration comedy one of the issues that preoccupied several of the Sons of Ben.
HARBAGE, ALFRED. *Cavalier Drama: An Historical and Critical Supplement to the Study of the Elizabethan and Restoration Stage* (New York, 1936). An indispensable survey, of which Ch. IV of Part One, "The Trend in Comedy," pp. 72–90, is still one of the best short discussions of its subject.
HILL, CHRISTOPHER. *Society and Puritanism in Pre-Revolutionary England* (New York, 1964). An historical survey that provides important background for an understanding of the situation of the Sons of Ben.

Selected Bibliography

HOLLAND, NORMAN N. *The First Modern Comedies: The Significance of Etherege, Wycherley and Congreve* (Cambridge, Mass., 1959). A highly readable critical study that helps place Restoration comedy in a new perspective needed by students interested in anticipation of this comedy by the Sons of Ben.

KAUFMANN, R. J. *Richard Brome: Caroline Playwright* (New York, 1961). The best critical study to date of an individual Son of Ben, a kind of model for future studies of the remaining Sons. Its demonstration that Brome's *The Love-sick Court* is a parody-burlesque of serious Platonic drama, rather than a middling effort to follow the vogue, is one of the most impressive of its several original contributions.

KERNAN, ALVIN. *The Cankered Muse: Satire of the English Renaissance* (New Haven, 1959). Contains some excellent discussion of Jonson's development of satirical comedy.

KNOLL, ROBERT E. *Ben Jonson's Plays: An Introduction* (Lincoln, Nebr., 1964). A most engagingly written critical study that will aid any future student of the Sons of Ben.

LAMONT, WILLIAM M. *Marginal Prynne, 1600–1669* (Toronto, 1963). A critical contribution to our knowledge of Prynne as prolific propagandist and polymath.

MUESCHKE, PAUL AND MIRIAM. *A New View of Congreve's Way of the World,* "University of Michigan Contributions in Modern Philology" No. 23 (Ann Arbor, 1958). This essay, together with a forthcoming similar one by the same authors on Etherege's *The Man of Mode,* provides the kind of model for detailed explication of a seventeenth century comedy that could be of great help to future analysts of individual comedies by the Sons of Ben.

PARTRIDGE, EDWARD B. *The Broken Compass: A Study of the Major Comedies of Ben Jonson* (New York, 1958). A brilliant analysis of Jonson's imagery that opens the way to a similar approach to the comedies of the Sons of Ben.

SQUIER, CHARLES L. "The Comic Spirit of Sir William Davenant: A Critical Study of His Caroline Comedies" (University of Michigan Ph.D. dissertation, 1963: see *Dissertation Abstracts,* XXIV, 2488–89). A model of the kind of detailed analysis that should be applied to other comedies of the Sons of Ben.

THAYER, C. G. *Ben Jonson: Studies in the Plays* (Norman, Okla., 1963). One of the most readable critical surveys of Jonson's work.

WEDGWOOD, C. V. "Comedy in the Reign of Charles I," pp. 111–37 of *Studies in Social History, A Tribute to G. M. Trevelyan,* ed. J. H. Plumb (London, 1955). Despite an understandable confusion of Brome's *The City Wit* and Mayne's *The City Match,* this essay is a lively and learned defense of the documentary value of Caroline comedy.

239

Selected Bibliography

Text for Teaching

SIX CAROLINE PLAYS, ed. A. S. Knowland (Oxford University Press: London, New York, Toronto, 1962). World's Classics No. 583. Contains a useful short introduction to Caroline drama followed by newly edited texts of Shirley's *The Lady of Pleasure* and *The Wedding;* Brome's *A Mad Couple Well Matched* and *The Antipodes;* Davenant's *The Wits;* and Killigrew's *The Parson's Wedding.*

Index

241

Index

Index

Joe Lee Davis is professor of English and chairman of the program in American culture, University of Michigan. He received his B.A. and M.A. from the University of Kentucky and his Ph.D. from the University of Michigan. He is the author of several books and many articles.

The manuscript was edited by Alex Brede. The book was designed by S. R. Tenenbaum. The type face used for the text is Linotype Granjon cut by Claude Garamond in the seventeenth century. The display face is Bembo originally designed for Aldus Manutius by Francisco Griffo in 1495.

The book is printed on Warren's Olde Style Antique white wove and bound in cloth made by Columbia Mills and paper from Lindenmeyr Schlosser Company. Manufactured in the United States of America.